WHITNEY
&
BOBBI KRISTINA

WHITNEY

&

BOBBI KRISTINA

The Deadly Price of Fame

IAN HALPERIN

GALLERY BOOKS

New York London Toronto Sydney New Delhi

G

Gallery Books
An Imprint of Simon & Schuster, Inc.
1230 Avenue of the Americas
New York, NY 10020

First Gallery Books hardcover edition June 2015.

GALLERY BOOKS and colophon are
registered trademarks of Simon & Schuster, Inc.

For information about special discounts for bulk purchases, please contact Simon & Schuster Special Sales at 1-866-506-1949 or business@simonandschuster.com.

The Simon & Schuster Speakers Bureau can bring authors to your live event. For more information or to book an event, contact the Simon & Schuster Speakers Bureau at 1-866-248-3049 or visit our website at www.simonspeakers.com.

Interior design by Jaime Putorti

Manufactured in the United States of America

10 9 8 7 6 5 4 3 2 1

Library of Congress Cataloging-in-Publication Data is available.

ISBN 978-1-5011-2074-9
ISBN 978-1-5011-2076-3 (ebook)

Dedicated to the unique spirits of
Whitney and Krissi

INTRODUCTION

The cable guy was running late when he rang the doorbell at approximately 10:20 AM on January 31 at the luxury town house in Roswell, inside the well-heeled gated complex of the tiny Atlanta suburb where Whitney Houston had lived before her 2012 death.

The door was answered by Max Lomas, who was apparently unaware that Bobbi Kristina Brown—his ex-girlfriend—had been expecting a service call. He went off to look for her. Moments later, he found Bobbi lying facedown in a bathtub filled with water. Hearing cries of help, his buddy Nick Gordon came running. As the two pulled Bobbi's body out of the bathtub, they were joined by Max's girlfriend, Danyela Bradley, who had stayed over the night before.

At 10:29 AM, while Nick performed CPR, Max phoned 911 to report that a girl had been found "drowning." In the nearly twenty minutes it took for paramedics to show up, the two men took turns attempting to revive the twenty-one-year-old young woman with whom both men had a tumultuous history. As Danyela looked on, terrified, she couldn't help but notice that the bathwater was ice-cold and that the girl had strange marks around her mouth and chin.

Just under twenty minutes later, paramedics arrived and transported the unconscious victim by ambulance to the nearby North

Fulton Hospital in Roswell. Less than an hour later, the world learned that Bobbi Kristina Brown was fighting for her life in circumstances that eerily paralleled the death of her famous mother, who had accidentally drowned in a bathtub nearly three years earlier, also facedown.

But when I received a call at my home in Miami on February 4 from someone with indirect ties to the case, the caller shared a cryptic piece of information:

"It looks like we have ourselves another Natalie Wood."

CHAPTER **ONE**

In February 1994, Whitney Houston was at the pinnacle of her career. Thanks to her work on the soundtrack to *The Bodyguard*, and its megahit single "I Will Always Love You," the awards and accolades were pouring in. On February 7, she attended the American Music Awards at the Shrine Auditorium in LA, where she swept a total of eight awards that evening. When Best Soul/R&B album was announced, she came rushing across the stage with a baby in her arms to accept the award. As she began her speech, little Bobbi Kristina— a pink ribbon in her hair—reached for the microphone. Before she could grab it, Whitney scolded her and went on with her speech. It was a portent of a life spent reaching for the spotlight in her mother's shadow, but never quite getting there.

Three decades earlier, Whitney Houston had also started life in the shadow of a performing mother.

Cissy Drinkard's parents were part of the first major wave of black Southerners to migrate north. In 1923, they relocated with three children from the seething racism of Georgia to a working-class, mixed-race neighborhood in Newark, New Jersey, to a home with their first indoor toilet. Cissy came along ten years later, the last of eight children, at the height of the Depression. Her father was one of the lucky ones whose strong back served him well in a steady series of jobs repairing roads and pouring iron to keep his family fed and clothed while many around them went hungry.

Devout Christians, the family attended the African Methodist Episcopal Church where voices raised in music and prayer could be heard day and night, not just on Sundays. Their devotion helped the family get through their overwhelming devastation when Cissy's mother lost two sets of twins at birth in succession. Giving birth to twelve children by the time she was thirty took a tremendous toll on Delia Mae Drinkard's health. At age thirty-four, she suffered a massive stroke that left her in a wheelchair with brain damage and impaired movement in her arm and leg. Not long afterward, the tenement building where they lived in a cramped apartment was engulfed in flames, destroying all the family's possessions. The fire proved a mixed blessing when city services relocated the Drinkards to a better neighborhood and a new church.

Cissy was only five years old when her family began attending the St. Luke's A.M.E. Church, where, she later recalled, you could feel the "force of the Spirit and the music" from the moment you stepped inside its doors. Their old church had a piano, but St. Luke's had cymbals, tambourines, and even a washboard to accompany the joyous clapping and syncopation that rang through its pews. It was the first time Cissy began to experience music as something spiritual, and, along with her brothers and sister, she wholeheartedly embraced it. When her father heard them singing together, he decided they had something special and made them practice at home for hours at a time. Sometimes Cissy didn't feel like practicing and would run outside and hide behind the car, but her father would always find her and threaten her with a beating. And, although he wouldn't hesitate to take his hand to the other children, Cissy was his "baby," and she was always spared.

Cissy recalls these first few years in the new neighborhood as the happiest times of her young life. But in May 1941, a dark cloud would descend on the family when Delia Mae suffered another stroke. As the children gathered at the window to watch their father bring her home from the hospital in her wheelchair, they watched instead as he arrived alone and sobbing. An aunt shouted out, "Your mother is dead." Cissy would never recover from the emptiness and sorrow that came with losing her beloved mother at such a young age. The only thing that kept the family from falling apart, she recalls, was music.

Her father would often come home from his job late at night, only to wake the children and ask for a song. Soon, the Drinkard family was being booked to sing in churches and gospel programs in New Jersey and even New York. Although her father permitted them to listen only to gospel music, Cissy and her sister would sneak Billie Holiday and Dinah Washington records onto their old Victrola or duck out to the local teen spots and listen to the jukebox. As they danced to the blues, they dreamed of singing in the nightclubs across the river that their father had warned them were filled with sin and temptation.

After her father announced he was getting remarried and that Cissy would come to live with him and his new wife, Viola, she remembers running out of the house in tears and ending up at St. Luke's despairing about the hardships that had been visited on her. As she heard the voice of the reverend preaching to the congregation, and the voices of the choir reverberating, she describes an epiphany where, for the first time, she shared her father's vision of the purpose of singing. Gospel music was a ministry, "an end in itself," spreading the Word of the Lord through song. She knew where she wanted to devote her life.

Meanwhile, the Drinkard Singers were starting to make a name for themselves getting gigs all up and down the Eastern seaboard. Traveling the gospel circuit, they regularly opened for established acts such as the Swan Silvertones and the Dixie Hummingbirds. Booked to accompany the Soul Stirrers, sixteen-year-old Cissy met their lead singer, Sam Cooke, and fell for his devastating good looks. He proposed, and she was tempted, but in the end, his fast life and secular music was incompatible with the values of her devout family, which considered such a lifestyle a form of backsliding from the church.

As manager of the Drinkards, Cissy's older sister Lee Warrick (her daughters would later change the spelling to Warwick)—determined to keep the group far from the "temptations" of popular entertainment—rejected a number of recording deals, national road tours, and even TV shoots. But some offers proved just too tempting to turn down, especially the opportunity to appear at Carnegie Hall with the legendary Mahalia Jackson—a performance so raucous that Jackson threatened to call the police to empty the hall if the crowd didn't settle down. But even an appearance on the world-renowned stage couldn't convince Nicholas Drinkard to loosen the tight grip he firmly believed was necessary to keep his children on the straight and narrow. To the family patriarch, music served only one purpose—to preach the Word. Cissy's talents would be put to better use directing St. Luke's choir and helping others to express their gift to the Lord. Reluctantly, Cissy agreed to take over the grueling task with what she called "a firm hand" while "taking no mess."

In 1952, the family received yet another blow when Nicholas was diagnosed with stomach cancer. A week later he was dead, and Cissy was an orphan at eighteen. Rudderless, she turned to alcohol and partied almost every night in the dens of sin from which she had always been sheltered. Her faith unshaken, Cissy still found herself in church every Sunday morning and still determined to lead the choir in order to honor her father's memory. But her heart was no longer in St. Luke's, which held too many painful memories of a happier time.

The Drinkard Singers had performed on a number of occasions at the New Hope Baptist Church in the University Heights section of the city and had always enjoyed its welcoming vibe. Together, the family made the decision to leave St. Luke's and make New Hope their new spiritual home. Cissy felt rejuvenated at her new place of worship and before long was directing the choir that would one day produce a superstar named Nippy.

During her young life to date, Cissy had turned down more than one marriage proposal and beaten back the advances of countless men. But now, freed from the strict reins and moral compass of her father, she let her guard down. Wooed by a handsome construction worker named Freddy Garland, she agreed to his hasty marriage proposal after dating for a little more than a month. Looking back, she would explain that she rushed into marriage because she was "lonely," especially since all her brothers and sisters had by then started families. At age twenty-one, the two tied the knot at a ceremony held at New Hope attended by her family. It was a colossal mistake. Within months, Cissy came to regret her decision and was on the verge of leaving Freddy when she found out she was pregnant. Stuck in a loveless marriage and with a baby on the way, she weighed her options and foresaw only years of misery. Without looking back, she packed up her belongings one day and moved in with her sister.

She was already starting to show when the Drinkard Singers got the call that would change Cissy's life. The quartet was invited to appear at the Newport Jazz Festival—the biggest in the world at the time—with Mahalia Jackson and Clara Ward. The reception to their rollicking performance that day was overwhelming—they were nearly mobbed by the huge crowd—and within days, Lee received an offer for the group to sign with RCA Victor, making them the first gospel group ever to sign with the prestigious label. Four months later, Cissy gave birth to a boy named Gary. She was now a single mother.

In 1958, the Drinkards released their first album, *A Joyful Noise*, which received some radio play though the sales were not spectacular. Among those who were most impressed by their sound was a young Elvis Presley—then at the height of his career—who invited the group to record and tour with him. Shocked by his brazen sexuality, Lee immediately rejected the offer. Rock and roll was incompatible with the Spirit of the Lord, she insisted.

Not long afterward, the group was invited to perform a weekly televised gospel show from Symphony Hall in Newark. Watching from his living room one Sunday morning, a truck driver named John Houston was struck by the look of the group's beautiful lead singer. Determined to meet her, Houston made his way to the hall and introduced himself to Cissy following the broadcast.

When she laid eyes on the tall, light-skinned man who, like her father, was part Native American, she was immediately struck by his looks. "He was gorgeous," she recalled. It dawned on her that she had seen him once before, when she was fourteen and he was an army MP searching for an AWOL soldier in the tenement next to hers. At the time, she and her friends thought he was the most handsome man they had ever seen. Now here he was, asking her out on a date.

Having attended a Catholic prep school on a scholarship, John Houston was well read, sophisticated, and "drop dead funny." Separated from his first wife, he was thirteen years older than Cissy, and her sisters most decidedly did not approve, calling him a "cradle robber." But Cissy was hooked, and before long, the two were inseparable. Still a devout Christian and leader of the New Hope Choir, she knew she was "doing wrong" when she moved into an apartment on Eighth Street with John. But life was hard as a single mother, and John loved kids.

His divorce wasn't final, so marriage was out of the question for some time, but John drove taxis when he wasn't driving the big rigs, and he was a good provider to Cissy and Gary. He loved gospel music and fancied himself something of an impresario. Lee didn't want anything to do with him. There was no way he was going to mess with the Drinkard Singers. But attending New Hope on Sundays, he couldn't help but notice Cissy's two talented nieces—Dionne and Dee Dee Warwick—who sang with the choir she still directed. The two girls had gotten together a little quartet they called the Gospelaires. Acting as their informal manager, John got the group some gigs at local gospel shows. They would frequently travel to the Apollo Theater, across the river in Harlem, for amateur night. One night backstage, he offered his group's services to a musician seeking background singers for a recording session featuring Sam "The Man" Taylor.

Before long, Dionne and Dee Dee were working with some of the biggest names in music, including Elvis's songwriters Leiber and Stoller, the Coasters, Dinah Washington, and the Drifters. John Houston had become a full-fledged player at the center of the action, but he had set his sights firmly on another act a little closer to home. As he saw the Warwicks soar as background singers, he knew that the real money was to be made with solo acts. And he had just the one in mind. Convinced that Cissy could be a star if she went out on her own with him opening doors, he worked on her day and night. But she firmly resisted. Recalling her father's disdain for popular music, she wouldn't betray his memory, or her calling, just to make money. In between the Drinkard gigs, she had a steady job at the RCA plant and was content. Besides, she later recalled, she was stubborn. She wasn't going to do something just because a man wanted her to do it. She was also about to be a mother again. Michael Houston was born in 1961 and now she had young two boys at home.

Yet John had not given up. Dionne was booked for a session with Scepter Records, but John had double-booked her for another session with a rockabilly star named Ronnie Hawkins, who was being touted as the next Elvis. Finding himself in a jam, John begged his girlfriend to step in just this once. Reluctantly, Cissy agreed. Immediately she was hooked. She knew her sisters would disapprove, but she managed to rationalize her decision. She decided she could be *in* the world of secular music without being *of* that world. Before long, she was singing backup with her nieces on a Drifters album that was destined to be a classic. At one of these sessions, Dionne was discovered by Burt Bacharach, who was instrumental in signing her to Scepter—the first stepping-stone to her hugely successful solo career. By December, she had her first top-ten single. And that same month, Cissy discovered that she was pregnant once again. She prayed it would be a girl.

CHAPTER **TWO**

Within hours of the news that Bobbi Kristina had been discovered, barely breathing, in the bathtub, the disparate branches of Bobbi's family began to descend on Atlanta. And it seemed appropriate that the city had once been known as the epicenter of an epic civil war. Since Whitney's passing, it seemed a civil war had been simmering within the family. Now it was about to erupt.

The first indications that all was not well came when an Atlanta spokeswoman announced to the press that Bobbi Kristina had been found by her "husband," Nick Gordon, and a friend at around 10:20 AM. Indeed, Bobbi had Instagrammed a photo of her and Nick wearing "wedding bands" in January 2014 under the hashtag #HappilyMarried.

Following the news that Bobbi had been hospitalized, her father, Bobby Brown, immediately flew from Los Angeles to be by her side—on a private plane lent to him by his close friend, the Hollywood personality Tyler Perry. The producer and star of the popular Madea franchise had also supplied a plane to fly the body of Bobbi's mother, Whitney, from Los Angeles to a funeral home in New Jersey in 2012.

Arriving in Atlanta on Saturday, Bobby issued a media statement before ducking into the Roswell hospital through a back entrance to be by his daughter's side. "Privacy is requested in this matter," he said. "Please allow for my family to deal with this matter and give my daughter the love and support she needs at this time."

Inside, a distraught Brown kept a nearly twenty-four-hour vigil in the room where other members of the family had also gathered. Although there was no love lost between Bobby and Whitney's tight-knit family, they managed to put aside their differences to consult with medical staff on Bobbi's condition. Cissy, closely following developments back in New Jersey, would not arrive for another six days, though her daughter-in-law Pat Houston kept her apprised by phone.

Brown continued his vigil, standing over Bobbi in the intensive care unit, stroking her hair and murmuring "baby girl." According to a member of the staff, he could frequently be seen singing gospel hymns near her bedside, often joined by members of Whitney's family. He even joined in a rendition of Whitney's signature tune, "Greatest Love of All."

The medical prognosis was not good. Tests showed that Bobbi—who had likely been unconscious for minutes underwater—had little brain function and was unlikely to recover. Tight-lipped about her condition, medical staff let it be known to the press that she was "fighting for her life" but refused to provide any more details.

At the same time, it became evident that both sides of the family were spending as much or more time consulting lawyers and publicists as they were the doctors.

Infuriated by the description of Nick Gordon as Bobbi's husband, her father had his attorney issue an unequivocal statement to the gathered media: "Bobbi Kristina is not and has never been married to Nick Gordon," Christopher Brown of the firm Brown & Rosen insisted. At the same time, they let it be known that their office was "currently investigating the events that led to the hospitalization of Bobbi Kristina."

The words struck onlookers as strange. Why was Bobby's lawyer conducting an investigation rather than leaving the matter to law enforcement authorities?

In fact, Roswell police had been conducting their own investigation practically from the moment the ambulance took Bobbi Kristina away. Within an hour, they had questioned Gordon and Max Lomas as well as the XFINITY cable technician who had arrived at the house that morning. Word soon leaked that they didn't like what they had heard. Nor did they necessarily believe that the incident that left Bobbi in a coma was an accident. Less than a week after Bobbi was pulled out of her bathtub, police officials made no secret of the fact that they were pursuing an investigation. And, although a number of media outlets reported that Nick Gordon had become the target of the investigation, my own sources informed me that the evidence pointed to more than one suspect and that the evidence was murkier than was being reported.

Officially, the police would only say that "the matter may or may not result in criminal charges being brought against individuals." Nick and Max had already lawyered up. But as long as Bobbi remained alive, it remained an open question whether police would end up laying charges of homicide or merely attempted murder against their suspect should they determine that foul play was involved.

Meanwhile, the world was watching the tragedy unfold, and Twitter was ablaze with celebrities sending their thoughts and prayers:

La Toya Jackson, who knew from personal experience what the family was going through, was one of the first to weigh in:

"Let's All Send Love Light & Prayers To Bobbi Kristina Brown! Wishing Her A Healthy & Speedy Recovery!"

Social media, in keeping with its tradition, had witnessed more than its share of cruel comments and jokes about Bobbi's condition. One of the tamer ones was:

"I guess it's true then that all little girls turn into their mothers eventually."

Others were outright racist. Responding to the sick barbs, Brandon Williams tweeted:

"People are really out here making jokes and laughing at Bobbi Kristina? That's sad. Pray for that young woman. Send positive energy her way!"

Mariah Carey, who had recorded a well-known duet, "When You Believe," with Whitney, offered:

"My thoughts and prayers continue to be with Bobbi Kristina. Sending love and support to the family. God Bless."

Lady Gaga sent out a message to millions of her Little Monsters:

"Praying for Bobbi Kristina. Monsters let's all together send our love & healing energy to Whitney's daughter. World send her strength."

Meanwhile, as conspiracy theories and accusations swirled about the events that left Bobbi in a coma, the Reverend Al Sharpton issued his own plea: "Let's all pray for Bobbi Kristina. Let's not speculate on what happened, let's ask God to intervene."

Whitney's longtime friend Missy Elliott revealed that Bobbi's mother had once asked her to look out for her daughter. "Bobbi is like a little sister to me," she said. "I have been very close to her mother. One thing that her mother said to me before she passed away was to make sure Bobbi Kristina was straight, so my prayers for healing [are] that she comes out and be around people that love her."

CHAPTER **THREE**

It wasn't an easy birth. Cissy was laid up at home for almost two months after she gave birth to Whitney Elizabeth Houston on August 9, 1963. Having saved up some money from her increasingly frequent recording sessions, John's first task was to find a house in a better neighborhood. In the fall, they closed on a nice house on Wainwright Street in a section of Newark with brick row houses occupied by young families. There was enough left over after the down payment to put in a new kitchen and living room.

The family was thrilled to move out of the old third-floor walk-up. Cissy's parents had always preached the importance of making sure your kids did better than you. With the move, they had truly moved into the middle class.

With Gary now in school and Cissy working a day job at the RCA plant, John stayed home with young Michael and the new baby, who Cissy recalled was always up to mischief even before she could walk. John took to calling her "Nippy," after a comic book character who attracted trouble, and soon nobody called her anything else.

An early starter, young Whitney was walking by six months and would constantly tease the family's German shepherd Thor, who they acquired when they moved to the new neighborhood. By the time the baby turned one, John's divorce finally came through, paving the way for him to marry Cissy.

Meanwhile, Dionne Warwick had started her solo career, which would eventually see her become one of the most successful female artists of all time. Dee Dee soon followed, signing a deal with Mercury, leaving Cissy to make a growing name for herself as a background singer on studio session work. For some time, at John's urging, she had been looking to start a group of her own, and by 1966, she had assembled the core of the quartet that would become known as the Sweet Inspirations. The Sweets were not looking to become the next Supremes. Their forte was background vocals—a musical art form that was still in its infancy. Most background session acts were trios, but Cissy had added a fourth voice to sing an octave lower than her own and create a distinctive sound. With the new sound, recalled John Houston, "They began to wipe out all the other background singers." At first, the women went into the studio to sing background vocals for whatever solo artist the studio assigned. But in 1967, Atlantic Records was toying with creating a new sound for a rising star named Aretha Franklin. As a young girl, Cissy had listened to the radio sermons of Aretha's father, the Reverend C. L. Franklin, known as the "Million-Dollar Voice." On occasion, the Drinkard Singers had appeared on the same bill as Aretha when she was touring the gospel circuit but still a relative unknown. Now, Atlantic had big plans for her and the Sweet Inspirations were chosen to be a part of those plans.

Previously, background singers were expected to arrive at the studio at the appointed time, do whatever the producer told them, and disappear. But Atlantic gave Cissy and the Sweets the freedom to spend hours in the studio working out the background parts on Aretha's songs and experimenting with different variations. The Sweets, she recalls, became known for a certain musical "punctuation" that would come to characterize the songs on which they were featured. If the singer, for example, sang the line "Do you love me?" they would come back with a rousing "Yes, I do."

Her years singing in church had taught her that the listener had to *feel* the song, and now she put that background to good use. With the Sweet Inspirations backing her up, Aretha exploded onto the charts with a steady stream of early hits, including "Chain of Fools," "I Never Loved a Man," and Cissy's favorites, "Natural Woman" and "Ain't No Way." On the latter tune, Cissy worked in a high solo behind Aretha's lead vocals, ensuring an unusually large profile for a background singer. Such flourishes soon got her and the group noticed, and they were given the opportunity to record their own singles.

Though their specialty was backgrounds, suddenly it seemed that everybody wanted them. That same year, the Sweets went into the studio to back up former Them singer Van Morrison, who had recently gone solo and was recording a new single, "Brown Eyed Girl."

Its success cemented the group's reputation for what she called "taking a record over the top and making it a hit." Meanwhile, Aretha had asked the group to back her on tour, and Cissy's grueling schedule meant that John was left to care for the children much of the time.

While she was on tour one night in Las Vegas, she called home to discover that Nippy, now four years old, had fallen while playing with her brother and got a wire coat hanger stuck down her throat. When she was rushed to the emergency room to extract the object, doctors told John that the hook had just missed perforating her vocal cords.

Nineteen sixty-seven was also the year that Newark erupted in race riots as angry disaffected black youth went on a violent looting rampage through the streets. The worst of the rioting took place a fair distance from their neighborhood, but it was close enough for the family to see the smoke and hear the gunshots. Soon after, they started looking for a new home in the suburbs, but the only way they could afford a move was for Cissy and the Sweets to continue touring. With John working only periodically, they depended on Cissy's income.

The tour dates down south were particularly difficult, given Jim Crow attitudes that still permeated the region. "We found racism on the road at just about every turn," Cissy later wrote, recalling that they were often turned away from hotels or restaurants because of their race or encountered open hostility.

By 1969, the Sweet Inspirations were in high demand. After working on sessions with Dusty Springfield in Nashville and Jimi Hendrix in New York the year before, they got a call from Elvis Presley, who had heard the Drinkards at the Newport Jazz Festival years earlier. He was preparing to headline the International Hotel casino, and he wanted the Sweets to back him.

While Cissy was captivated by his "drop dead gorgeous" looks, John established a rapport with the King and his crew—spending hours chatting about the business at the hotel coffee shops between shows. The information he gleaned from these sessions about the industry, she recalls, would prove to be invaluable once Whitney's career took off.

John's charm was legendary. Cissy recalls him once asking, "Now Elvis, are you sure you're not black? 'Cause you sure got a lot of rhythm, man." Elvis would retort that John looked a little like his daddy. Although she complained that she often got bored performing the same shows over and over night after night, Cissy also established a rapport with Elvis, who loved gospel music and enjoyed having four devout church ladies backing him up. One day, he told her that the sound of her improvised countermelodies made him think she was squirrelly. That became the King's nickname for her. When he gave the group diamond bracelets to thank them for their work, hers was inscribed "To Cissy" on one side, and on the other, it simply said "Squirrelly."

Singing with Elvis for two months, Cissy missed the kids terribly, but she and John had decided that Las Vegas, still known as Sin City, was no place for children. Back in New Jersey, their friends Phyllis Hardaway and Ellen White—known as Auntie Bae—looked after the kids. Six-year-old Nippy, she recalls, spent most of her time watching TV or listening to her favorite singer, Michael Jackson. But the older kids were finding the separation difficult. Michael in particular often burst into tears for no reason.

Returning home in the fall of 1969, Cissy and John managed to spend some quality time with the children, but the road beckoned. The money was good, but tensions were beginning to form in the group, as the other members wanted to wear revealing costumes onstage like the other background acts. But Cissy's moral upbringing kicked in. "I was onstage to sing, not bounce around and flaunt my business," she later recalled.

Preparing to go back on the road one day, Cissy was packing the car when she spotted the kids playing nearby. As she reached to give Michael a kiss, he pulled away and started sobbing. Joining them, the other children burst into tears as their mother looked on in devastation. That's the day she made the decision to quit the Sweet Inspirations.

For years, John had been clamoring for Cissy to embark on a solo career. This was the opportunity he had been waiting for. He successfully pitched Cissy to Charles Koppelman, an industry stalwart who had signed the Lovin' Spoonful in 1965 and was now running the music division of a new label, Commonwealth United. With an advance of $15,000, John and Cissy went looking for a new house. They found just the place in the respectable suburb of East Orange just up the Garden State Parkway from Newark.

For the first time, each child had their own bedroom and, best of all, a big backyard pool to while away the sweltering New Jersey summers. The pool soon turned into a neighborhood gathering place where Gary, Michael, and Whitney entertained their growing legions of friends. And as kids came and went, so too did the clothes and toys that Cissy bought them. She theorized that they felt guilty that they had so much and were eager to share the bounty with others. Whitney was particularly generous.

One day, Nippy was watching Michael Jackson performing with his brothers on TV, when she announced that she was going to marry that boy, adding that she was going to become a big star and buy her mother a house.

Although Cissy loved her boys, Nippy was her pride and joy. Something about her manner—loving, friendly, trusting—stole Cissy's heart. When she took her on errands, she recalls little Nippy marching right up to strangers to wish them good morning. When her mother tried to explain why that wasn't a good idea, the girl would dismiss her concerns with "Oh, Mommy."

She thought everybody was her friend, Cissy recalled. That's why it was especially heartbreaking for her when she later discovered a different reality.

Embarking on her solo career, Cissy was given a song to sing called "Midnight Train to Houston." It didn't seem right to her, so she decided to tweak the title and change "Houston" to "Georgia." Hamstrung by a lack of promotion, the song received limited airplay, to the constant frustration of John, who told everybody who would listen that it would be a huge hit if they would just put some money behind it. Three years later, Gladys Knight and the Pips recorded the song, and it struck gold.

Meanwhile, the solo career of Cissy's niece Dionne was exploding. Her single "I Say a Little Prayer" had just sold one million copies—one of nineteen top one hundred hits Dionne would enjoy during the sixties, making her the second best-selling female vocalist after Aretha Franklin. The family was excited for her success and none more so than little Whitney and her brothers, who were often invited to join their aunt on her private plane as she jetted around the world on tour. Cissy continued to record with Aretha, who Nippy called Auntie Ree when she accompanied her mother to the Atlantic studio one day. "Cissy brought her to one of my recording sessions," Franklin later recalled. "She was around 9 or 10. I think Cissy had instructed her to be very quiet because she didn't say too much after that. She was just very quiet and very attentive."

Contrary to popular belief, Franklin was never her godmother, but rather an "honorary aunt." Her appointed godmother was in fact the singer Darlene Love, whose best known song "He's a Rebel" went to number one in 1962. Love remembers once visiting the family when Whitney was young and sharing a bed with the young girl. "I was pregnant at the time, and she'd go, 'What do you want, what do you want?' There was a store on the corner where she'd run down the street and buy fruit for me. So charming from Day One," she told *Rolling Stone*.

Nippy had started attending school at Franklin Elementary, where she was frequently bullied because she came to school in expensive dresses, while the other girls wore jeans. Cissy had threatened to "whoop Gary's butt" years earlier when she found out her oldest son failed to fight back when a schoolmate attacked him. But Whitney pleaded that she didn't like confrontation. She just wanted to be friends. Her mother, however, was determined to open her eyes to reality. "That's not the way the world is, baby," she recalls telling her. "Sometimes you just have to tell people to kiss your ass and keep on walking." When groups of mean girls occasionally chased Whitney home, her older brother Michael would often stand up to them. But when Cissy witnessed such a confrontation one day, she invited the girls to whip her ass first if they wanted to take on her daughter.

Whitney would later recall the trauma of being bullied. "In grammar school, some of the girls had problems with me," she later recollected. "My face was too light. My hair was too long. It was the black-consciousness period and I felt really bad. I finally faced the fact that it wasn't a crime not having friends. Being alone means you have fewer problems. When I decided to become a singer, my mother warned me I would be alone a lot. Basically, we all are. Loneliness comes with life."

Once she learned to ignore the other girls' taunts, Whitney focused on her studies, in which she excelled. John's mother, Elizabeth, had been a teacher, and now, that's what Whitney said she wanted to be. Every day, she'd gather her brothers in front of a toy chalkboard and pretend to teach them while they went along with it. When their attention strayed or they giggled, Cissy recalls, Nippy would pick up a ruler and smack them on the head with it as they burst into laughter.

In the early seventies, many public schools were beginning to experiment with progressive education theories that discarded the rote learning of the past and encouraged children to learn independently. Franklin Elementary was no exception. When Whitney was in the sixth grade, the school adopted an open-classroom curriculum where children were allowed to wander from room to room, and classes were often held outside or in the halls, while kids worked on projects of their choosing and studied at their own pace. As a firm believer in traditional education, Cissy did not approve of these so-called progressive methods and began exploring private options. She was impressed by a Catholic all-girls school in Caldwell called Mount St. Dominic Academy and raised the idea with Nippy, who she assumed would welcome a more disciplined academic environment, especially in light of the bullying at Franklin. But Whitney was horrified at the idea and pleaded to remain in public school.

One day, Cissy arrived at Franklin to drop something off and found a chaotic scene, with kids running around and yelling in the open classroom. When Whitney saw her, she'd later recall that this was the moment she "knew my ass was on the way to Catholic school."

Cissy was still actively involved at New Hope Baptist Church and would bring the kids every Sunday. Whitney was often reluctant to go at first, but she gradually came to enjoy the church, where she eventually started singing in the choir when she turned eleven. Her mother believes she welcomed a place where, unlike school, nobody made fun of her clothes or her hair.

In later years, Whitney only occasionally talked about her religious faith, but her mother reveals that Nippy was "saved" at New Hope and that she later told Cissy that she had "accepted the Savior into her life and heart."

When her grueling schedule permitted it, Cissy would act as

choir director, and Whitney would later recall that watching her on Sundays was the catalyst that made her want to become a singer.

"When I used to watch my mother sing in church, that feeling, that soul, that thing—it's like electricity rolling through you," she said in 1993. "If you have ever been in a Baptist church, when the Holy Spirit starts to roll and people start to really feel what they're doing, it's incredible. That's what I wanted."

She soon abandoned any previous ambitions she had harbored. "I wanted to be a teacher," she told *Rolling Stone*. "I love children, so I wanted to deal with children. Then I wanted to be a veterinarian. But by the age of 10 or 11 when I opened my mouth and said, 'Oh God, what's this?' I kind of knew teaching and being a veterinarian were going to have to wait. What's in your soul is in your soul."

Growing up around some of the greatest singers of the generation clearly had a profound impact on the young girl. "Being around people like Aretha Franklin and Gladys Knight, Dionne Warwick, all these greats, I was taught to listen and observe," she later recalled. "It had a great impact on me as a singer, as a performer, as a musician. Growing up around it, you just can't help it. I identified with it immediately. It was something that was so natural that when I started singing, it was almost like speaking."

Cissy was not enamored of the idea of her daughter becoming a professional singer. She told her stories about the sleazy side of the business and encouraged her to do her singing in church. Privately, she had her doubts that a girl who was so easily bullied could withstand the harsh side of the music business.

But Nippy was determined and if she really wanted to learn to sing, Cissy was going to make her do it the way her father trained her, provided she followed her mother's strict rules and routine. Daily rehearsals at home plus choir every Sunday soon started to pay off. Looking back, Cissy believes she was harder on Whitney than she would have been with someone else's kid, always demanding she aim higher. Developing a rigorous routine, she drilled into her the importance of learning the melody and enunciation. She could be a harsh taskmaster, and Nippy was often frustrated. In her memoir, Cissy remembered Nippy complaining after enduring particularly harsh criticism from her mother. "Mommy, you make me feel like I want to go through the floor, like I'm never going to be good enough."

When she was fourteen, Whitney was finally ready for her first solo, which took place one Sunday at New Hope with a recital of the hymn "Guide Me, O Thou Great Jehovah." The response was electrifying. They recognized a gift from God when they heard one. "I was scared to death," she later recalled. "I was aware of people staring at me. No one moved. They seemed almost in a trance. I just stared at the clock in the center of the church. When I finished, everyone clapped and started crying. From then on, I knew God had blessed me."

———

Whitney hated her strict new school, with its rules and routine. She implored her parents to let her switch to the public middle school, and John was open to the idea, but Cissy was adamant. The discipline would do her good.

She hated the school so much that she rarely participated in extracurricular activities.

"She wasn't even in the school chorus," recalled her Saint Dominic classmate Maria Pane. "She would sing ditties during lunch hour and hum a bit. She had a very sweet, angelic voice."

When she was thirteen, the family had a scare when John had a heart attack at home after he'd returned from driving Cissy to a gig at a Manhattan jazz club. He pulled through, but things weren't the same after that. Something in his personality changed. Cissy put it down to a combination of a midlife crisis and the frustration of a black man trying to make it in a white man's world. "Like so many black men, he was angry at the world, bitter about being denied," she wrote. Soon, he was taking his anger out on her, even though their marriage had been a happy one until that point. Much of the tension, she believed, stemmed from his fervent desire to push her into a solo career. He could have made her a star if only she had wanted it and stopped being so stubborn. Instead, Cissy was largely content with being known as the best backup singer in the business.

Both Cissy and John lamented the racism of the business that kept black acts largely confined to rhythm and blues and out of what she would describe as an "exclusive white club where only the Sinatras and the Streisands were allowed to enter." She cited the black music divisions of most record labels as a prime example of how black acts were kept down. After the heart attack, John seemed to blame her for his own lack of success. What was once a happy home became a frequent scene of loud arguments, fights, and recriminations. The two were sleeping in separate bedrooms and barely talking. Eventually, John would move out. Cissy later believed that the domestic breakdown had a devastating effect on her children. Whitney had always been a daddy's girl, and she had come to appreciate how much her household differed from that of her friends. For all intents and purposes, John had been the house husband for most of Nippy's young life and Cissy the breadwinner. After her rise to fame, Whitney would frequently cite John's unique role in her upbringing.

"My Dad is the backbone of our family," she told *Jet* in 1986. "Any problem that I've ever had he's always been there for me. . . . If my mother had a recording session, he would stay home, dress me and do my hair. He would put a beautiful dress on me with tube socks, like sweat socks. And my hair would look kind of crooked but it was cute. He was a very affectionate and loving dad."

The children witnessed almost daily fights between their parents and the acrimony took its toll before John finally moved out. "For a while they stayed together for our sake," Whitney recalled. "Finally they realized that the only way for them to stay friends was to split. It was strange not to have my father there but he lived just ten minutes away. Besides, even if you're not together physically the love never dies."

For Whitney, music and church became a refuge from the household tension. Cissy was stricter than ever at choir practice, prompting Nippy to storm out on more than one occasion, announcing that she was quitting. When she was fourteen, John gave her permission to enter a local teen singing competition. Whitney sang Barbra Streisand's "Evergreen" and placed second. The first-place winner won with the song "The Greatest Love of All," which would ironically become Whitney's signature tune a decade later.

Not long afterward, Cissy was scheduled for a backup session on a single that Michael Zager was recording for a new album. Zager later told Fox News how he encountered Whitney:

> I was producing an album with Cissy and the night before one of the background singers canceled. So I asked Cissy who she wanted to get and she said I'm going to bring my daughter Nippy. She was fourteen years old. I said, 'Are you sure you want to bring in a fourteen-year-old?' She said 'Don't worry about it.' So Nippy showed up to the studio in her school uniform and she was very, very quiet. She got up and I couldn't believe my ears when she opened her mouth. It was beyond belief.

The resulting single, "Life's a Party," would mark Whitney's professional debut. Impressed by her poise and professionalism, Cissy began bringing her daughter along to sing backup at the Manhattan jazz clubs like Sweetwater's and Mikell's, where she would often appear on weekends. One night, Cissy lost her voice and was going to have to cancel a Mikell's gig. She asked Whitney to go on in her place. Terrified, Nippy demurred, but her mother knew she was ready. This was the moment that Whitney had been waiting for, and she was determined to make the most of it. The crowd responded with a tremendous ovation.

"I was pretty nervous," she recalled. "I was scared to death. It was fun. I just fell in love with it."

From that point on, Whitney would often accompany her mother to gigs, usually singing background, but every once in a while, Cissy would step aside and give her a solo. One thing Cissy and John agreed on, however, was that Nippy was not going to embark on a professional music career under any circumstances until she finished school.

But as it turned out, music wasn't the only professional career that beckoned. In 1979, Whitney backed up Cissy at a benefit for the United Negro College Fund at Carnegie Hall and attracted considerable attention when her mother brought her out to sing a chorus of "Tomorrow" from *Annie*. The next day, they were walking along Seventh Avenue when a *Vogue* photographer approached sixteen-year-old Whitney and asked her if she was interested in modeling. He had been at the Carnegie Hall gig the night before and was captivated by her look and poise. He mentioned a new modeling agency called Click that was looking for teen models.

Cissy gave her okay, and they headed to the address the photographer had given them. Two hours later, Whitney was offered a modeling contract.

A whirlwind schedule of photo shoots soon followed, landing her in the pages of *Vogue*, *Glamour*, *Cosmopolitan*, and *Mademoiselle*. In 1981, she would land on the cover of *Seventeen* magazine—one of the first black women to ever achieve this feat.

"From the beginning, the camera and I were great friends," she later recalled of her modeling career. "It loves me, and I love it."

Despite her success as a model, however, she still had not given up her original dream.

CHAPTER **FOUR**

It was clear that there had been no change in Bobbi Kristina's condition, despite the occasional unreliable report from one family camp or another that she had opened her eyes or that she was making "progress." She had already been moved from the North Fulton Hospital in Roswell to the ICU of Emory University Hospital in downtown Atlanta that housed state-of-the-art equipment, but her prognosis appeared bleak.

On the other side were wild media reports revealing that Bobbi had been declared "brain dead" and that the family had decided to take her off life support on February 11, the anniversary of her mother's death.

This was the last straw for Bobby Brown, who issued a terse statement through his attorney:

The false reports that continue to appear in print and on the Internet are egregious, false and will be dealt with at an appropriate time. In particular, the false reporting of TMZ, The National Enquirer, The Atlanta Journal Constitution and the Daily Mail (UK) citing police sources, family sources and Bobby Brown himself, will receive my attention. The desire to be 'first' has clouded the judgment of many reporters as they forgo accuracy. This is a criminal investigation and the integrity of that process requires silence.

One report that was most decidedly not a rumor concerned Brown's own family, who had assembled to throw him a party for his forty-sixth birthday on February 5 at the W hotel in midtown Atlanta.

The clan, some of whom lived in Atlanta, had been keeping Bobby company all week as he kept vigil at his daughter's bedside. Evidently, they were looking to unwind as they gathered at the upscale hotel. Exhausted from his ordeal, Bobby left the festivities around midnight. An hour later, 911 received a call that a brawl had broken out. "There is a group that's fighting at the bar and they won't leave," reported the caller. The caller said there were no weapons involved but that a member of the crowd had "used a glass at the bar as a weapon and cut somebody in the face." He said the fight involved eight to ten people. When police arrived, they discovered that Bobby's sister Tina Brown had hit her son Shayne over the head with a bottle. The dispute apparently started over a valet parking ticket. According to the police report, "Mr. Brown stated that while arguing with his mother, she spit in his face and hit him on his head with a glass bottle." Onlookers reported that Tina took a swing at her son when he called her a "crackhead." After declining to press charges, he drove himself to the emergency room, where he was treated for lacerations and given five stitches.

Ten years earlier, Shayne had been involved in another incident in Atlanta, when he and his cousin were stabbed during a fight at a bar around one thirty in the morning. Bobby Brown had reportedly been present when the incident occurred but was not involved in the altercation. These incidents, it turned out, were just the tip of the iceberg in the never-ending saga of the Brown family.

Two days after she assaulted her son, Tina was rushed to a hospital emergency room, complaining of numbness in her right side. She was diagnosed with a vascular blockage and irregular heartbeat.

"She's just overwhelmed by the stress of Bobbi's medical crisis," a family rep explained.

The day after the hotel brawl, Cissy arrived in Atlanta for the first time. For a week, members of the Houston and Brown family had visited Bobbi's ICU unit in groups of two or three, while Bobby stayed by her bedside much of the time. "He's so upset, he can barely put one foot in front of the other," reported one visitor who observed Bobby grieving at his daughter's bedside. But Cissy's arrival necessitated a new arrangement since there was no love lost between her and her former son-in-law whom she reportedly held at least partially responsible for her daughter's death even though she publicly denied it. A visitation schedule was now reportedly worked out that would ensure the two adversaries never had to cross paths.

It soon became apparent, however, that there was at least one thing Bobby and Cissy agreed on. Whether or not he had anything to do with Bobbi Kristina's state, Nick Gordon was bad news. The Houston and Brown families agreed to make common cause. The first order of business was to remove Gordon from the town house where he had lived the high life with Bobbi since 2013. Pat immediately made provisions to have the locks changed and notify security that Nick was to be barred from the complex. If he was spotted on or near the premises, they were to call police immediately.

As Bobbi lay comatose, doctors performed neurological scans three times a day, searching for signs of recovery—testing for brain activity, response to painful stimuli, or dilation of pupils. After the doctors debriefed Bobby, he shared the news with family members gathered in an outer room, but so far, there has been no good news to report.

So far, the Atlanta police had been tight-lipped about the results of their own investigation, but bits of information were beginning to leak out. *TMZ* reported that law enforcement officials believed drugs were involved in whatever circumstances led to Bobbi lying facedown in a bathtub. But during an initial search of the town house, they failed to find any drugs on the scene. That's because they were only looking for items that "were out in the open," the entertainment site reported. But during a second and more thorough search of the premises, police allegedly told the family they found illegal substances and seized a number of items.

Indeed, reports were starting to filter out that Bobbi and Nick had a long history of drug use so it wasn't a difficult stretch to assume that narcotics were involved.

As these kinds of reports came fast and furious, I was preparing to fly to Atlanta to start my own investigation, but first I needed to get the lay of the land and separate facts from rumors. My connections in the Houston camp were telling me that the hospital was nearly a fortress and that the family was keeping information very close to their vests. The most they could share at this point were unconfirmed rumors.

I was referred to a former Atlanta homicide detective who I was told could steer me in the right direction. When I made contact, he told me he would do some digging and get back to me. Forty-eight hours later, he shared his thoughts.

"This is an unusual situation," he explained, "because the victim is lying there unconscious in a hospital bed, which makes it very difficult for police to get what they need." He said the medical staff would have done a basic blood test when Bobbi arrived which would have determined whether there were drugs in her system and what kind. But there are limitations.

"What worries me is that the longer she lies there, it means her wounds are healing. If she eventually dies, it will be much more difficult for an autopsy to reveal what happened and to get to the bottom of the case."

He believes that if police are looking at a suspect and already have strong evidence, they or the district attorney may be waiting to see whether Bobbi dies to determine the charges.

"If she dies, they may be able to make homicide depending on the circumstances, but if she pulls through, the most they might have is a drug charge. It really makes a difference in a case like this."

Next, I made contact with a British reporter named Sharon Churcher, whom I've worked with before. She had been in Atlanta, covering the story since shortly after Bobbi was found. In this case, she's working for the *National Enquirer*, which may not have the best reputation in journalistic circles but, like the British tabloids, it has deep pockets and is willing to pay its sources when necessary.

Sure enough, Sharon managed to land an interview with the mother of Danyela Bradley, who was present at the house when Bobbi was found.

Holed up in an Atlanta hotel, Marlene Bradley told Churcher that she had been in touch with Danyela, who revealed some of what happened in the house that morning. Danyela was dating Max Lomas and had been staying at the house with Bobbi while Max and Nick were out all night partying. She claims Danyela told her that it was Max who dragged the body out of the bathtub. She told her mother, "It makes no sense. [Bobbi Kristina] was completely naked. She was in a tub of ice water. I can tell you she didn't put herself in the tub. No woman would take a bath in a tub of cold water. She would be dead if it were not for us. Max and I gave her CPR."

According to Marlene, "Danyela said to us, 'I want to tell you what happened but I can't tell you. It's so messed up.' She insinuated to us that she doesn't think it was an accident."

Danyela revealed that the police are looking at Lomas as a suspect because of his past, but she insists he "didn't do anything but save [Bobbi Kristina]." She claimed that Nick was the last person to see Bobbi alive.

Marlene also suggested that there might have been a sixth person at the house that morning besides Bobbi, Nick, Max, Danyela, and the cable installer.

She also revealed that her daughter shared stories about Bobbi's relationship with Nick. "Danyela heard Nick screaming and yelling. They fought constantly."

Finally, her daughter confided, "Krissi does all the drugs that Whitney did and more, including heroin. She uses anything that is put in front of her."

Marlene would not reveal where Danyela was staying since the incident but said that she remains "very upset." And very suspicious.

"From the way she's been talking, she believes Nick did something to [Bobbi Kristina] before she was found. I truly believe that she believes that Max is innocent, but we are worried that Danyela is trying to protect Max because she believes she is in love with him."

Indeed, it would appear that Marlene was aware of the kind of company that Danyela kept before the incident and was already very concerned about her association with Max Lomas, who is six years older.

Just over two weeks before Bobbi was found in the bathtub, Roswell police were dispatched to room 239 at the InTown Suites—an extended-stay hotel on Hembree Road—on suspicion that Lomas was forcibly confining Danyela.

In the police report of the incident, dated January 14, Officer M. Matthews wrote, "I was advised by Sgt Desrosiers that family members were worried about Danyela Bradley being held against her will by Maxwell Lomas, who was possibl[y] drugging her so she would not run away."

When police entered the apartment, they discovered Max, Danyela, and a friend, plus something in the air.

"When we approached the door I could smell a strong odor of fresh marijuana," Matthews reported.

After a search, Max Lomas was arrested for possession of a

firearm/knife, possession of marijuana with intent to distribute, and possession of the prescription drug Xanax. After Max was led away, another officer noticed a lump beneath the blanket on the bed.

"I moved the blanket back and revealed a Glock model 23 40-caliber handgun," wrote Officer Rooker. "I checked the gun for safety and found it to be loaded with a round in the chamber." Danyela informed him the gun belonged to Max. Rooker immediately called the precinct to obtain a search warrant for the premises.

Detectives Williams and Nagel arrived a little later with a signed warrant. They discovered "a large amount of marijuana under the bed and 1000s of Ziploc baggies commonly used to package marijuana. On the shelf of the nightstand was an electronic scale," the police report states. They also found a pill bottle containing "10 Xanax bars."

The other man found in the room with Max and Danyela was Duane Tyrone Hall, age twenty-four, who Danyela's mother told Sharon Churcher had been in the town house with Max, Nick, and Danyela when Bobbi was discovered in the bathtub.

Two days later, as Bobbi lay in a coma, Roswell police pulled over a gray Toyota Camry for a lane violation. When they searched the car, they found marijuana residue in the center console, though no charges were filed. The occupants of the vehicle happened to be Nick Gordon and Duane Tyrone Hall.

Meanwhile, it was reported that the police were anxious to interview Max Lomas again but that he was insisting on an immunity deal before he talked.

CHAPTER **FIVE**

By age fifteen, Whitney was juggling school and fashion shoots with regular weekend appearances onstage with her mother and even the occasional recording session. She had already graduated from Click to the much more prestigious Wilhelmina Models agency, and she was getting regular shoots modeling the preppy fashions of the time.

The sudden attention may have been going to her head, and occasionally her mother had to take her down a notch, like the time when she kept her offstage for two weeks to punish her for being "boastful."

Also when Whitney was fifteen, Cissy began a long artistic association with Luther Vandross, who would prove to be a significant influence on the young girl. Vandross was impressed by her unique voice and wanted to produce Whitney as a solo act, but Cissy thought it was too soon. "I wanted her to finish school first, because I knew if she got started in the business, there'd be no stopping her," she later explained.

A year later, she brought Nippy along to do background vocals for Chaka Khan's new album. Soon after, Whitney accompanied her mother to Tokyo, where she had been invited to participate in the Yamaha Popular Song Contest. It was an exciting life for a teenager. A little too exciting, Cissy thought.

Her sons were starting to get in trouble, and she blamed herself for not being around more. Gary had been hanging around with a bad crowd and had started using drugs, which would eventually derail a promising athletic career after he played a year in the NBA. Now, Michael was acting out, and as it turned out, he too had started dabbling in drugs.

Wanting her daughter to start living a normal life to keep her grounded, Cissy encouraged her to volunteer at the playground of a local community center, which soon led to a summer job as a camp counselor. And that's where she met Robyn.

Robyn Crawford was eighteen when sixteen-year-old Whitney arrived to volunteer at the East Orange Community Center, where she was working a summer job. The teenager introduced herself as "Whitney Elizabeth Houston." That's when she knew Whitney was special, she later recalled. Not too many people introduced themselves with their middle names. "She had peachy colored skin and she didn't look like anyone I'd ever met in East Orange, New Jersey," Robyn remembered.

For her part, Whitney remembers that when she befriended Robyn, the bullying she had endured from other girls came to an abrupt end.

"I didn't like to fight," she told *Ebony*. "I was not outspoken and really outgoing. Robyn was. They always wanted to whip me for no reason. So once Robyn became my big sister, all that ended."

If Whitney and Robyn hit it off from the moment they met, Cissy was not happy about their friendship and was not afraid to show it. "I had a bad feeling about that child from the first time I saw her," she later wrote. Cissy found Robyn an abrasive young woman who didn't hesitate to share what was on her mind. She was certainly a startling contrast to her sweet churchgoing daughter. "As I would later learn, she was also gay, although that had nothing to do [with] why I didn't like her," Cissy later revealed. Years later, Oprah Winfrey asked Cissy why she didn't like her daughter's friend. "She just spoke too disrespectful sometimes like she had something over Nippy, you know? I didn't like that at all," she told the talk show queen.

Robyn had just graduated from Clifford J. Scott High School, where she was an all-state basketball player. Before long, she would be offered a basketball scholarship to Monmouth University.

As Cissy watched her daughter's friendship with Robyn intensify, she fretted. "I didn't want her to lead my daughter to places that I didn't think were good for her," she recalled. In no uncertain terms, she told Robyn that she didn't want her around her daughter. "There wasn't much I could do though," she conceded. "Kids have a mind of their own. When they get older, they want to experiment with all kinds of things." Whether or not Cissy detected the possibility of a sexual relationship at that point, the other kids appeared to.

"It just seemed odd, these two girls always together," a community center regular told Whitney's biographer Jeffery Bowman. "They even started to look alike. It got to the point where you couldn't tell where one ended and the other began. They would walk arm-in-arm in public. It all seemed somewhat odd. When they were together, they'd act as if no one else was even in the room. They had their own world. People didn't understand it."

Eventually, the nature of the girls' relationship began to spark gossip among the girls who had once bullied Whitney.

"I remember one particularly nasty fight," a friend of Whitney from East Orange told Bowman. She continued:

Someone accused Whitney of being a "dyke." [The person said] she knew for a fact that she and Robyn were lovers. Whitney's eyes flashed with anger. "Oh you do, do you," she shot back. The next thing I knew, Whitney had this girl pinned up against the wall. She was all up in her face. "If I ever hear you spreading gossip about me, it'll be the last time you ever do," Whitney warned her. After word of that got around, it was just understood that you didn't mess with Whitney Houston.

The friend said Robyn was equally tough.

"There were counselors who would quickly walk the other way when Robyn came into a room just because they were afraid they would accidentally say the wrong thing, or imply the wrong thing. Basically, it got to the point where you just let Whitney and Robyn alone."

And whether or not Whitney was a lesbian, there is no question that Robyn was. At the time, according to Bowman, she had evidently reached a breaking point when she perceived that Whitney was trying to dodge the rumors. A friend told him that there was a showdown where Robyn confronted her friend. "Look, Whitney," she said, "if you can't handle the fact that people think we're lesbians, if that's so goddamned offensive to you, then fine, we just won't be friends anymore. See you round. It's been fun. Later."

Their brief separation broke Whitney's heart, recalled the friend. Eventually, she apologized to Robyn and promised that they would be friends no matter what anybody said.

Cissy believed that Whitney was drawn to Robyn's independence and her disregard for what other people thought. Did she have an inkling that the two might be more than just friends? "Nippy never shared details of her personal life with me about things like that," she reveals. "But I do know that Nippy and Robyn cared a lot about each other."

During those years, Cissy always rationalized Whitney's lack of interest in boys by the fact that she and John had strict rules governing their daughter.

"She didn't date young. I didn't allow it. Period." Cissy explained. "But she did go through a rebellious teenage phase, mostly small stuff. . . . She was lazy, stubborn and opinionated. When she was 16, I told her she wasn't going to make it to 17 because I was going to kill her."

It wasn't long after Whitney started hanging around Robyn that things reached a boiling point at home between John and Cissy. One day, as they were having a shouting match, Cissy recalled in her memoir, John threatened to walk right out the door. Watching the scene that had become a regular occurrence around the house, Whitney finally snapped. "Daddy, if you're going to leave then just *do* it!" she shouted in tears. "Just stop arguing and leave."

Soon after that, John finally moved out. A little while later, Whitney did the same. After graduating from St. Dominic's in 1981, she simply announced one day to her family that she was leaving. It wasn't so much the idea of her youngest child cutting the apron strings that upset Cissy, she later wrote. Instead, it was her decision to move in with Robyn.

"She knew how I felt about Robyn, but she was determined to live with her anyway," Cissy wrote. Resigned to Nippy's decision, she was determined not to lose her daughter completely. There was at least one thing about Robyn that she could respect. "We had our love for Nippy in common and though we rarely agreed, we were at least able to keep things from being too uncomfortable when we were all together." And even though they now lived only twenty minutes apart, Cissy was not welcome to visit Nippy at her new apartment. "She kept me at arm's length with regard to her personal life. I could feel her pulling away." They would still talk on the phone and see each other at gigs, but she missed Nippy terribly. Years later, Whitney would reveal that she missed her mother, too, and longed to pick up the phone and tell her.

Now that Whitney had graduated high school, she was finally free to pursue her passion. Now that John had moved out, he and Cissy got along much better and he would still drive her into Manhattan for gigs. John was especially excited about Whitney's potential and he was determined to see her make it big. Cissy was not so sure. She wanted her daughter to have a college education. "But her talent was not to be denied," she recalls. Together, they made the decision to hire a management company to ready her for stardom.

Tara Productions had been managing the career of Dionne Warwick, who asked them to take a look at her talented young cousin. Before long, Tara's head, Danny Gittelman, was bowled over by Whitney's four-octave voice and was determined to help guide her career path. He arranged acting and elocution lessons and shopping trips as far away as Boston and Providence for clothes that would sharpen her image.

When she was nineteen, Tara arranged for her first lead vocal on an album by the group Material, led by bassist Bill Laswell. She contributed a song called "Memories," which the *Village Voice* would call "one of the most gorgeous ballads you've ever heard."

A year later, she sang in a TV commercial for Canada Dry ginger ale dressed as a waitress. She was still modeling but she was beginning to hate it.

"Modeling was really degrading," she later recalled. "They were always on me, picking at my appearance. It was not a life that I wanted to live."

Believing she was finally ready for the spotlight, Tara arranged for Whitney to perform in a series of industry showcases. Gerry Griffith, an A&R rep for Arista Records, had been impressed by Whitney's voice for some time:

> I went to see one of our own artists that was performing at the Bottom Line in New York. And the head of promotions at my label, Richard Smith, and I were sitting at the same table and had no idea that Cissy Houston was being backed up by her son and daughter—her daughter obviously being Whitney. Three or four songs into the show, Whitney stepped out and she sang about two or three songs. Afterwards Richard said to me, "Man, you should really sign this girl!" and I was like, "She's really special, but she's awfully young and I just don't think she's ready."
>
> So one and a half years went by and I heard through the grapevine that she was being signed to Elektra. A friend of mine who is not even in the music industry called me and asked if I

knew who Whitney Houston was, and I said, "Yeah . . . why?"
He said, "Well, she's signing with Elektra," and I said, "Oh no!"
So I called Whitney's manager, Gene Harvey, and Gene said,
"Well, we're talking to them but we haven't signed yet, so why
don't you come down and see her at Seventh Avenue South this
weekend?" That's a club in New York. So that was the second
time I saw her perform. And I already knew the family, I knew
Cissy before then because I would always see her at her man-
ager's office.

She knew me and I knew her so it was an easy introduction.
And I was like, "Look, I really want to present Whitney to Clive
so let's see what happens," and she said, "Fine." So the next day I
went into Clive's office and said, "I'm going to showcase a great,
beautiful female artist for you and I need a budget." He had no
idea who she was. He said, "Fine, what do you need?" and I told
him and I put the showcase together. We rehearsed for roughly a
week, and showcased her for Clive and that's the way the whole
thing came about and that's why I say I didn't actually discover
her, but that I saw her in a club and the rest is history.

––––––

In 1983, Clive Davis was already a legend in the business with a
reputation for spotting talent. As head of Columbia Records in the
late sixties and early seventies, he had discovered Janis Joplin, Earth,
Wind & Fire, and Aerosmith, along with a host of other major acts.

In 1973, he was suddenly fired—reportedly because he charged
his son's bar mitzvah to his expense account. He maintained that the
alleged infraction was the fault of the label's head of artist relations,
who had been in "cahoots with a mobster" to doctor invoices and
generate kickbacks.

One of his earliest tasks as an executive at Columbia had him
incurring the wrath of Bob Dylan when he had to inform the icon
that he would have to remove the song "Talking John Birch Society

Blues" from his new album because it contained a potentially libelous line about John Birchers holding "Hitler views." Dylan went ballistic.

He had better luck with another of the label's acts, Janis Joplin, when he was preparing to offer her band, Big Brother and the Holding Company, its first record label. She was so grateful that she offered to sleep with him. Her manager, Albert Grossman, delivered the news when he arrived to sign the deal. "You know what Janis would really like to do?" announced Grossman. "She thinks it would be only fitting and proper that she ball you to cement the deal. That would be her way of showing this is a more meaningful relationship." Davis politely declined.

Once Joplin exploded onto the charts, Davis had the idea of playing one of her songs for Broadway legend Richard Rodgers, composer of *Oklahoma!* and *The Sound of Music*. When he played Rodgers Joplin's cover of "Summertime" from *Porgy and Bess*, the veteran composer was singularly unimpressed. "If this means I have to change my writing, or that the only way to write a Broadway musical is to write rock songs, then my career is over," he lamented.

Now, with his rock and roll days behind him, Davis had turned his sights to forging or reinventing the careers of artists like Dionne Warwick, Carly Simon, and Aretha Franklin.

He readily agreed to check out this new act; Griffith had assured him Whitney could hold her own with the assemblage of female talent that had become his forte. It didn't hurt that she came from an impressive musical pedigree.

Years later, he'd describe seeing Whitney sing for the first time to *People*.

"It was at a club called Sweetwater's in 1983. She was doing back up singing for her brother and mother Cissy, and then did two solo songs that were essentially her 'audition' for me," Davis recalled. "One of the solo songs? 'The Greatest Love of All,' which had previously been recorded by George Benson. To see this young 19-year-old find meaning in that song . . . she was bringing it to a whole other level that I had never heard before."

He called signing her a no-brainer. "I said, 'She will be for the next generation what Lena Horne was for her generation.'"

Arista wasn't the only company present that night to offer her a contract. In fact, Elektra had come in with a higher advance than Davis was offering. But Cissy was impressed by the amount they had set aside for promotion. John wanted to take the higher offer but he knew how Cissy's own career had stalled because of lack of promotion. In the end, neither Cissy nor John were the ones to decide with whom their daughter signed. Whitney was in charge of her own destiny and she just trusted Davis more than the others who had been courting her.

Years later, in a *Rolling Stone* interview, she recalled the events that led to her decision:

> *I did showcases and invited record-company people. People were interested in me from the time I was fifteen—it was kinda like they were just waiting for me to grow up. Everybody put their bids in. So I sat down with my managers and my parents, and I remember this long, drawn-out meeting. "What are you gonna do? Who are you going to go with?" I remember stopping the meeting and saying, "I gotta take a break." I went into another room and sat in a chair, and my mother came in after me and said, "You know, this is very difficult, but I'm going to tell you the truth: You should go where you are going to get the best out of it. Meaning, let's say a company offers you a contract, and they're saying: 'Whitney, you can choose the songs. You can produce the songs. You can do whatever the hell you want to do.' As opposed to Arista, with Clive Davis saying: "We'll give you this amount of money, and we'll sit down, and as far as the songs you want to do, I will help you. I will say: 'Whitney, this song has poten-*

tial. This song doesn't.' So my mother was saying to me, 'You're eighteen years old. You need guidance.' Clive was the person who guided me."

Arista executive Ken Levy recalled that Davis was extremely excited about his new discovery. "He talked about Whitney the way he talked about Janis Joplin. He was from the world of great singers. He's enchanted by powerful voices."

When the day finally came to put her name on the contract, Whitney arrived at the office dressed in a Levi's sweatshirt and jeans. Arista vice president Roy Lott recalled the occasion, describing her as a work in progress. "Just a regular kid," he said. "Not squeaky-clean, but a regular kid." Talent agent Ben Bernstein, who was tasked with arranging her promotional tour, told *Rolling Stone* that "Everyone would've been thrilled to sell a few hundred thousand albums."

Not long after she signed with Arista—just two weeks shy of her twentieth birthday—Whitney made her national television debut on *The Merv Griffin Show* alongside Clive Davis, who gushed about her natural charm. "You've either got it or you don't got it," he told Griffin before bringing out his new protégée. "She's got it." The influential talk show host revealed that he had accompanied Davis to the initial Sweetwater's showcase and had been equally bowled over by her talent.

Arista was determined to cultivate Whitney slowly rather than rush into the recording studio. Carefully nurturing her image, they arranged some television appearances including a spot singing with Jermaine Jackson on the soap opera *As the World Turns* and a cameo on the sitcom *Give Me a Break* with Nell Carter.

In 1984, Arista brought her into the studio to record a duet with Teddy Pendergrass on the song "Hold Me," which climbed to number five on the R&B charts.

As Arista carefully cultivated her image, Cissy was there every step of the way and she didn't hesitate to intervene if she didn't approve. When a designer was brought in to create a revealing wardrobe for Whitney's live appearances, her mother thought it made her look like a stripper.

"You can put all that crap back," she barked. "She is not shaking no butt, showing no skin, nothing like that!"

Arista had assembled a stable of their best songwriters and producers to produce the material they believed Whitney would turn to gold.

But even before she stepped into the studio, Whitney's onstage performances were beginning to generate media attention. "She is talented with tremendous potential," wrote the *New York Times*. *Billboard* magazine agreed, opining, "Whitney has the pedigree and the style to be a major vocalist." The *Village Voice* took notice of the growing buzz. "Sensational word-of-mouth has been going around about Whitney Houston. She has a big voice, the kind that makes you laugh and weep at the same time."

It was clear Clive Davis knew what he had in Whitney but he wasn't taking any chances. He had set aside an unprecedented $250,000 to produce her debut album, and he was determined to do it right.

Arista had recently signed Michael Jackson's brother Jermaine to the label. None of the other brothers had been particularly successful as a solo act but when the Jacksons announced that they would be uniting for the 1984 Victory Tour, the label wanted a Jermaine Jackson album ready to capitalize on the hype the tour was certain to generate.

The album would contain two duets. One featuring Jermaine and Michael on "Tell Me I'm Not Dreaming" and a second featuring Jermaine and Whitney on "Take Good Care of My Heart." When it was released in 1984, the album hit the top twenty, and Whitney had taken her first steps to conquering the charts.

But she was far from content to sing on other people's albums.

Whitney was growing impatient to record one of her own. Arista, however, had its own plans for their new find, and they were sticking to the strategy they had carved out from the beginning.

Whitney's manager, Gene Harvey, later recalled how he and Davis were determined to cultivate their plan carefully.

"It was a matter of searching for the right material and producers," Harvey told the *Los Angeles Times*. "It was Clive's philosophy and ours that we not push this girl out there right away. We decided to wait and do the best job that we could, and if it took a little longer, so be it. It was a matter of searching for the right material and producers."

It proved to be a smart strategy. While for decades black artists had been pigeonholed into R&B and soul, since 1981, there had been an important breakthrough led by artists such as Michael Jackson, Prince, Tina Turner, Lionel Richie, and other black musicians who had been dominating the *Billboard* charts and finally proving to executives and radio programmers that "black music" was an outdated concept.

"It worked out great," Harvey recalled, "because pop radio became more accepting of black music. As Whitney debuted, all the circumstances were there."

Whitney had come along just at the right time and Davis appeared to know what he was doing. They appeared to click from the beginning. Even Cissy was astounded at how much freedom the veteran executive gave her daughter to help choose the songs that were right for her. But Whitney was also impressed at how well she collaborated with this white Jewish guy in a suit.

"It's uncanny how much Clive and I think alike," she noted. "If he likes a song, it's almost 100 percent sure that I will too."

During the course of 1984, she worked on the album that Arista had scheduled to hit stores in 1985. In preparation for its release, they scheduled a promotional tour that saw Whitney flying all over the country to generate advance buzz. It was the longest she had ever been away from her family and she was desperately lonely.

But she was also excited at what lay ahead.

CHAPTER **SIX**

I had more than a little experience investigating the mysterious circumstances surrounding the fall of celebrities. For whatever it was worth, I had gained a reputation shedding light on the death of grunge icon Kurt Cobain and the downfall and eventual death of Michael Jackson. But in those cases, I had spent years establishing contacts, sifting through the minutiae of evidence, and piecing together the pieces of the puzzle that culminated in their final days and eventual demise. Now, time wasn't on my side.

I was determined to discover if possible what happened to Bobbi Kristina Brown before she woke up or passed away. I knew from experience that police were often hamstrung by the desire of their superiors to protect local celebrities. Sometimes they are starstruck—from frequently associating with the star in question at local functions—while other times they are simply determined not to let the image of their city be tarnished by having it associated with the sleaze and sordid circumstances that often surround the lifestyle of said celebrity. Years after I accused Seattle police of a rush to judgment in declaring Cobain's death an "open and shut case of suicide," the retired police chief, Norm Stamper, acknowledged that they had indeed failed to investigate other possibilities and said that if he was still chief, he would reopen the case.

Although I once had extensive contacts in Whitney Houston's camp—stemming from a brief collaboration with her father more than a decade ago—many of them had long since departed the scene, some following Whitney's death in 2012, most years before. Few could shed any light whatsoever on Bobbi Kristina, whom they had known only as a child. As I prepared for a trip to Atlanta, I alternated between mining my old contacts and establishing new ones in Georgia who could smooth the way for my investigation on the ground. I had an indirect tie to the Atlanta police—someone who first alerted me to the fact that the circumstances of the drowning were suspicious—and I had managed to glean some secondhand information about the state of the investigation in Roswell, but everything was still very sketchy.

Based in Miami, I have been fortunate in that this is the city where a number of Whitney's old camp have chosen to spend their winters. One of these figures is a British bodyguard who calls himself "Mugs," who had arranged security for a number of Whitney's appearances over the years. When we met for lunch in South Beach, he revealed that he was introduced to Whitney for the first time not in England but in Grosse Pointe, Michigan, where she was staying. They hit it off, and she eventually hired him to do security for a number of events, concerts, and private parties.

He claims that he met Nick Gordon only twice, once in Miami and once in Atlanta, but had no idea at the time who he was or what his association with Whitney was.

"He was weird, socially awkward," Mugs recalled. "He wore very expensive clothes but he seemed shy. He always had some food in his hand that he was munching on. I really didn't know what to make of him. I thought he was just there as a hanger-on. He was weird."

The burly bodyguard expressed regret that he didn't know Whitney during her golden years. When he encountered her for the first time, she was already "a wreck."

"Unfortunately she refused to get the right help," he said. "She had many demons that were going to destroy her life. I saw through that right away."

She was at her worst, he claimed, when he did security for three of her London concerts in spring 2010:

> *It was a comeback tour that turned out to be a career killer. She was in no shape to get onstage. I couldn't believe they let her onstage. It was so sad. I saw her backstage, I saw her at the hotel, I saw her at the arena rehearsing. It was sad. Whitney was drugged up. She didn't seem to know where she was. Michael Jackson had died a year earlier and I got to see him rehearsing during his final months in London at the same venue. To me, he truly seemed to be in better shape than Whitney. I didn't see it coming. After seeing her in that condition a year later, I felt sad, I knew Whitney didn't have much time left, she was going to join Michael soon. It was just so sad.*

On a number of occasions, I asked him about Bobbi Kristina, but each time, he looked like he was fighting back tears. The truth is, I was a bit taken aback to see someone who looked like him on the verge of crying. Finally, he composed himself and described her as the "sweet-est kid I ever met."

After Whitney died, he claimed Bobbi had no guidance and just lost control. He said the Bobbi of the last couple years had nothing to do with the sweet girl he first met when she was six. I tried to determine if he was basing this on recent media reports or if he has had contact with Bobbi since 2012, but he broke down and said he couldn't talk about her anymore.

Having also worked for Amy Winehouse, he said he finds it difficult to deal with the celebrity "madhouse."

"You get attached to them and they go off the deep end and you lose them. I can't deal with it anymore. It's too sad," he lamented.

———

One of my tennis partners told me he knows a club promoter, Jeffy T., who knew both Whitney and her daughter. We met for drinks.

Jeffy recalls meeting both Bobbi and Nick for the first time in Manhattan a few years ago at a downtown hip-hop event:

They were young, very shy. I thought they were brother and sister. Someone pointed Bobbi Kristina out to me and I said, "Damn, too cool." I was a big Bobby Brown fan growing up. He was my idol. I went over to them and started talking, you know, about small things, and about how big a fan I was of both her parents. They were really nice, down-to-earth but very shy. The next time I met them was during Grammy week [in 2014]. I noticed them walking down Melrose doing some shopping. I went up to them and said hi. Gordon looked different; he looked like a grown man, but rougher than the first time I saw him. I was worried when I saw Bobbi Kristina. She looked too thin. She didn't look happy. We exchanged pleasantries, and Nick told me things were good and that they were headed to Miami soon. I gave them my number and told them I'd hook them up there. I never heard from them again.

Neither meeting provided much insight, nor was I getting very far digging into the events that led to Bobbi Kristina's near drowning. But at least both these contacts had some association, however minute, with Whitney and her family. That's more than can be said for my neighbor, Eva Ritvo.

Eva is one of Miami's leading psychiatrists and a well-known author who is frequently featured on the *Today* show and even in the *New York Times* for her insights into "difficult" people. She has also treated a number of prominent celebrities. When I mentioned in passing what I was working on, she offered to provide a professional opinion that might give me some guidance in making sense of the events. I was a little skeptical, thinking that her analysis of someone she has never met might be akin to a séance or the predictions of a tarot reader, but I was open to hear what she had to say. One thing I had to admit when she issued her verdict days later was that she had clearly done her homework.

"When thinking about Bobbi Kristina it would seem that many factors contributed to her tragic accident," Ritvo began.

> First, there is the uncanny coincidence of her drowning in the bathtub just days before the three-year anniversary of her mother's death in the same way. More than one hundred years ago Freud coined the phrase repetition compulsion, a psychological phenomenon in which a person repeats a traumatic event or its circumstances over and over again. Next, there is the question of substance abuse. We know that a tendency to abuse drugs and alcohol is inherited and Bobbi Kristina had two parents with drug and alcohol problems. Moreover, she was exposed to their drug use during her childhood, also leading to an increased likelihood of her having similar difficulties.

> Bobbi Kristina also had to cope with the tremendous stress of growing up in the limelight. The pressure of constantly being watched and criticized by others is difficult on adults but even harder on children who tend to be more sensitive to the comments of others. [Her mother's] divorce is another stress this young woman endured at age thirteen. Adolescence is a difficult time for most children, and parents who are divorcing are often caught up in their own psychological turmoil and their parenting skills may decrease.

> Next, we have the depression from which she most likely suf-

fered. Her depression probably was increasing as the anniversary of Whitney's death was approaching. Mental health experts have shown that the impact of losing a mother has long-lasting implications. The earlier the loss, the more significant the impact. Depression is the most likely outcome and it is clear that Bobbi Kristina was depressed.

And lastly, she had been involved in a car accident four days before the near drowning. She may have suffered a head injury leading to a delayed concussion or bleed that contributed to her unresponsiveness. In 2013 she had a seizure followed by a loss of consciousness that might also be the cause of this tragic event. Bobbi Kristina had tremendous loss in her life: the early divorce, estrangement from her father, and the untimely death of her mother. Nick Gordon filled many roles for her. After Whitney's death, their relationship took on a new form and they became boyfriend and girlfriend and not surprisingly this created friction within Bobbi Kristina's extended family.

In addition to the family challenges and loss, Bobbie Kristina has lost multiple friends. Her best friend died of a heroin overdose in March 2014 and another friend died in August 2014 of a brain bleed following a car accident. These major losses undoubtedly impacted her and may have contributed to her having a death wish and a conscious or unconscious desire to join them. Her accident follows many losses from her inner circle.

Nick Gordon is reported to be a controlling figure in Bobbi Kristina's life. Both her father and grandmother expressed concern over Bobbi Kristina's choice to consider him as her husband.

I was especially interested in hearing her take on Bobbi's relationship with Nick. "What do you make of their apparent engagement so soon after Whitney's death?" I asked.

"It is highly unusual for a sibling-type relationship to turn romantic," she revealed. "Even non-siblings reared in close quarters such as a kibbutz in Israel show lower rates of marriage than would normally be expected. Familiarity may breed love but our genes intuitively know that cross-mixing our genes offers our offspring a better chance of survival and we are not attracted to family members."

Meanwhile, as Bobbi remained comatose back in Atlanta, new unconfirmed reports were dribbling out about the investigation.

Nick Gordon—undoubtedly on the advice of his lawyer—refused to talk to the police about the events of January 31. Now homeless and without the seemingly endless money supply he had become accustomed to from Bobbi's monthly allowance, he was clearly without the means to strike back against the endless negative media reports that were painting him as somehow responsible for his girlfriend's dire condition. Presumably, with sufficient resources, he would have hired a publicist to clean up his image. Instead, he turned to social media, which he and Bobbi had frequently used over the years to apprise the world of their relationship.

On February 1, the day after Bobbi was found, Nick had been photographed leaving North Fulton Hospital. It was also the day Bobby arrived from LA to be at his daughter's side. It appeared to be the last time Nick was allowed anywhere near the woman he still professed to be his wife. *Radar Online* reported that on that visit he had to be forcibly ejected from the premises. Their source didn't witness what started it but they heard a scuffle coming from inside Bobbi Kristina's unit. "About maybe two to three minutes later, [a family member] came back with [Nick] and they had their hands on him, like holding on to him, and you could see that everybody was distressed. Officers arrived on the scene and physically escorted him from the floor. The whole incident was very upsetting."

Although the report was unconfirmed, Nick started issuing increasingly desperate tweets aimed at Bobby Brown, pleading to be allowed by Bobbi's bedside:

"Real talk let her hear my voice she will wake up" [sic], *he tweeted in mid-February.*

"If anything happened to Krissi I wouldn't be able to handle it. I'm strong but not strong."

"Man to man I love your daughter . . ."

"I don't know why you won't let me see her . . ."

"Your daughter is going to hate you when she wakes up. It's not like you know her anyways [sic].*"*

"What's her favorite color? What's her favorite smell, movies, food. You don't know."

"Crazy how all the Browns came to the hospital when this went down," Gordon tweeted on February 23.

"I've been with her 24/7 watching over her and mom. Bobby left when it got heavy."

"I can't wait till she wakes up and dismiss all of the negative thoughts. There is a reason why her mom made me promise to look after her."

"I've been to the hospital bet you didn't know that with Tyler Perry my baby's lawyer and a couple of AUNTs," he tweeted on February 23, apparently referring to his February 1 visit prior to being ejected.

He also shared photos of a new tattoo bearing Bobbi's name along his forearm.

"Healing just fine like my baby," he posted with a photo of the tat.

Stepping up his offensive, he went on a further tirade against Brown, implying that money was Bobby's only motivation for his concern over Bobbi's welfare.

On February 21, Brown's lawyer finally responded to Nick's accusations, revealing that Gordon had been given an opportunity to visit Bobbi if he agreed first to tell her father what happened on the day his daughter was found. So far, Nick had refused to do so.

"Obviously Mr. Gordon is not as desperate to visit Bobbi Kristina as he wants the world to believe," Christopher Brown told the E! network. "At least not desperate enough to inform Bobby Brown, in writing, what happened to Bobbi Kristina."

In response, Nick's lawyers issued a statement:

"Mr. Brown is not law enforcement," his lawyers said. "However, in response to requests from law enforcement, Mr. Gordon and others have made statements. All Mr. Gordon wants from Mr. Brown is permission to see Bobbi Kristina. And again, Mr. Gordon is willing to meet privately with Mr. Brown to discuss this."

Most of the family remained tight-lipped about what they had been told by medical and law enforcement authorities. Presumably, Bobby had been apprised of their findings to date but he was not sharing information with anyone outside the family. That's why the public took notice when Bobby's sister Leolah Brown gave an interview to Atlanta's Fox 5 news—the first time a family member had spoken publicly about Bobbi.

Leolah, who had once worked as Whitney's assistant, was unequivocal, predicting that "Nick Gordon will 110 percent be charged" for a crime.

Asked by a reporter what evidence the police have against him, she responded, "I'm not going to comment on that but I believe Nick Gordon will be charged with this. I *hope* that he will be charged with this as well. Soon. I really do."

For the first time, Leolah also revealed that Bobbi's condition might not be as dire as had been reported to that point. The reporter pressed her about recent reports that the family was planning to take Bobbi off life support.

"There are so many signs showing us that she will be okay in spite of what people are saying over the Internet. Krissi is fine as I sit here before you today."

Asked if doctors had told the family she's improving, Leolah replied, "Yes ma'am . . . We know that she's opening her eyes. That's true, and there's a few more things that she's doing but Krissi is doing well right now. She is."

She also revealed that she suspected as far back as two years ago that harm might come to her niece and repeatedly tried to reach out to her "a couple of times," but her help was never well received.

"I saw this coming," she revealed. "I told Krissi not to trust anybody, and I meant that."

Her prediction that Nick would be charged caused a sensation, but Nick quickly reiterated on Twitter that he would be cleared of suspicion when Bobbi recovered.

"When she wakes up and tells the truth I wish I could see the look on your faces," he tweeted.

So far, the only reliable source to hear Nick's version of the events of January 31 appeared to be documentary producer Daphne Barak, who had befriended Bobbi and Nick while working on a production with them in 2012. CNN had reported that police were looking into bruises found on Bobbi's body when paramedics found her on January 31.

Barak revealed to TV host Nancy Grace that she had spoken on the phone with Nick, who told her that he explained the origins of those bruises to police.

"They asked him about injuries on the chest and he told them it was when he was doing the CPR," Barak told HLN's Nancy Grace. "She was very tiny. He was very frustrated to save her so it made sense to me," Barak added.

Barak said she believed that Nick and Bobbi were very much in love. "These two young people—he was everything for her, she was everything for him," she told Grace.

Soon afterward, another person stepped forward to publicly

defend Nick from the accusations swirling around him. Bobby's nephew Jerod Brown posted a tweet that Nick immediately retweeted on his account:

> *"I really felt if she was in danger she would've told me. She only spoke highly of @nickdgordon . . . never downed him only uplifted him #Facts."*

Still, if Nick had nothing to hide, Bobby Brown wasn't the only one to wonder aloud why he was refusing to give his version of events. The suspicion escalated when it was reported by the *Atlanta Journal Constitution* that Gordon's lawyer had filed a temporary restraining order in Fulton County Superior Court to prevent police from carrying out a search warrant for footage captured on his in-home security camera. The *Atlanta Journal Constitution* obtained documents showing that the restraining order also sought to keep the company that owns the surveillance system from complying with a police search warrant.

"The Search Warrant violates the Fourth Amendment in that it is overly broad and seeks private data 'without limitation,' and fails to narrowly limit the scope of the data sought by date or other characteristics," reads the filing.

"On February 12, 2015, Nest notified via email its customer, Nicholas Gordon . . . that it had received 'legal process' for data and documents related to the account and that it intended to comply."

Nick's lawyers protested, saying, "There is an insufficient link between the crime alleged in the search warrant, specifically 'possession of a controlled substance.'"

After a backlash resulted from Nick's apparent attempts to interfere with the police investigation, his lawyers announced that they were withdrawing their petition.

Employees from a Roswell strip mall and bank close to Bobbi's town house had already reported that police had confiscated footage from their surveillance cameras taken on the day Bobbi was discovered.

Nick again took to Twitter to address the backlash. *"I've talked to the cops no lawyer,"* Gordon tweeted. *"If Roswell Detectives know how to do there [sic] job everything is cool. #don't fabricate."*

To this point, the media reports were so unreliable and conflicting that most observers had no idea what to believe. Every day, it seemed, another theory was floated about what had happened on that January morning. Watching from my base in Miami, and trying to determine how to begin my own investigation, I was as confused as ever. But then I picked up *People*, which is pretty much the only reliable media outlet when it comes to celebrity reporting. The magazine is so meticulous about its fact-checking that it usually refuses to print unconfirmed rumors. The resulting coverage is therefore not as sensational or interesting as its counterparts but is rarely if ever wrong. Therefore, I immediately took notice when the weekly reported the results of its own investigation on February 21.

"Bobbi Kristina Brown was under the influence of drugs the morning she was found unresponsive in her bathtub, a source familiar with the details of the situation tells *PEOPLE*."

The magazine revealed that "multiple sources" who know Bobbi confirmed that she was a habitual user of heroin, cocaine, and Xanax in the months before her near drowning. She was also a heavy drinker.

"One of the sources who saw Brown regularly says she often appeared to be high, slurring her words and seeming incoherent," the account continued. A source told the magazine that Bobbi had been "in and out of rehab" since Whitney died. She was "distraught" over the upcoming third anniversary of her mother's death, which only served to "fuel her addiction."

"How thin she had gotten is an indicator," a friend told *People*. "This girl was trying hard, but she didn't have any support system. She was still dealing with a lot of grief over her mother."

CHAPTER **SEVEN**

The anticipation was excruciating. It had seemed like forever since she had signed her name on the Arista contract, and Whitney was itching for the album to finally be released. She wasn't the only one. A number of company insiders wondered why it was taking so long. But with Davis's track record, they trusted that he knew what he was doing.

Arista publicist Barbara Shelley was particularly impatient. She had shepherded Whitney on the West Coast leg of the promotional tour, where Whitney was showcased to radio and industry insiders prior to the album's release. The response was tremendous. But still, there was no sign of the album, and no word of when it would see the light of day. Both Davis and Harvey later rationalized the delay by saying that they wanted to make sure it was perfect. But Shelley revealed that there was a lot of second-guessing going on behind the scenes.

"So much care went into this album that it didn't seem like it would ever come out," she recalled. "When the album was completed, Clive was still having second thoughts. He was afraid that there were not enough hits to compete with Whitney's talents. He finally succumbed to the pressure of this personal decision. Should he keep this girl's talents under wraps any longer? Or, should he release an album that he knew was good, but was it good enough for Whitney's talent?"

She revealed that Harvey was calling Davis every day to discuss what Whitney should wear on the album cover and other minutiae.

While most albums have one producer, Davis had assembled a variety of talent to put together the kind of tracks he believed would best suit Whitney's voice and style.

Narada Michael Walden, who would later coproduce the soundtrack for *The Bodyguard*, had been laying down tracks on Aretha Franklin's new album, when he got a call from Gerry Griffith, asking to produce a song for Whitney. Walden had worked with Cissy years before and had first met Whitney when she was thirteen. But he had no idea what she was capable of. Griffith assured him it would be worth his while.

"He told me, 'You need to make time for her. She is going to be a major artist,' Walden recalled.

Once he told me that, I knew he was serious. So, I slowed down. When I first heard her open her mouth in New York on the song, I was like, "Yeah. She's bad." She was so confident. She came back in to where I was sitting to hear the playback of the song, and she was looking at me. She was real confident. She was looking at me, and I was looking at her. After that, we went out for a slice of pizza. She started talking about how her album was coming along and how she was doing. I had to be really careful that she didn't think I was hitting on her because she was so beautiful. I was married, but nevertheless, I didn't want her to think I was hitting on her, so we could become good friends, which we did. She was 20 years old at the time. You could tell that her mother really got her into vocal shape and that she listened to Aretha Franklin, Gladys Knight, and all the great ones before her. She took something from each of them, but she worked really

*hard to get her own sound. Her mother really passed the torch on
to her. Her mother, Cissy, was a genius.*

Finally, the moment was at hand. Whitney was giddy with excitement and also very nervous. On February 14, 1985, *Whitney Houston*
was officially released, though it had been shipped to stores the month
before and had already garnered some attention. And although Arista
had assumed it would rocket up the charts right out of the box, at
first, sales were disappointing. Had Davis lost his magic touch? Was
his new find all hype?

By March 30, the album had debuted on the *Billboard* 200 chart
but at an unimpressive 166.

Cissy attributed the slow start to the preponderance of ballads
that were meant to be a showcase for Whitney's unique voice. That,
she recalled, may be why the album failed to gain traction at first.

But if the album-buying public were slow to catch on, the critics
were bowled over.

Rolling Stone believed the songs themselves were mediocre and
"featureless" but described their singer as "one of the most exciting
new voices in years . . . her interpretive approach is what sets her
apart." Predicting that the artist is "en route to a big career," Whitney Houston, the review concluded, "is obviously headed for stardom, and if nothing else, her album is an exciting preview of coming
attractions."

Likewise, the *LA Times* reviewer was hardly enamored by the
track list, but he too was captivated by Whitney's voice. "Neither the
frequently listless arrangements nor the sometimes mediocre material
of this debut LP hides the fact that Houston is a singer with enormous
power and potential." The *New York Times* was impressed by both the
album and the singer. "Along with an appealing romantic innocence,
she projects the commanding dignity and elegance of someone far
more mature." Finally, the *Village Voice* savaged the songs themselves
as "schlock" but again singled out Whitney's "sweet, statuesque voice."

And just when it looked like Whitney's debut was going to fade away, something happened. First, the single "You Give Good Love" started getting radio play, and slowly but surely the album climbed the charts. By early summer, it had reached number one on the R&B charts. Then, by August, it had clawed its way to the top ten on the *Billboard* album chart. It was an auspicious debut for a twenty-one-year-old singer but not quite what Arista had expected, especially after the time and money the company had invested in their young phenom.

Whitney had hit the road to promote the album, but the venues were still relatively small. She received some increased exposure that summer when she toured as the opening act for Jeffrey Osborne, who had written one of the songs on her album.

When the Grammy nominations were announced, Whitney and her record were up for three honors but were conspicuously left out of the important category Best New Artist—a category that had been won over the years by such artists as the Beatles, Carly Simon, Bette Midler, and Natalie Cole, among other future superstars. On the other hand, some past winners had quickly fizzled, such as Bobbie Gentry, singer of the one-hit wonder "Ode to Billy Joe" and Taste of Honey, known only for their disco hit, "Boogie Oogie Oggie." Because of Whitney's recordings with Teddy Pendergrass and Jermaine Jackson the year before, it was ruled that she didn't fit the criteria as a "new" artist. Cissy was mildly annoyed at what she considered a snub, believing her daughter was being "punished" for nothing. But Clive Davis was furious. He wrote a letter of protest to the Academy, claiming that on the two 1984 recordings, "Whitney was simply an unknown vocalist making a 'cameo' appearance on just one of eight or nine songs contained in a major artist's album. She was not even a member of a continuing artistic duo. Whitney was merely a featured vocalist, not the artist, and certainly not the focal point of the song." However, Michael Greene, chairman of the Academy, was unbending.

"The rule that disqualified Whitney is perfectly clear," he wrote.

"It reads: 'An artist is not eligible in the best new artist category if the artist had label credit or album credit, even if not as a featured artist, in a previous awards' year.'"

To many observers, it appeared that Davis was simply stirring up controversy for the sake of publicity, especially since he made sure to release the correspondence to the media and penned his own commentary about the snub in *Billboard* magazine, which referenced some of the many honors that had been rolling in for months.

> *How is it that a recording artist can be voted Favorite New Female Artist by the readers of* Rolling Stone, *named Newcomer of the Year in music by* Entertainment Tonight, *Top New Artist by* Billboard *and not be considered a candidate for 'Best New Artist?' . . . It is a conspicuous injustice that Whitney will not be getting her shot. . . . When someone comes along and makes an impact such as Whitney has, it'll come as a big surprise to quite a few people that, according to the rules of NARAS, sometimes new isn't New.*

Whatever the case, his high-profile campaign appeared to work, because sales began picking up significantly in advance of the 1986 Grammy ceremony. It also didn't hurt when she won two American Music Awards in January 1986.

By the time Whitney stepped onto the stage to accept her only Grammy of the evening—for Best Female Pop Vocal Performance—on February 25, *Whitney Houston* had already sold two million copies and spawned three top-ten singles, including two number ones. Before her award was announced, she had delivered a live heartfelt rendition of one of those singles, "Saving All My Love for You." The musical royalty present that night loved it.

When the big moment arrived a little later in the evening, it seemed fitting that the presenter happened to be Whitney's cousin, Dionne Warwick, who did a little dance of excitement as she pulled the winner's name out of the envelope while her co-presenter, Julian Lennon, looked on.

As Whitney took the stage in a poofy red gown, she looked out at the audience as if fighting back tears and exclaimed, "Can you believe this?"

With a crucifix around her neck and her mother in the audience, she delivered what appeared to be an off-the-cuff speech, as if she hadn't been expecting the honor:

"First I must give thanks to God who makes it all possible for me. To my mommy and daddy, the two most important people in my life. My managers Gene, Seymour, and Steve. . . . To everybody at Arista. . . . Clive, you are the best. You are the best. Oh my goodness. I love you. God bless you. Thank you."

Album of the Year that night went to Phil Collins for *No Jacket Required*. Whitney failed to win in the other category for which she was nominated, Best Female R&B Vocal Performance, but appeared thrilled when the winner was announced as her Auntie Ree, Aretha Franklin.

By the time the ceremony was over, it was clear that Whitney was destined for the top. Sure enough, two weeks later, the album vaulted into the number one spot on the *Billboard* charts, completing its improbable rise fifty weeks after it was released. Only *Fleetwood Mac* a decade earlier had taken longer to reach number one, at fifty-eight weeks. And the best was yet to come.

By Grammy time, the album had already garnered three top-ten hits, but there was one particular song that had inadvertently not been released as a single. Clive Davis had heard Whitney sing "The Greatest Love of All" that night at Sweetwater's the first time he saw her. What struck him most about the performance was that he had originally commissioned the song for the soundtrack of the Muhammad Ali biopic, *The Greatest*. But for whatever reason, he argued against including the song on her debut album. It was, in fact, one of the few creative disagreements he had with Whitney during the recording process. Only after some persuasion by the song's composer, Michael Masser, and Whitney herself, did he agree to include it.

When the initial reviews came in, many critics singled out the song as one of the bright lights in an otherwise mediocre array of material. Singling out the song in his *New York Times* review, Stephen Holden noted that "Houston sings it with a forceful directness that gives its message of self-worth an astounding resonance and conviction" and called the song "a compelling assertion of spiritual devotion, black pride, and family loyalty, all at once." *Rolling Stone* also paid attention, writing that as the song builds, "Houston slowly pours on the soul, slips in some churchy phrasing, holds notes a little longer and shows off her glorious voice."

Still, Davis deliberately excluded it from the list of singles Arista chose to release in 1985. Only in April 1986, after the album had hit number one, did he consent to releasing it, but only as the B-side to the single "You Give Good Love." It was an auspicious decision. The song quickly became a radio staple, and it catapulted to number one on the *Billboard* charts, where it remained for three consecutive weeks. When Davis won accolades for his role in the creative process behind *Whitney Houston*, he never explained his reticence.

Although he hadn't let on, Davis had in fact initially been very anxious by the slow start of the album, on which to some extent he had staked his reputation. When it finally hit number one, it appeared that he had been vindicated.

By midyear, *Whitney Houston* had been certified as sextuple platinum, signifying sales of more than six million copies, and was the most successful debut album in music history. By that point—between March and June 1986—it had spent a total of fourteen non-consecutive weeks at number one on the *Billboard* charts, only one week less than the record held by Carole King's 1971 effort, *Tapestry*.

"Through all this, Whitney and I honestly couldn't believe how well things were going," Davis recalled in his 2013 memoir, *The*

Soundtrack of My Life. "Whatever success I'd had before, nothing was comparable to this. Whenever we would see each other, she knew what was on my mind and she would volunteer, 'I'm pinching myself!' And I knew she meant it."

As the album just kept on selling, Davis came to feel that they were simply "swept along by the momentum" and that the success of the album was just taking on a life of its own.

For her part, Whitney tried to heed Cissy's lifelong admonition against being boastful.

"You know, it gets to the point where the first couple of million you go, 'Oh, thank you, Jesus!,'" she told *Rolling* Stone about the album's phenomenal success. "I mean, let's face it, you make a record, you want people to buy your record—*period*. Anybody who tells you 'I'm makin' a record 'cause I want to be creative' is a fucking liar. They want to sell records. As it went on—and it went *on*—I took a very humble attitude. I was not going to say, 'Hey, I sold 13 million records—check that shit out.' My mother always told me, 'Before the fall goeth pride.'"

As the acclaim just kept pouring in and Whitney was heralded as a full-blown superstar, it was difficult not to let the success go to her head. She appeared riled that much of the positive media attention was focused on Davis's role in her discovery and the creative process. When *Rolling Stone* asked her if it bothered her to read that Davis was her Svengali, she confessed:

"Sometimes it did when critics would say that Clive told me what to do and how to do it, because that's all bullshit. I don't like it when they see me as this little person who doesn't know what to do with herself—like I have no idea what I want, like I'm just a puppet and Clive's got the strings. That's bullshit.

"That's demeaning to me," she continued, "because that ain't how it is, and it never was. And never will be. I wouldn't be with anybody who didn't respect my opinion. *Nobody* makes me do anything I don't want to do. You can't make me sing something I don't want to sing. That's not what makes me and Clive click."

Indeed, Davis was anxious to capitalize on her success and get her back into the studio to record a second album. In fact, he had been assembling material in consultation with Whitney before her debut album was released, but it stayed on the charts so long, they didn't want to do anything to jeopardize its run.

When things finally calmed down in fall 1986, Whitney headed back into the studio to start recording the follow-up to her successful debut. Narada Michael Walden, who mixed many of the tracks on *Whitney Houston*, recalled preparing to start on the second album:

"After a first album, most acts have a sophomore jinx, and I said to her, 'Are you nervous?' She said, 'No. If they loved me the first time, they'll love me now.' I was really taken aback by her confidence. But she was right."

The touring and promotion had been grueling, but her family stayed close and made sure she stayed grounded.

"I'm proud of the way she handles herself," her father told *People*. "When she's onstage she belongs to the audience . . . but 15 minutes after she's off, she's my kid again."

Whitney herself insisted that she wasn't letting the sudden fame change her. She credited Cissy for keeping her levelheaded and reminded people that this wasn't her first experience with the show-business lifestyle:

"We got to ride in limousines, fly from one place to another, the California thing, but Mom made sure it was something we were grateful for—an opportunity we had that others didn't," she recalled. And although she was enjoying her success, she appeared annoyed at being the new poster child for young black women.

"I'm not wild about people looking at me as a role model," Whitney said. "What I do have is a talent I got from God. I'm me. That's all."

Cissy never talked publicly about the troubles her two sons faced, but she expressed cautious optimism that Whitney would not succumb to the temptations of the celebrity lifestyle.

"There's so much mess out there—drugs and all that kind of business," she said. "But Whitney is very levelheaded, and I hope and pray . . ."

With the success of the album came money. A lot of it.

With her new wealth, Whitney decided to buy a house—a massive five-bedroom mansion in Mendham Township, about thirty miles west of New York City.

At $2.7 million, the new estate required at least three household staff to maintain. At first, Cissy was thrilled with the purchase. Her daughter was still living with Robyn at the apartment in Woodbridge, and the two were still inseparable when Whitney's schedule permitted, though Whitney was cagey when the media asked about her private life. In a 1986 *People* profile, she appears to have deliberately misled the reporter about her living arrangements.

"Her 'lavender apartment,' as she describes it, is just half an hour from her childhood home in East Orange, and her only roommate there is Misty Blue, a Turkish Angora cat. 'He's the only man in my life at the moment,' Houston says. 'I don't have the kind of time it takes to nurture a relationship the way I'd like to right now, and I'd never attempt to jump into one unless I had that time. Besides, I'd always be worried about what he was thinking when I was gone.' "

Cissy believed the new house would finally give her an excuse to move away from the human roommate that she knew had in fact been living with her daughter for more than four years. In fact, she thought the new house would be a place she could finally settle down and one day start a family. To her dismay, Nippy immediately invited Robyn to move in with her in Mendham Township, which was even farther away from East Orange than the Woodbridge apartment had been—a residence that Cissy had never visited.

It helped soothe her feelings when her daughter bought her a luxury condo at the same time.

Cissy admitted she didn't like Robyn—who nicknamed her "Cuda," short for Barracuda—any more than she had before but was resigned to letting her daughter make her own choices.

"Besides," she wrote, "I didn't hate Robyn; I was just concerned about what I perceived to be her influence on Nippy."

With Whitney's newly minted fame came newfound scrutiny from the public and the media. Arista publicist Kenneth Reynolds remembers the first time Robyn's relationship with Whitney came on the radar.

"Robyn was very much a protector, Whitney's guardian," Reynolds told *Vanity Fair*. "Whitney had gone on a promotional tour without Robyn in 1985. When she came back, we were going to the National Association of Black-Owned Broadcasters Convention, in Washington, D.C. [Whitney's manager] Eugene Harvey went to Arista and said the company should buy Crawford an airline ticket to the convention. 'Because Whitney missed her,'" Harvey told him.

"I got up and closed my door and I said, 'Gene, the airline ticket costs $79 for Robyn to fly to D.C. and stay in the room with Whitney. Don't make a big fuss about it at the company. All you need is a bunch of straight, macho radio jocks finding out that Whitney wants Robyn on the trip.'

"Anyway, pretty soon the whole building was buzzing about it." When Whitney arrived at the convention, he said, disc jockeys and program directors from across America were all buzzing about it, too. "And that was the big weekend when rumors about Whitney's sexuality started."

CHAPTER **EIGHT**

The circus was coming to town. After the initial frenzy following Bobbi's hospitalization on January 31, most of the media had packed up and left rather than enduring a seemingly endless waiting game with virtually no news filtering out of the hospital or police headquarters.

So when *TMZ* reported that the Brown family was filming a reality show, there weren't a lot of reporters around to verify the bizarre turn of events. A correspondent for the site's syndicated daily TV show announced on March 3 that some of Bobby Brown's family—though not Bobby himself—have been shooting a reality show. The show had allegedly been in the works before Bobbi's near drowning but with the family descending on Atlanta to visit her in the hospital, several members of the family had been talking about the ongoing tragedy on camera as it unfolded. While Brown continued his daily bedside vigil by his daughter's side, he was reported to have been unaware that his siblings Tina, Leolah, Tommy, and their kids were "setting up shots" to talk about what was going on with Bobbi. The show noted that Bobby's wife, Alicia Etheredge, was "livid" at the news.

Bobby's lawyer immediately issued a statement appearing to deny the report:

"There is no Brown family reality show that is in production which chronicles Bobby Brown, Bobbi Kristina or the medical emergency she presently faces at Emory Hospital," stated Chris Brown. But when asked whether other family members might be involved in such a production, he failed to close the door, simply noting that "extended family members are not my clients."

News that Bobby's brother and former manager, Tommy, was involved was particularly intriguing, because he was instrumental in the catastrophic reality show *Being Bobby Brown* that aired on Bravo in 2005 and inflicted significant damage to the public image of both Bobby and Whitney.

Meanwhile, it appeared that Nick Gordon was slowly going off the deep end. Still banned from Bobbi's bedside, he had launched a full-fledged rant against her father on February 23. Nick tweeted:

"I have to remain strong for me and REALbkBrown."
"Bobby seen his daughter 4 times in the last 5 yrs. Now him and his family want Whitneys $$$ which belongs to Krissi or Cissy."

He also accused the Browns of "death threats" against him.

Appearing to realize that his Twitter attacks against Bobbi's father were getting him nowhere, he finally softened his tone for the first time on March 2 and tried a different tactic. He tweeted:

"I forgive you @KingBobbyBrown much love I wish we could get together and deal with this as fam."

Then on March 3, the day before Bobbi Kristina's twenty-second birthday, he posted a tweet that caused considerable alarm:

"I'm so hurt I wanna do myself in. I know I have to [stay] strong."

Some observers interpreted his tone as a bid for sympathy; others posited that he sounded suicidal. He had appeared calm by the next day, when he posted a tweet marking Bobbi's twenty-second:

"Happy Birthday baby I wish I was there with you to hold you and be by your side."

But by then, Dr. Phil was already riding to the rescue. The day after Nick's emotional tweet, it was reported that his family had reached out to the pop psychologist Phil McGraw, who had made a name for himself with regular appearances on *Oprah* during the nineties. McGraw had come to Oprah's attention in 1995, when her show hired his legal consulting firm to prepare for the infamous Amarillo Texas Beef trial, in which she and her production company were sued by the beef industry because of disparaging comments she and a guest had made about beef during a mad cow scare.

His subsequent appearances on her show made him such a fixture that he was given his own TV show in 2002 in which he specializes in using his folksy pop psychology to discuss and address the problems of his guests, including celebrities.

In one of the most infamous and widely criticized events of his career, McGraw notoriously visited Britney Spears in her hospital room during one of her mental breakdowns, prompting her parents to accuse him of exploitation and a "betrayal" of their trust.

Now it was reported that the TV personality would be arriving in Atlanta to sit down with Nick and his mother to address his problems. Although the show had been known to pay for appearances, and many assumed the apparent stunt was a cash grab by Nick, a family "insider" explained that "Nick is under intense pressure and not being allowed to visit Bobbi in the hospital is just horrible. Dr. Phil will be conducting an interview with Nick, and he won't be paying for it."

Instead, McGraw was said to be "arranging ongoing mental health services for Nick" paid for by the show.

Almost immediately after hearing news of the bizarre turn of events, Bobby's sister Leolah condemned the idea and publicly urged Dr. Phil to reverse his decision. In an open letter posted on her Facebook page, she wrote:

Dr. Phil,

With all due respect,

Nick Gordon is under investigation for the attempted murder of my niece Bobbi Kristina Brown.

We have strong evidence of foul play. Until this investigation is completed by law enforcement, I would ask that you or anyone else not provide this individual a platform to spin this situation to his benefit.

If Nick Gordon does not have the courage to speak with my brother Bobby Brown and/or law enforcement about what happened the day my niece's body was found in a bathtub, he does not deserve to have a platform to speak to anyone of your caliber until this investigation is concluded.

Respectfully,

Leolah Brown

Later, she posted a follow-up in the same vein:

Nick Gordon is very disrespectful and inconsiderate! Especially to my family. Moreover, he has done things to my niece that I never thought he had it in him to do!

With the police still remaining tight-lipped about their investigation, Leolah's revelation that Nick was being investigated for "attempted murder" appeared significant. As a supposed family insider, she would presumably know what was going on at a time when the public was still being completely left in the dark. Two weeks earlier, she had revealed to a local station that she "hoped" Nick would be charged. Now she was suggesting that such a charge could be imminent and that there was actual "evidence" of "foul play."

But Bobby Brown's wife, Alicia, told *TMZ* that if you "put a microphone in front of Leolah, she'll talk about anything" and that "she has no facts at all about what's going on with Bobbi Kristina."

Moreover, it was revealed that Leolah had made the talk show rounds in 2012 claiming that Whitney was the victim of foul play. Jacky Jasper, of the blog *Hollywood Street King*, revealed a letter Leolah had sent him in 2012 when he asked for an interview:

> *Jacky, I have some information that will blow the roof off, but I need to get paid.*
>
> *If Pat [Houston] and them can get paid from* Star *and* Enquirer *magazines, so should I. I can prove Whitney was murdered—I know what really happened.*
>
> *I'm not going to do the interview with you, because I need to get some money for my story. Put me in contact with* Star *and* Enquirer, *they pay. That's the only way I'm talking.*

So much for the first significant clue that I thought would lead me in the direction of the truth. But it wasn't long before I finally found one more reliable.

CHAPTER **NINE**

If her first album had been slow to catch on, her second rocketed to the top at a dizzying speed. Released in June 1987, *Whitney* debuted at number one, the first time in history that a female recording artist had achieved that feat and only the fourth artist in total after Elton John, Stevie Wonder, and Bruce Springsteen. And when it stayed there for eleven consecutive weeks, it was obvious that the success of the first album was no fluke.

As with her debut, the critics weren't particularly bowled over. The *New York Times* complained that the songs were "formulaic," writing, "*Whitney* plays everything safe. It uses three of the debut album's producers. . . . There are bouncy, tinkly songs aimed at teenagers, and slow tunes aimed at sentimental adults, as before. Even the album title fits in with an Arista Records custom of separating female singers—*Dionne, Aretha, Carly*—from their last names." *Rolling Stone* also panned it, calling the album "smug, repressive and ridiculously safe. . . . The formula is more rigorously locked in than before, and the range so tightly circumscribed that Houston's potential seems to have shrunk rather than expanded." Again, most reviewers singled out Whitney's voice.

But if the press were lukewarm, the public had no such reservations. Not only did the album fly off the shelves from the outset, but after she hit the road on a sold-out concert tour, an astonishing four singles hit number one as well. Although she was the first female recording artist ever to achieve this feat, Michael Jackson's *Bad* had in fact scored five number ones. But when added to the streak from her debut, she had now achieved seven consecutive number ones. Neither Jackson nor the Beatles nor any other artist in music history had ever accomplished this milestone.

And suddenly Whitney was being mentioned in the same breath as those iconic artists, especially when *Forbes* revealed its list of the top-earning musicians of 1987. Whitney earned $44 million that year, just behind Madonna but ahead of her idol Michael Jackson, who earned a million less.

The media, however, wasn't yet ready to equate commercial success with greatness. There were complaints that the success had in fact been "manufactured," and once again Clive Davis was being given credit for the achievement.

Whitney, however, regularly bristled at such suggestions and was quick to set the record straight when it was suggested that her success was the result of a carefully cultivated image that *Time* credited to Arista's "Svengali strategies."

"They didn't have to make me over," she countered. "There would be no *Whitney Houston* without Whitney Houston."

As Whitney hit the road, the press couldn't help notice the striking woman who was always at her side. Robyn had been put on the payroll as her executive assistant as far back as 1985 when she gave up a basketball scholarship at Monmouth University and dropped out to be with Whitney. In fact, the liner notes on *Whitney Houston* included her friend in the acknowledgments. "Robyn, what an assistant! I love you and I guess all you need to do is stay in my life, Nip." On her new album, her name appears in the notes once again. "Robyn, you are my friend and you are also quite an assistant. Be strong, for you are a child of the almighty God and you walk in his love and in his light. I love you, Whitney."

In his 1987 profile "The Prom Queen of Soul," Richard Corliss of *Time* was the first reporter to take note of Robyn and the widely circulated rumors—what he calls the "tattle mill" that she and Whitney were more than just friends. Describing her as "tall, slim and severely handsome," he notes that the two shared an apartment and quotes Whitney calling her "the sister I never had."

Robyn dismissed the rumors, telling Corliss, "I tell my family, 'You can hear anything on the streets, but if you don't hear it from me, it's not true.' "

For her part, Whitney appeared to issue a non-denial denial:

"My mother taught me that when you stand in the truth and someone tells a lie about you, don't fight it," she told Corliss. "I'm not with any man. I'm not in love. People see Robyn with me, and they draw their own conclusions. Anyway, whose business is it if you're gay or like dogs? What others do shouldn't matter. Let people talk. It doesn't bother me because I know I'm not gay. I don't care."

The surprising mention of lesbian rumors in a magazine as prestigious as *Time*—not, after all, known as a gossip rag—appeared to signal to the mainstream media that it was okay to broach the subject of Whitney's sexuality, although some reports suggested that the Arista publicity machine was anxious to give Whitney a chance to douse the rumors for fear they would hurt record sales and encouraged other publications to bring it up.

In a 1987 cover story, for example, *Us* magazine brought up the subject with Whitney and her mother. Whitney began by downplaying the glamour of her new success: "I really do ordinary things with my life," she said. "I eat, sing, sleep, play tennis, play with my cats. Being alone is very important to me but when I'm with my friends I laugh, joke, fool around, act normal."

When pressed about stories circulating about her personal life, she said, "Why should people know everything? There have to be surprises."

Interviewed for the same article, Cissy was anxious to talk about the people who were out to "bruise" her daughter by spreading false stories about her.

"I tell her, 'If you're on a firm foundation, no one can destroy you whatever they say. She knows that and I think she's learning that you cannot even give credence to those things that are not true by talking about them."

She shared her belief that some of the talk still bothered her daughter but advised her not to "pay attention to that crap."

Cissy then assured the reporter that "Whitney does want to get married and have babies. It's just a matter of finding the right time and the right person. She's got to find someone who loves her for herself, not for her money or anything."

Whitney had never before publicly talked about dating men. Suddenly, after the *Time* article, she went out of her way to paint herself as a nice heterosexual girl.

"I've had boyfriends all my life—very good-looking and very fine young men," she told *Ebony*. "And I've had great relationships. But I've never been one to have five relationships at the same time. I get no enjoyment out of that. You know, I was raised as a Christian, and my mother was very strict with me as far as boys were concerned. She told me that the way to a man's heart is not by opening your legs. You let him get to know you first.

"All that stuff has stayed with me, and it has worked for me, because it has allowed me to know that this is mine!" she said, pointing at her body. "It is better to preserve yourself because nobody likes anything that's old and worn out."

As the question of her relationship with Robyn became a regular staple of media interviews, she became adept at addressing the rumors with nonchalance.

"Robyn is my oldest and dearest friend," she told *Essence*. "People used to say we were gay when we went in East Orange because when you saw Robyn you saw me, and when you saw me you saw Robyn. We were that tight, you know? So this thing has kind of followed us. And half the time we'd say, 'Fuck it, if they think we're gay, let 'em think we're gay.'"

———

Eddie Murphy and Whitney Houston had something in common. Like Whitney, the gay rumors about Eddie had been circulating for years, ever since the former *Saturday Night Live* comic burst onto the Hollywood scene in the early eighties. It was whispered he had a penchant for transvestites, a rumor that later exploded into the public consciousness in 1997 when Murphy was pulled over by police on Santa Monica Boulevard with a transvestite prostitute. But in the late eighties it was still just gossip making its way around town and threatening to derail a successful career.

Suddenly, around 1988, Whitney was being photographed with Murphy at a number of events and gave interviews where she suggested they were together. In one profile for *Ebony*, she showed off a 5.5 karat diamond ring that she claimed had been given to her by Murphy.

Explaining that Arsenio Hall had introduced her to the actor three years earlier, she revealed, "We've been dating ever since."

"I can recall going to a party years ago at Bubble Hill, which was Eddie's estate in New Jersey and Whitney was there as his date, girlfriend, whatever," recalls talk show host Wendy Williams in a documentary about Whitney, scrunching up her nose in sarcasm. "I just don't think that was a real relationship."

"Bear in mind we're not talking about 2012 where gay marriages are becoming legal pretty much around the world. This was not a time when you could be out and proud in Hollywood and have much of a career," explains NBC entertainment correspondent Ashley Pearson in the documentary.

In 2014, Murphy finally came clean. "I was never dating Whitney," he revealed. "She was a friend of mine. I may have gone to dinner with her a few times, but it was never like we were dating—we were never boyfriend and girlfriend. We were very friendly acquaintances. She was a beautiful person. I hear a lot of people talking about her sense of humor, and she really did have a great sense of humor. She was a funny girl."

And the Arista publicity machine was working overtime to ensure that reporters knew that she was hanging out with Murphy. Although the tabloids still trumpeted the lesbian rumors, there was a distinct change in tone in the mainstream celebrity press. Eddie Murphy was frequently mentioned in the celebrity profiles during this period, which sometimes saw Whitney on the cover of three magazines in the same month. And when the public appeared to have a hard time swallowing the reports of Whitney and Eddie together, suddenly she was linked to the football star Randall Cunningham and hanging around his NFL team the Philadelphia Eagles. Before long, hundreds of media accounts reported that the two were dating. Others suggested that Cunningham and Murphy were just a few of her many suitors but that she had in fact previously been engaged to Jermaine Jackson, who worked with her on her debut album. After Whitney's death, a *New York Post* entertainment reporter revealed that Whitney once told him she was dating "the brother of a big star," obviously referring to Michael Jackson and, by implication, Jermaine. And yet when Whitney walked the red carpet at the whirlwind of awards ceremonies and events where she was constantly photographed, she never brought a date. Instead, she would usually arrive on the arm of her father, her brother Michael, or Clive Davis.

Still, the rumors about Robyn had for a time been successfully supplanted by articles with such headlines as "Whitney and the Men in Her Life."

New York talent-management consultant Michelle Callahan describes the way image consultants handle such matters.

"I can imagine that if she were going to consult anybody about that if it were true, that they would advise her you don't have to say anything about it which again would be another thing to have to hold inside. We're trying to sell records not you, not the real you, the image of you," she says.

Whitney herself was often outspoken on how her image was distorted.

"It's really strange," she told *Rolling Stone*. "Michael Jackson said it best: You become this personality instead of a person. That's what's strange about this image business—the more popular you become, the weirder they want to make you. I read some stuff about myself in the last year—it's like 'Who the fuck are they talking about?' . . . But the media always distorts shit. It's never, never what I said; it's never how I said it; it's never how I thought that person perceived me. It's always some other crazy shit—which is why I don't like doing interviews. Because they lie. They just outright lie."

Like it or not, however, Whitney went along with the time-tested if distasteful process that plays an integral part in the molding of any celebrity, let alone one who was rapidly catapulting into the ranks of megastardom.

"Once in a blue moon, a new artist emerges who simply *takes over*, in utterly decisive and undeniable fashion," trumpeted *Billboard*, to explain the phenomenon that Whitney had become.

For her industry handlers, there were hundreds of millions of dollars at stake. For her family, there were new houses, cars, trips on private planes, red carpet events, and the glamour and excitement that come with traveling in the court of music royalty.

It was a lot of pressure for a twenty-three-year-old to handle, and it was taking an enormous toll.

As she catapulted to superstardom, Whitney liked to profess that she wasn't succumbing to the celebrity lifestyle or letting fame get to her.

"It hasn't changed my life," she insisted to one reporter. "I'm just busier than I've ever been in my life. I'm basically the same. I still think the same as I did before 'Whitney Houston' came about. I think the same and I still have the same values."

She made it a point to let it be known that she had no intention of moving to Los Angeles or Manhattan to live the glamorous life associated with celebrity. Instead, she was intent to stay close to home in New Jersey and experience a "normal" life. This, she explained, would help keep her grounded.

"I'm able to go out," she told USA Today about her decision to resist a move to LA. "I can go to the mall. People don't bombard me. It's important to me to be human. Everybody thinks I'm a superstar, but I know the real deal."

She was fond of stressing how her upbringing and Christian values helped her resist "temptations." In later years, when Whitney's drug use became common knowledge, pundits and fans liked to believe it was Bobby Brown who led her astray. But there is a mountain of evidence that shows that with fame and success also came her first foray into drugs long before she met Brown.

Cissy had long known that her sons Michael and Gary had a drug problem. But she refused to believe that Whitney could ever fall into that trap even after she read an interview in which her daughter talked about her "partying." So she claims it came as a shock when none other than Robyn Crawford came to her one day and expressed concern that Whitney was using drugs. Robyn admitted that they often used together but that "Nippy likes it a little too much." Soon after, Cissy recalls in her memoir, she approached Whitney to ask about her drug use. Her daughter's response? "Oh Mommy. You don't need to worry about that," she said, claiming that Robyn was "overreacting."

She reveals that John later told her that he, too, was worried about his daughter during this time. And even though he knew about his sons' problems, he told a family friend that it was Whitney he was most worried about.

Years later, Michael Houston admitted that it was he who first introduced Whitney to cocaine. "I think probably the first time we ever, she ever did it was probably, you know—but you gotta understand, at the time, the eighties, it was acceptable," he told Oprah Winfrey in 2013. "In the entertainment industry it was just like, available. It wasn't like a bad word like it is now. You know what I'm saying? We didn't know. We just didn't know."

And yet there's no indication that her drug use ever rose to the level of abuse during this period. Nor is there any evidence that her professions about leading a normal life were simply a disingenuous attempt to mold a wholesome image for public consumption.

In the thousands of articles and profiles written about her during her rise to fame, there is a surprisingly distinct dearth of references to the word *diva*—a word that would frequently be leveled at her a decade later.

My first and only encounter with Whitney Houston came in the summer of 1988, when I was living in London. At the time, I was a musician and frequently collaborated with a South African man named Robert Sithole, who was living in political exile in the UK. Sithole had the distinction of being one of the world's greatest pennywhistle players. Whitney was in town to perform at Nelson Mandela's seventieth birthday party concert at Wembley Stadium. That week, Whitney showed up at a party hosted by an antiapartheid group where Robert and I were performing. After our set, Whitney came over to tell Robert how she was blown away by his playing. She had never before seen a pennywhistle, and he gave her a quick lesson, letting her try it out. She said something about how she loved the sound, and it was too bad it wouldn't fit in with her music. I didn't have much interaction with her other than small talk, but I was struck at how gracious she was to everybody present that evening. I remember thinking she was a class act. If I didn't know who she was, I would never have guessed she was one of the world's most famous celebrities, then at the peak of her success. She was with a small entourage, but I have no idea if Robyn was with her that night, because I had no clue who she was at the time.

Indeed, after all the drama that came later, it is easy to forget that Whitney used her sudden success and fame to dedicate herself to some of the causes that she held dear. In 1988, she launched the Whitney Houston Foundation for Children. And unlike many celebrities who turn to philanthropy to burnish their public image, it was clear from the outset that Whitney was passionate about the cause. The foundation's mission was to improve the lives of homeless children and kids suffering from HIV or cancer. She raised millions for the cause and traveled tirelessly to promote the foundation's mission. But more importantly, she became one of a small array of celebrities who helped raise public awareness around HIV issues during the peak of the AIDS crisis. Her own passion for the issue reportedly stemmed from the death of a male friend from the disease during the eighties. It was a subject rarely discussed in the black community, making her voice all the more important. Acting as the foundation's president, Cissy also did important humanitarian work during this period.

In addition, Whitney performed countless benefits and raised money for a number of organizations close to her heart, including the NAACP and the United Negro College Fund. She was a steadfast and outspoken opponent of apartheid and refused to do any business with any company with ties to South Africa.

At a time when her handlers were clearly nervous about the rumors about her sexuality, Whitney also sang at numerous benefits to raise money for organizations battling AIDS, including Gay Men's Health Crisis.

"Sadly, there is a stigma associated with people afflicted with AIDS," she said at the 1991 Reach Out and Touch UK HIV/AIDS Vigil in Hyde Park. "Even as we speak, it is sweeping away our children, our families, our loved ones. Our world must continue through research to work towards finding a cure."

It is likely that it was this high-profile advocacy rather than her purported lesbianism that made her a darling of the gay community throughout her career. Aside from my own encounter, I am struck by the fact that virtually everybody I have spoken to who met or was close to Whitney used words like *sweet, warm, generous, humble,* and *giving* to describe the Whitney Houston of the eighties and early nineties.

And for those who knew her and experienced her magnanimous spirit during those golden years of her career, it made what happened next all the more tragic.

―――――

Whitney's work with the foundation—and the fact that she simply needed a break after the whirlwind of the last few years—was one of the reasons almost three years would go by between the release of her second album and the time she hit the studio to release the follow-up album, *I'm Your Baby Tonight*, which would not see the light of day until late 1990.

During the interval, those around her could sense a backlash brewing that threatened to derail her status as the world's most successful female recording artist.

Cissy claims she had sensed trouble as early as 1986, when MTV started playing her videos in regular rotation—unusual at that time for a black female artist—and that her wide exposure on the network signified to some people that her music wasn't "black enough."

On the first season of the Wayans brothers' satirical comedy TV series *In Living Color,* Kim Wayans would parody Whitney's pop ballad–heavy album *I'm Your Baby Tonight* in a way that some observers interpreted as implying that she had no rhythm and therefore is too white.

"Whitney was never trying to be white," writes Cissy. "She just wanted to sing, to share her God-given talent and be herself. If they didn't like it that she didn't take off her clothes and shake her ass and all that mess, well—that was their problem."

Occasionally, Whitney herself brought up the subject in a defensive manner. "Sometimes it gets down to that, you know?" she complained to Katie Couric on the *Today* show. "You're not black enough for them. I don't know. You're not R&B enough. You're very pop. The white audience has taken you away from them."

Speaking to *USA Today*, she again referenced the supposed criticisms: "I would think that black people would be proud," she says. "I don't sing music thinking this is black, or this is white. I just sing songs that I think and hope everybody is going to like."

And yet it was rare that the interviewers themselves broached the subject of whether Whitney was sounding too white. There was just one subject that still seemed to be on everybody's mind, despite all the publicity about the various men she was allegedly dating.

In an appearance on the TV series *Ebony Showcase* in 1999, the interviewer told Whitney that she recently did a radio call-in show in Detroit. She claimed that thirty calls came in that day and everybody wanted to know "Is Whitney gay or not?"

"Whitney is not gay. That is the story about that," the singer responded emphatically. "I'm particular, that's all. I'd rather wait you know instead of spreading myself too thin. I don't know why people think that you have to be running around with every Tom, Dick or Harry there is. I was not raised that way. I just wasn't. Nobody in my family was. That is the basis for that but (exasperated sigh) Whitney is not gay. The only gayness I feel is when I'm happy honey. That's it. That's all that matters."

On April 13, 1989, Whitney attended the third annual Soul Train Music Awards at LA's Shrine Auditorium, where she was nominated for Best R&B Urban Contemporary single for her song "Where Do Broken Hearts Go"—the fourth single from her second album. The year before, at the same ceremony, she had won the award for Best

Album–Female and lost Best Music Video to Janet Jackson, but this time she was up against Karyn White, Anita Baker, and Vanessa Williams for only one award on a night when Baker was heavily favored to sweep the evening for her acclaimed 1988 release, *Giving You the Best That I Got*.

She had been well received at these awards on two previous occasions. But when the nominations were called out in her category and Whitney's name was mentioned, a smattering of boos rang out among the crowd, which consisted of a who's who of black music industry heavyweights. Robyn sat beside her as she endured the indignity. It was even later claimed that the Pointer Sisters were among those booing their peer and that the words *oreo* and *whitey* were flung from the balcony but no such contemporary account exists. Although that night would later mark a much more significant milestone in Whitney's life, the booing would be widely cited as evidence that there was a growing backlash among African Americans against Whitney because of the perception that she was "too white." The incident failed to garner much mention at the time, but when her third album was released and its sales lagged far behind her first two, some would look back to that night as evidence that she was perceived as a sellout by some. In a May 1991 profile, *Ebony* would later reference the booing, noting, "Black disk jockeys have chided her for not having soul."

Leona Price, a radio syndication rep, was in attendance at the Shrine Auditorium that evening, and she has a different take on what went down than the conventional narrative:

> First of all, it's simply not true that the crowd booed her that evening. It would be accurate to say that there were some boos but much more cheering than booing, the cheers were louder. I can't speak for those people but I think it's bullshit to say that they were booing because she was too white or wasn't black enough or whatever, as people have said. That simply wasn't the attitude

of the black community at that time. You had Whitney being this major force; she was as big as Elvis or the Beatles and her success was this point of pride for the community. If you remember, Michael Jackson actually lightened his skin to look whiter for Chrissake and even then the black community didn't turn against him or accuse him of selling out. Maybe later with the pedophile stuff but that was a different thing. So why would they turn against Whitney just because some people perceived she didn't have enough soul or whatever it was? No, if anything bothered people it was the whole lesbian thing. That is something that definitely had some people turned off. I think a lot of people didn't believe the talk but a lot certainly did. I remember you'd have men making these crude jokes about her and "carpet munching"; things like that and they'd be sniggering. And the women also talked about it in a negative light. Not everybody but it was there. You'd hear it in the beauty shops and salons for sure, people would talk and gossip. I think if people were talking about her being not black enough, that was code for her being gay. It definitely hurt her but she was still being played on black radio so there was an audience no matter what.

Was African-American homophobia genuinely a factor in the so-called backlash?

In 2008, author Terrance Dean penned a memoir, *Hiding in Hip Hop: On the Down Low in the Entertainment Industry—from Music to Hollywood*, detailing his encounters with closeted gay men in the music and film industries. Dean, who is black, possessed the credentials and credibility, having worked for more than a decade with industry heavyweights such as Spike Lee, Rob Reiner, Keenan Ivory Wayans, and Anjelica Huston, and with production companies ranging from Paramount to Warner Bros. and Sony Pictures. He reveals that a wide range of very prominent figures from hip-hop moguls to rappers, actors to musicians, are hiding in the Hollywood closet and that industry insiders go out of their way to hide these secrets for fear of jeopardizing their profits.

Dean is particularly eloquent on the subject of homophobia in the black community and its effect on closeted African-American stars. He argues that it is far riskier for black celebrities to come out than white stars. Interviewed by *Time* soon after the book's release, he pointed to some concrete examples.

I think for whites it has been more accepting because you look at the presence of Ellen DeGeneres, Rosie O'Donnell, Melissa Etheridge, they've all been accepted. When they came out, the community rallied behind them and encouraged them, and they were empowered. Unfortunately in the black community it seems that if you come out, you risk jeopardizing your career because we do not discuss sex or sexuality in our community. It's seen as taboo. The more masculine you present yourself, then we will love you, accept you, praise you. The more effeminate you are, we tend to shy away because we don't want to be seen with you, we don't want to be guilty by association. Even if [a person] is not gay, but because a friend is, that person will stop associating with them because they don't want people to think that's what they do.

A year later I would discover poignant evidence of this phenomenon—a discovery that would shed important insight on the life and career of Whitney Houston.

CHAPTER **TEN**

Who needs to turn on a TV set to watch the reality show allegedly being produced by the Brown family? As the clan gathers in Atlanta to offer support to Bobby in his time of anguish, the ongoing antics of his extended family are presenting their own real-time reality show right before our very eyes.

Before the spectacle of Leolah Brown's unsubstantiated accusation against Nick Gordon about his Dr. Phil appearance could dissipate, along comes her nephew Jerod Brown, suggesting that the police are barking up the wrong tree, looking at Gordon—a mere appendage of Whitney's family—as a suspect. Instead, they should be looking at actual honest-to-goodness relatives.

In a March 9 post on his Facebook page, he levels an astonishing charge against Whitney's sister-in-law Pat Houston, who has acted as executor of the late singer's estate since her 2012 death in a Los Angeles hotel bathtub that the coroner had ruled was caused by drowning, with heart disease and cocaine use as contributing factors:

> *Auntie Whitney was murdered not drowned. That's a fact. Now the whole bathroom plot shows up again w/Bobbi Kristina's situation. C'mon are you people that bold to perform this act again*

on my family? And the public believes whatever these people put in their faces, I mean it is convincing if you're not on the inside. However, I will let it be known Kristina has always had suspicion about Pat Houston. Soon evidence will be handed over to assist this investigation.

As the ridicule poured in about this apparently baseless conspiracy theory, Jerod took to Facebook again to preempt a predicted attempt by his uncle to shut him up by referencing some of the conspiracy theories leveled by Michael Jackson's sister after his 2009 death:

La Toya Jackson was considered crazy for standing for her brother (Michael) because she knew the truth. I will not stand down anymore. My bloodline is on the line and we no longer will be hush hush! I know people got jobs on the line, and some are afraid to speak up, and my uncle Bobby might even put another statement on me about remaining quiet, But somebody will pay for the death of auntie Whitney. Kristina is UNTOUCHABLE! THIS ISNT THE FIRST TIME THIS ACT WAS ATTEMPTED. BUT THIS WILL BE THE LAST TIME! THEY MIGHT COME FOR ME BUT SOMEONE HAS TO STAND FOR WHATS RIGHT. THIS ISNT ABOUT MONEY, FAME, OR ATTENTION . . . THIS IS ABOUT MY FAMILY. BOBBI KRISTINA WILL PULL THROUGH BECAUSE SHES A CHILD OF GOD. SO WITH THAT SAID CONTINUE TO #PRAYFORBK AS WE NOW FIGHT FOR #TrueJusticeForWhitney

A few hours later, after being subject to more ridicule, Jerod attempted to soften his previous postings:

I never said Pat Houston was a murderer. I said Krissi has had suspicion of her (when it came to her money & her mom).

The fact still remains, Auntie Whitney's case needs to be reopen #PrayForBK

If all this wasn't unfolding against the tragic backdrop of a young woman fighting for her life in a hospital bed, it would almost be fun to watch. But I had no time to pay much attention to this clan of clowns. I was finally on my way to Atlanta to attempt to make some sense of the unfolding drama and separate the facts from the nonsense.

CHAPTER **ELEVEN**

It is fashionable to dismiss rumors about the sexuality of celebrities as tabloid gossip or as nobody's business but their own. Others believe that entertainment figures belong to the public whose patronage supplies their livelihood and so their lives deserve to be open to scrutiny. For me, it's never been that simple.

When I published my first book with Max Wallace in 1998, casting doubt on the circumstances behind the 1994 death of Kurt Cobain, it may have seemed to some people on par with the recent accusations leveled by Jerod Brown suggesting that Whitney Brown had been murdered. In actuality, most of the book focused on discrediting the myriad conspiracy theories circulating about who may have murdered the grunge icon. In the end, I simply shed light on the hastiness of the suicide verdict and called for authorities to reopen the investigation. The *New Yorker* called the book a "judicious presentation of explosive material."

In fact, the book's central theme was not in the end the murder conspiracy theories but the exploration of a phenomenon that surfaced following Cobain's death. In the weeks and months following his reported shotgun suicide, at least sixty-eight young people— mostly teens—committed "copycat suicides."

Youth suicide was a subject that haunted me and my coauthor, whose young cousin had killed himself years before on the day of his law school graduation, leaving a note to his deeply conservative, religious parents announcing that he was gay and that their homophobia had helped drive him to suicide.

The link between homophobia and youth suicide has in fact been long documented with jarring statistics to bolster the link. The Suicide Prevention Resource Center has estimated that between thirty and forty percent of LGBT youth, depending on age and sex groups, have attempted suicide.

Suicide experts have argued that the lack of gay role models contributes to the problem. Some believe that gay public figures have an obligation to come out because of the impact it might have on struggling youth. Others decry the staggering number of conservative and religious figures—including a number of high-profile Republican politicians and countless Roman Catholic priests—who are not only closeted but who publicly spew venomous hatred toward gays and lesbians or oppose same-sex marriage to serve as a smoke screen to avoid suspicion.

Some activists are even dedicated to the questionable ethical practice of outing gay public figures, arguing that they have an obligation to serve as role models for gay and lesbian youth confused about their own sexuality or battling societal homophobia. When I was in school, I remember that I believed as common knowledge that the actor Rock Hudson was "married" to Jim Nabors, TV's Gomer Pyle. What was unusual is that this was the seventies, long before Hudson became the first major celebrity to be outed following his death from AIDS, supposedly surprising millions of people unaware that the heartthrob was gay. And yet I remember that all my friends and I had heard this story long before anybody had ever heard of AIDS. Following Hudson's death in 1985, a number of books were published about his life. With the release of each one, I remember eagerly searching the index in vain to find Jim Nabors's name and get to the bottom of this mystery.

Finally, a few years later, a biography was released that shed light on the connection. It seemed that in the early seventies, according to Hudson himself, a group of "middle aged homosexuals" from Huntington Beach sent out invitations announcing the marriage of Jim Nabors and Rock Hudson, who would subsequently be taking the name "Rock Pyle." Hudson later maintained that the invitation had been a joke, but considering that the public was blissfully unaware of the two stars' sexuality at the time (Hudson had spent his career deep in the closet), it seems more likely that it was a deliberate attempt to out them. It seemed to have worked, because years later none of my friends were at all surprised by the supposedly shocking revelation.

Indeed, nowhere has the debate about outing public figures been more pronounced than in Hollywood, where the celluloid closet has long sheltered a vast array of celebrities. In a roundabout way, this is how Whitney Houston first happened upon my radar in any significant way.

Early in the new millennium, I had been commissioned by Canada's largest TV network, CTV, to shoot a documentary about pilot season, following young Canadian actors trying to land their first roles in Hollywood.

My connections in Tinseltown were limited, so a friend hooked me up with a man whose own ties to the entertainment industry were legendary.

I first met Joe Franklin at his cluttered office near Times Square. According to *Guinness World Records*, Franklin was the world's "most durable talk show host," hosting the first ever TV talk show, which ran from 1950 to 1977 on WABC-TV and continued on radio for another three decades until his death in January 2015. In his nearly sixty years as a talk show host, Joe interviewed more than thirty-one thousand guests, including a virtual who's who of Hollywood celebrities. In fact, he is credited with introducing a number of future superstars, including a young Barbra Streisand, Woody Allen, and Michael Jackson, as well as the still obscure Elvis Presley before he ever appeared on *The Ed Sullivan Show*.

When I met him, his office was filled with a treasure trove of memorabilia from his incredible career. I sat for hours, listening to him spin tales about celebrities he had interviewed, including JFK, and advice about where I might begin my quest. By the end of my first of many sessions with Franklin, I was a little starstruck, especially when he shared a tidbit about Marilyn Monroe, with whom he claimed to have had an affair during the fifties. In fact, Franklin cowrote the first Monroe biography in 1953, *The Marilyn Monroe Story*, and he showed me all kinds of evidence demonstrating that the two did indeed have a brief fling.

I happened to have known Ava Gardner quite well during the latter years of her life in London, where I met her walking her corgis in Hyde Park. It is the only credible celebrity connection of my own that I could summon to the conversation. I brought it up after he told me about his long acquaintance with her ex-husband Frank Sinatra, whom he interviewed a number of times on his show. Ava once showed me a scar that she said had been given to her courtesy of Sinatra, who struck her in a fit of jealousy. She never told me what prompted his rage, but I later read a story about how Ol' Blue Eyes had allegedly walked in on her in bed with Lana Turner.

When I brought this up with Franklin, he shared a surprising revelation.

"Almost everybody in Hollywood is gay," he said with a straight face. "The rest are half gay." At the time, I dismissed his words as a joke or an exaggeration. But in a subsequent encounter, I brought up the claim and asked him to elaborate. He was all too willing to dish the dirt and share the names of a host of allegedly closeted celebs. I can't remember if it was him or me who first brought up Whitney Houston, but he told me he had interviewed her and Cissy many times over the years. By then, it was common knowledge that Whitney was a purported lesbian, so I think the subject came up when I listed the handful of celebrities I had heard were in the closet. Among these was Tom Cruise, who to my surprise Franklin told me wasn't actually gay, "just strange." But when the subject of Whitney came up, he immediately said, "That's an easy one," and proceeded to tell me why her name always surfaces at the top of the list.

"Why do you think that practically everybody in America has heard that Whitney likes women?" he asked. "It's because for years she hardly bothered to hide it. She was living openly with this woman and they'd be all lovey dovey in public even. That was quite unsual for a celebrity back then and even now," he says. "Then she finally dove into the closet and pretended it never happened but by then it was too late. Everybody knew." At the time, he compared Whitney to Rosie O'Donnell, who he said was an open lesbian during her early career in New York before she "pretended to be straight for a while."

At the time of our conversation, Whitney was only one of the many celebrities whose name Franklin brought up, and the truth was that I was less interested in the stories about her than some of the movie stars he dished about. But partly as a result of these conversations, I ended up changing the direction of my documentary.

Instead of a film about pilot season, I would eventually end up going undercover as a gay actor trying to make it in Hollywood. Franklin would soon supply me with a number of valuable contacts who would help pave the way for my project. Among these happened to be Whitney's father, John Houston, whom Franklin had known for almost four decades, including during the period when he had acted as the head of Whitney's company, Nippy Inc.

Franklin would, in fact, later play a role when I inadvertently came close to collaborating on a book and/or documentary about Whitney Houston—a project that collapsed before it was finalized when John died of a heart attack in February 2003.

I was first introduced to John by Joe Franklin when he called Joe, telling him he wanted to get his story out there. Joe told John he had an author/documentary filmmaker in his office and suggested to John that we collaborate. I spoke to John on the phone at length, and he seemed excited about the prospect of capturing his story on film. He told me the stories would make "world headlines" and that we'd both make a lot of money if it was done properly.

The first time we talked, he had been estranged from his daughter for some time for reasons I never fully fathomed. He was also embroiled in a bizarre lawsuit that saw him suing Whitney for $100 million to compensate him for supposedly helping clear her of a marijuana charge and for negotiating a $100 million record deal. It turns out that he actually had very little to do with the lawsuit, which had been filed through his company, John Houston Entertainment, by a figure who claimed to be John's business partner. At the time the action was filed, Whitney's spokesperson claimed that John, in fact, had nothing to do with the lawsuit.

Indeed, when I spoke with him, he seemed deeply hurt that the two were estranged, but it was clear that he had nothing but love for his daughter. Indeed, after John's death it was revealed that his $1 million life insurance policy named Whitney as the beneficiary. I'm still a little hazy about the timeline, but I was unaware of most of the details of the lawsuit until after he died.

He didn't appear to have an ax to grind against Whitney. Instead, it appeared he wanted to paint a picture of himself as a person who was instrumental in his daughter's success and felt slighted that he rarely received credit for her career. And yet he talked with nothing but affection for Whitney and even for Cissy. He confessed he had cheated on his wife and that he was the "bad guy," but our collaboration never got far enough off the ground for me to acquire many of those details.

In the one and only time I brought up Whitney's purported lesbianism, he told me, "I don't ask my daughter what goes on in her bedroom." He said that he respected Robyn, who had worked with him on the business side of Whitney's career and was very dedicated, but that they often clashed. He admitted that he lobbied very hard for his daughter to distance herself from her friend on a personal level.

"There's a reason this is called show business," he told me. "That woman was bad for business and I was in charge of the business. Cissy hated her for all kinds of reasons. She was a churchgoer so that had a lot to do with it, but for me it was hurting Whitney's image and sales that people believed they were together. It doesn't matter whether they were sleeping together, I can't tell you to this day, but everybody thought they were so that's what counted as far as I was concerned."

He admitted that there was a lot of "pressure" for Whitney to stop spending time with Robyn. "From all sides, everybody wanted her gone," he revealed, saying it may have also had to do with Robyn's overbearing personality.

At this time, Whitney was still married to Bobby Brown, and it was obvious that John despised his son-in-law, whom he seemed to blame for his daughter's troubles.

"She'd have been better off staying with Robyn," he told me at one point.

When I asked him if he thought Whitney took up with Bobby because of the pressure, John laughed.

"You don't know my daughter," he said. "Nobody tells her what to do."

Although the project never got off the ground, I had established some good contacts in Whitney's camp as a result of our brief collaboration, some of which proved useful when I later embarked on a project about Michael Jackson, who often traveled in the same circles. By the time John was in the ground, however, I never expected that I would ever again delve into his daughter's world.

———

By the time I changed the focus of my film, I had no intention of discussing Whitney Houston or her sexuality. My distributor had made it clear that for legal reasons, I had to steer clear of outing living celebrities. And yet time and again while shooting this project, I gained insight into the lengths that celebrities must go through to remain in the closet and the devastating emotional toll that comes with living a lie.

My first immersion into this world came about as the result of a contact supplied by a publicist named Melanie when I embarked on my mission to transform into a closeted gay actor and land a movie role. She arranged for me to attend a session of a weekly poker game in the Hollywood Hills with a group of insiders who call themselves the "Queers of the Round Table," who were apprised in advance of my mission. I was replacing a well-known former sitcom star—the only actor of the group—who couldn't be there that week because of a work commitment.

The first thing I tell them is that I don't believe the actor I'm replacing, a reputed womanizer, is really gay.

"Queer as a three-dollar bill," comes the reply from Lenny, the host, who works as a location scout for TV and movies. "He's an actor. What do you expect?"

"What's that got to do with it?" I ask.

"All actors are gay," comes the response, echoing what Franklin had told me but which I dismissed at the time as a joke. "Actually, that's not true, although a lot of people think they are. In reality, it's probably closer to seventy-five percent."

I still find the statistic hard to believe.

"Well, let me ask you this," says Karl, a set designer. "What percentage of male hairdressers do you think are gay? And figure skaters, ballet dancers, interior decorators, flight attendants?"

"Don't forget librarians," Lenny adds.

I think about it and concede that most of the men in those professions are probably gay, likely even more than seventy-five percent. But acting isn't the same thing, I tell them.

"Honey, you are naive," says Christopher, a script editor. "Acting is one of those trades where it just helps to be flamboyant, not to mention sensitive. Gay men are just drawn to it. Tell you what, go to any drama school in this country and talk to the boys. You'd be hard-pressed to find a single straight male. And what's more, it's obvious right away. Just about every student is a swishing queen."

"Here's a good rule of thumb," says Karl. "Take the résumé of just about any movie star and look where they started out. If they took drama in college, the odds are they're queer. If they started in theater or did a stint on Broadway, especially musical theater, bingo they're gay. And I'm not talking seventy-five percent, I'm talking ninety-five percent."

"Like who?" I ask somewhat skeptically.

This was the wrong question—or maybe the right one. It's like a verbal stampede, as all three of them start tossing out famous names, one after another, some of them A-list superstars. I'm not exaggerating when I say they went on for at least fifteen minutes.

Karl finally puts a stop to it. "You know, this might go faster if we just listed the heterosexual stars."

Then they start tossing out those names, and indeed the list is noticeably shorter. "Sylvester Stallone, Brad Pitt, Bruce Willis, Arnold Schwarzenegger, Mel Gibson, Hugh Grant, Colin Farrell." At the next name offered by Christopher, Lenny stops him.

"No, you can definitely cross him off the list. I know for a fact that he is fucking [well-known Hollywood producer]."

I suspect they're abusing my naiveté—or perhaps their list is merely wishful thinking—so I finally interrupt the litany. "First of all, half the people you mentioned are married." This prompts shrieks of laughter from my new friends.

"He's a babe in the woods," says Karl.

The three of them then decide to give me a tutorial on the way things work for a gay actor in Hollywood. "Like we said," Christopher recaps, "drama schools are almost all populated by gays, at least the men. That much is easy to prove because at that point in an actor's career there's no reason for him to hide it. In fact, at that stage, it's almost an advantage to be gay because a straight guy is in the minority. And, by the way, that's why the sexuality of most stars is common knowledge. At some time they were openly hanging out in gay bars or cruising online, and their 'secret' is common knowledge in a large segment of the gay community wherever [their hometown is]. By the time they head back into the closet after hitting it big in Hollywood, it's too late."

He then asks me to list the male Hollywood stars that are out of the closet. I can list them on one hand, with fingers to spare.

"Now, how is it possible that thousands of drama students—the overwhelming majority, in fact, and most Broadway actors are demonstrably gay, yet virtually every movie star is a raging heterosexual? The answer is, it's not."

Then they start with a history lesson. I expect they will begin with the obvious—Rock Hudson—but instead they use the example of James Dean, the ultimate male Hollywood sex symbol of the fifties who I didn't even know was gay. "Not only was he gay," explains Lenny, "but his sexuality, which he supposedly didn't even bother to hide, was causing shit fits at the studio. They'd had plenty of experience handling gay actors before, but here they had this incredibly bankable star, worth millions, and he was cavorting around town with every fag you could think of, including another one of their biggest stars, Montgomery Clift. They were terrified the news would get out and his box office potential would go down the crapper. So they pretty well forced him to start dating starlets while their publicity department went to work portraying Dean as a great cocksman."

"The stakes were huge," he continues, "and there was enormous pressure from the studio for Dean to get married. Their preference was Natalie Wood, who was perfectly willing to act as Dean's beard," but he explains that both Wood and Dean were apparently reluctant to go along with the phony nuptials.

It's here that I interject. Do they really think America was so homophobic that people would stop going to his movies just because they thought he was gay?

"Well, at that time yes, definitely. But that wasn't the real point with Dean," Lenny replies. "The fact is that part of his huge box office appeal was that American girls were so in love with him that they would go to his pictures over and over again. Ironically, gay men did the same thing, but that's just an interesting side fact."

Lenny then named a contemporary A-list actor and drew a parallel to Dean. "Look at [one of the top box office stars in the world]. At the beginning of his career, he had a lot of quirky roles and was never really seen as a leading man, so he didn't really bother trying to hide his gayness very much. But all of a sudden he starred in [hugely popular film] and almost overnight he became a sex symbol superstar. The studio surveys showed that fourteen- and fifteen-year-old girls were going to the movie over and over again, some as many as twenty or thirty times. And why? Because they liked to fantasize that they were his leading lady and that he was seducing them. If they knew he was gay in real life, that was all threatened. So, the next thing you know, he's dating supermodels and going to strip joints, while his publicist makes sure the news is plastered in every newspaper in the world. Funny, you never heard of him having a girlfriend during the first ten years of his career."

Christopher explains that it is not necessarily homophobia per se that keeps actors closeted today, but rather this phenomenon of both men and women attending movies to fantasize about bedding the star. "Look what happened to Anne Heche after she came out as Ellen DeGeneres's girlfriend. She had already been signed to star opposite Harrison Ford as his love interest in *Six Days Seven Nights*. When the film came out, it completely tanked. Not because it was terrible, but because men could no longer go to her movies and picture themselves boffing her. And not long after that, look what happened. Heche broke up with Ellen and, surprise, she's straight again."

Lenny interrupts him. "Well, it's not entirely true that homophobia has nothing to do with it. Look at all the black fags." He names a black comedian. "He's not really a sex symbol, he's a comedian, so technically he could come out, but if he does, he can say good-bye to his black fan base forever. Kaput!"

At this stage, I point out that the star is married. I can understand why he got married. He needed a beard. But what's in it for the woman, I ask.

"Ah, that's the sixty-four thousand–dollar question," says Lenny. "We spend a lot of time debating that very point and nobody can agree on the answer. In some cases, we know for sure that the women do it for career reasons. They are basically promised that if they marry a particular actor, they are guaranteed their own acting career will take off and they will be offered juicy roles because their new husband has so much clout with the studios. That much makes sense. What we don't know is how many of these women are actually lesbians."

Lenny explains that while the overwhelming majority of male actors are gay, the same is not necessarily true for females. "Hollywood is not like the women's golf or tennis tour," he jokes. "If seven to ten percent of women in regular society are dykes, then that's probably the percentage in Hollywood as well.

(Since this encounter, I came across a University of Maryland study that found that the Queers may be better informed about gay men in Hollywood than gay women. Despite its claims that only gay men are represented disproportionately, the study found that lesbians and bisexual women are actually eight times more likely to enter theater and film than their straight counterparts.)

"Now, we all know for sure who some of the famous dykes are," Lenny continues. He points to Jodie Foster, who for years had lived openly with her longtime girlfriend, though she had never officially acknowledged her sexuality. (Foster finally came out at the Golden Globes in 2013, long after this session.)

"And then there's Rosie O'Donnell—a perfect example. When she started out, she was as far from a leading lady as you can get. She made absolutely no attempt to hide her sexuality. When she was star-ring in *Grease* on Broadway, she began a longtime relationship with one of her female costars. Then she's hired to front a popular daytime talk show, watched by a lot of conservative Midwest housewives who wouldn't be very keen on watching a dyke host. Suddenly, she starts talking about the crushes she has on various male actors. She con-stantly refers to one in particular as her 'boyfriend.' Then when her lesbian friends call her on this, she tells them she's obviously joking, especially because the star in question is widely rumored to be gay. So the whole thing is an elaborate inside joke. Then [as the show is coming to an end], Rosie finally announces she is a lesbian."

Then there's the countless women who date or marry gay actors. "The most famous Hollywood beard today," says Lenny, "is [well-known Oscar-nominated actress], who has been reported to be dating a number of different A-list actors over the years. Everybody in Hol-lywood knows she's a dyke. You can be sure that if you see an item in the gossip columns reporting that she's dating some actor, then that actor is a fag." He shoots off the names of three famous actors, each of whom is reported to be a notorious womanizer. Sure enough, all three of them have 'dated' the actress in question within the previous few years.

"But what's in it for her?" I ask.

"That's easy," says Lenny. "Just as the gay rumors get dispelled whenever these actors are reported to be dating a beautiful woman—or more often when they are photographed with her in public—she gets to look like a breeder whenever it's reported she is dating this or that handsome actor. Meanwhile, she has been dating [another well-known Hollywood actress] for years with the public none the wiser. So, it's basically a win-win situation for a lesbian actress to date or marry a gay actor. But then there's another subject we can never agree on—bisexuality."

"There's no such thing!" yells out Karl.

"Oh, shut up," Lenny replies. He explains that nobody really knows how many of these gay actors are simply dating and marrying beards, and how many of them are actually bisexual. This debate, he says, has been raging since the beginning of Hollywood.

He cites the example of Cary Grant, one of Hollywood's greatest sex symbols. Grant, he says, was reportedly in love with the movie star Randolph Scott. "Literally *everybody* in Hollywood knew it. They would sit there in the Brown Derby till all hours, staring longingly into each other's eyes and holding hands. They even shared a beach house together. Yet Grant was married five times. His wives had to have known about him and Scott, not to mention his lovers over the years. One book claimed that he even had an affair with Marlon Brando, another rumored bisexual. So why would anybody marry him in the first place? Were they lured by the promise of the fabulous glamorous Hollywood lifestyle and the money, or by the potential impact on their own acting careers? After all, three of his wives were struggling actresses."

I actually remembered an incident in the early eighties when Tom Snyder interviewed Chevy Chase, and the former *SNL* star said of Grant, "I understand he's a homo." Grant sued him for slander and won, although details of the star's many gay affairs later emerged after his death in 1986. It raises the question, how does anybody prove anybody's actually gay, short of catching them in bed with someone of the same sex?

Karl mentions one of the world's most famous sitcom stars, who is gay and married. "They live in this huge mansion, but according to people who have been there, he and his wife occupy half the mansion each and they never have anything to do with each other. Very convenient, but again, why did she marry him? I hear that the way these things work is the woman agrees to put in a certain amount of time before filing a divorce. In exchange, she is guaranteed a platinum credit card for the whole marriage and a generous settlement after the divorce. Hell, I'd marry some rich dyke looking for a beard. She wouldn't have to ask me twice.

"Then there's [recently married superstar actor], who's a little too close to being outed publicly for his own comfort. The story goes that he actually interviewed a series of women and offered them a huge sum of money, not to mention prime roles, in exchange for staying married to him for a certain number of years."

He continues, "The saddest part of the Hollywood closet for the gay stars who aren't bisexual is that they live a life of perpetual sadness. They can never really have an open relationship, so they end up having sex with high-priced Hollywood call boys for two grand a night."

"Unless Scientology gets its hands on them," Lenny says.

The mere mention of Scientology piqued my interest, because I had already embarked on an investigation of the alleged cult for a previous version of my film and had managed to film a tour of their famed Celebrity Centre with an actress named Jennifer Holmes and a cameraman named Miles. The tour had been particularly interesting because of an incident that took place while the centre's Vice President Greg LaClaire was showing us around.

As he extolled the virtues of the religion, a movement in the bushes distracted me. When I peered closer, I saw that there was a cameraman filming us, which resulted in the bizarre spectacle of our video cameras focusing on each in a surreal showdown. When I asked LaClaire what was going on, he seemed a little sheepish but had a ready explanation.

"He's just my guy, because we might use this someday, somehow," he explains, creeping me out.

Now, as the subject of Scientology comes up in this unlikely setting, I ask my host what the religion has to do with anything.

"Well, if you pay them enough money and you're gay, they promise to convert you," Lenny explains. "Or so I hear."

CHAPTER **TWELVE**

The moment of truth is at hand. On March 11, 2015, Dr. Phil McGraw was set to finally air the Nick Gordon interview he had conducted a few days earlier. The show had already leaked some of the details of what went down, and producers suggested that Gordon had been "out of control," even violent, during the taping. Having arrived in Atlanta days earlier, I eagerly waited to see whether the interview would shed any new light into Nick's persona or provide clues as to whether he was capable of the acts of which he was being accused. Would this be anything more than a ratings-grabbing publicity stunt? I had my doubts.

The episode, "Bobbi Kristina's Boyfriend, Distraught and Out of Control: The Nick Gordon Intervention," kicks off with an interview with Nick's mother, who flew to Atlanta from her home in Orlando, Florida, supposedly unbeknownst to Nick. And almost right away Michelle Gordon clears up a falsehood that has been reported literally thousands of times since Bobbi ended up in the hospital.

The media had been reporting that Nick came to live with Whitney when he was twelve and Bobbi was eight. The story had it that she "raised" Nick as an adopted son and that he was like an older brother to Bobbi since childhood before the couple's relationship turned romantic soon after Whitney's death.

But to Dr. Phil, Michelle revealed that she kicked Nick, now twenty-four, out of the house when he was eighteen and that he came to live with Whitney some time after May 2008. Contrary to what has been widely reported, Michelle did not know Whitney. They were not "friends." Rather, Michelle claims, Bobbi Kristina had met Nick and become friends with him in school.

Right away, this explains why I have been unable to find any evidence that Nick was raised by Whitney as her non-adopted son, despite weeks of attempting to track down details of this arrangement or witnesses who could confirm the unusual living arrangements. It simply isn't true, nor is their subsequent romantic relationship as creepy or "incestuous" as the media has been portraying it for weeks.

Michelle proceeds to deliver another surprise. She reveals that Nick was in a nearby room when Whitney was found unconscious in her LA hotel bathtub in 2012. When he heard an assistant scream, he ran in and found Whitney on the bathroom floor, where she had been dragged out of the tub. "At that point, she was on the floor and he administered CPR to her," Michelle says. "And he called me when he was standing in front of her body. And he just couldn't understand why he couldn't revive her. He said, 'Why? Why couldn't I do CPR on her? I couldn't get the air in her lungs?'"

Not a single eyewitness account of the singer's death ever mentioned the presence of Nick Gordon, so Michelle's revelation comes as quite a shock, especially because three years later he supposedly performed CPR on Bobbi when she was found in a bathtub under similar circumstances.

When McGraw asks what Nick told her about the circumstances surrounding Bobbi, she says,

Krissi, Nick, and Max [Lomas] went out Friday night and they went to a party or a club and they were drinking. They got home very early in the morning on the Saturday. Krissi and Nick had an argument and Nick walked away from the argument, went

to another bedroom to fall asleep and Krissi went up to her room
and drew a bath, a bubble bath. From what I understand, what
Nick's telling me, the cable guy came over. Max let the cable guy
in the house and he needed to enter into the bathroom for some
kind of access. Max found her. He pulled her out of the tub and
he doesn't know how to do CPR. So he went to get Nicholas
and Nicholas was able to do the CPR on her for fifteen minutes
and police arrived and they didn't help him.

"Nobody helped him until the [paramedics] got there, which I don't understand," she says, fighting back tears.

Asked whether Nick has shared with her how this has affected him, she says, "Nicholas continually expresses how much he failed Whitney because Whitney asked Nicholas to protect Krissi and Nicholas has always felt like he was a protector of Whitney and Krissi. He says if Krissi dies it's going to be his fault because she should have survived due to his CPR. He blames himself for all of this."

McGraw interrupts to explain he needs to know what's in Nick's head, because "he seems to be unraveling in a really bad way from what I've seen and understood."

Michelle reveals that he has told her many times lately that he is going to kill himself and "he's tried" by "taking pills" two weeks before. He had apparently shared this with his younger brother, Jack, and told him not to tell anybody. She then called the person with whom Nick has been staying and asked him to confiscate his stash of pills, including Xanax, for which he allegedly has a prescription.

The show then cuts to video footage somewhere in the same hotel of Nick, in an inebriated and likely drugged-up state, babbling to his "publicist."

McGraw reveals that he has been "told" that Nick accompanied Whitney and Bobbi Kristina to rehab at least three times during her final years when she was seeking treatment for her drug problem.

"I believe Whitney wanted to keep them all together as a family so she took Nicholas. Everywhere her and Krissi went, Nick went. They were never separated. They were always together," Michelle says. She maintains that her son didn't have a problem at that time but that she assumed Bobbi Kristina did. Dr. Phil is astonished at this revelation.

"Wow, I've never heard of that," he says. "I've been doing this for thirty-five years and I've never heard of anybody taking a posse to rehab."

She claims that in recent phone conversations her son has sounded intoxicated and told her he wants to die.

"He's just full of pain and hurt and he wants to see Krissi. He told her he just wants to hold her hand and rub her feet. He said he can't take it anymore. He doesn't want to live."

Asked why she thinks he's being blocked from seeing Bobbi, she responds, "It's her father. His pride and selfishness. He won't let Nicholas see Krissi because of his pride and his feelings toward Nick."

Asked whether she believes the family believes he hurt her, she replies, "I don't believe the Houston side believes that. I don't know about the Browns. My son would never try and hurt Krissi. I don't care what they think. My son would never hurt anyone."

"From what I've seen, what I've tracked, what I've learned, I was scheduled to come here and interview Nick because he wanted his side of the story out," announces McGraw. "He feels like he was being vilified in the press, he was being seen as some monster that had done terrible things and that he wanted to tell his side of the story. Why he wanted to be with her, wanted her to feel his presence, hear his voice if it could help in some way. He wanted to tell his story. And in the time between when that was scheduled and when we got here he has deteriorated so far, I don't believe he is in a position to do that interview."

The show cuts to footage of Nick curled up in a fetal position on the bed, crying, "I miss Krissi."

Then McGraw reveals that in the last forty-eight hours, Nick has gone "exponentially downhill" to the point that he is in "this building screaming that he wants to die and he's just out of control. At this point, I don't think he has any chance of turning this around on his own."

He then delivers the dramatic line that had been featured in previews all week leading up to the show:

"Your son, left to his own devices, will be dead within a week!"

Returning from a commercial, McGraw tells a distraught Michelle that he no longer intends to conduct an interview but "an intervention." His life hangs in the balance, and Dr. Phil fears that he will either kill himself or drink himself to death if he doesn't get help.

He announces that he intends to leave her for a few minutes and go find Nick in the hotel and "bring him down here one way or another." When he gets here, he tells Michelle, their "one mission" is to get him to agree to go to an inpatient rehabilitation center.

"Everything is set up," he tells her, "but you and I have to get him there and we don't take no for an answer."

Minutes later, McGraw enters Nick's hotel room and asks him how he's doing.

"I'm good, man," he says, shaking the doctor's hand. Leading him down the corridor, he asks the glassy-eyed young man whether he's been drinking. Nick reveals that he has had "two shots."

Asked how he's feeling as they enter the elevator, Nick says, "I'm feeling like I miss Krissi and Whitney." He rolls up his sleeve to show McGraw the tattoo of Bobbi's name that he had done a few days after she went into the hospital.

Sobbing, he pleads, "Please don't put this on TV. I'm weak." Arriving back at the suite, he sees Michelle. "Mommy, oh my gosh, oh my gosh," he exclaims as he throws his arms around her. "I'm so sorry for everything."

Composing himself, he turns to McGraw and says, "Let's do this. I'm good, I'm good, I'm good." As his mother hugs him, he whimpers, "Momma, I would never hurt anybody. I love people. I love babies, everything."

Steeling himself, he turns to the camera, rolls up his sleeves to display his tattoos, and says, "All right. Here we go."

Before McGraw can begin the interview, Nick announces that he's been drinking and doing Xanax but that he's "been sober besides that." He admits he's been drinking a lot as the show cuts to footage of him in his hotel room, slurring his words.

He tells McGraw, "My heart hurts, I have panic attacks." Reminded that he threatened suicide (on Twitter), he responds, "If anything happens to Krissi I will."

The next ten minutes continue in this vein, with Nick periodically crying and storming out of the room, then returning moments later and talking about his pain over Krissi.

At one point, he rages, "I hate Bobby Brown. It's to the point I'm getting frustrated."

Finally, Dr. Phil brings in two men from Willingway rehab center, where Nick has agreed to go for treatment. "Please help me see Krissi," he pleads. After he finally agrees to leave, he has one last change of heart. "What if Krissi calls my name and I'm like three hours away? My name will be the first she calls, so . . ."

McGraw pledges that "If that happens, I, Dr. Phil, will get a chopper on the ground at Willingway and we will fly you back to the facility. That's my commitment to you."

In response, Nick promises, "I'll be sober. I'll be clean. I'll be a good person." He then heads off to rehab.

It's a compelling, albeit disturbing, hour of television that was definitely worth the wait. But after it was over, I was left with some thoughts. First, Nick managed to get through the entire show without ever being asked to explain what happened on the morning that Bobbi Kristina was found. Instead, his mother supplies the version of events he told her, giving no one the chance to question any contradictions or inconsistencies. It is clear from Dr. Phil's narrative that Nick had never agreed to come on and talk about the events of that morning. Instead, "his side of the story" meant he would be allowed to deliver the same plea he has been issuing on Twitter for weeks—asking to see Bobbi. It makes sense, given the fact that his lawyers okayed his appearance, and they would likely never have given the green light to anything else, but it is disingenuous and even misleading to suggest he was ever going to give his side of the story.

The show marked the revelation that he now has a publicist, Josey Crews, who is pictured briefly in the broadcast and is undoubtedly the person who engineered this appearance. Crews is a former editorial producer for CNN and *Good Morning America* and now heads an obscure publicity agency in Atlanta. My guess is that he recently approached Nick, offering to do free publicity to improve his image. His name first appeared in connection with the case on March 3, just prior to the taping, when Nick tweeted, "I have the best publicist in the world." Indeed, Crews appears to have done a masterful job, because Nick comes off as a sympathetic and tragic figure without ever having to explain himself or account for the events of January 31.

But the thing that struck me most after watching the broadcast is the fact that throughout the show, only one photo of Nick with Whitney was ever displayed, over and over again—a photo of the two of them and Bobbi during what appears to be near the end of Whitney's life because of her ravaged appearance. They displayed the same photo at least ten times, despite the fact that Nick claims the trio was inseparable for years and traveled everywhere together. There are, in fact, countless photos of Nick with Bobbi taken after 2012, including a number displayed during the Dr. Phil episode but only that one single shot of the three of them together. It makes me wonder if Nick exaggerated the nature of his relationship with Whitney, whom he claims to have regarded as his second mother.

His penchant for exaggeration may explain the final revelation that Dr. Phil delivered for the cameras as the credits rolled:

"After our interview taped," he announces, "the Houston family reached out to us. They say that Nick Gordon did not perform CPR on Whitney Houston and the police report reflects that."

CHAPTER THIRTEEN

Did Whitney really marry Bobby Brown to reestablish her credibility in the black community or to finally silence the lesbian rumors that were starting to impact her career? Would somebody really go as far as to discard a happy, fulfilling relationship for the sake of money or fame? We may never know the answer to Whitney's motivations for discarding Robyn, though only the most naïve or disingenuous observer still believes they were simply friends—an absurd notion that beggars belief.

By the time I completed my investigation into homophobia in the entertainment industry, however, I knew that celebrities are often willing to go to much more desperate lengths to remain in the closet than simply marrying a person of the opposite sex.

As I pursued the undercover quest for my documentary more than a decade ago, few phenomena shocked me more than the role played by the Church of Scientology in maintaining the celluloid closet—something that first came to my attention while playing poker with the Queers of the Round Table.

After a peremptory investigation, I learned that part of the appeal of Scientology for some celebrities is its alleged promise that it could turn a gay person straight through an elaborate and expensive science fiction–inspired regimen.

Although there were literally thousands of anti-Scientology sites on the web, I didn't trust any of them to supply an objective view of the religion, because most seemed to have an ax to grind. Instead, I turned to a 1991 cover story about the church in *Time*, one of the world's most respected and credible media outlets. Judging by the headline, however, the article did not at first glance appear to be all that objective: "Scientology: The Thriving Cult of Greed and Power."

The article, by award-winning journalist Richard Behar, makes no bones about its view of the church, which Behar claims was founded by L. Ron Hubbard to "clear" people of unhappiness. Scientology, writes Behar, portrays itself as a religion but "in reality, the church is a hugely profitable global racket that survives by intimidating members and critics in a Mafia-like manner."

However, in the decade leading up to the article, he writes, prosecutions against Scientology seemed to be "curbing its menace." In recent years, he continues, hundreds of longtime Scientology adherents—many charging that they were mentally or physically abused—have quit the church and criticized it at their own risk. Some have sued the church and won; others have settled for amounts in excess of $500,000. In various cases, judges have labeled the church "schizophrenic and paranoid" and "corrupt, sinister and dangerous." The article calls Hubbard "part storyteller, part flim-flam man."

Born in Nebraska in 1911, Hubbard served in the navy during World War II and soon afterward complained to the Veterans Administration about his "suicidal inclinations" and his "seriously affected" mind. Nevertheless, Hubbard was a moderately successful writer of pulp science fiction. Years later, church brochures described him falsely as an "extensively decorated" World War II hero who was crippled and blinded in action, twice pronounced dead, and miraculously cured through Scientology. Hubbard's "doctorate" from "Sequoia

University" was a fake mail-order degree. In a 1984 case in which the church sued a Hubbard biographical researcher, a California judge concluded that its founder was "a pathological liar."

Behar warns that the church, which at the time of the article boasted seven hundred centers in sixty-five countries, threatens to become more insidious than ever.

But that really wasn't the part of the article that interested me. Instead, the passage that caught my eye involved one of the church's most famous members: John Travolta.

The church's former head of security, Richard Aznaran, told *Time* that Scientology ringleader David Miscavige repeatedly joked to staffers about Travolta's allegedly promiscuous homosexual behavior. Travolta refused to be interviewed, and his lawyer dismissed questions about the subject as "bizarre." But two weeks later, Travolta coincidentally announced that he was getting married to a fellow Scientologist, actress Kelly Preston.

According to the article, "High-level Scientology defectors claim that Travolta has long feared that if he defected, details of his sexual life would be made public."

"He felt pretty intimidated about this getting out and told me so," recalled William Franks, the church's former chairman of the board. "There were no outright threats made, but it was implicit. If you leave, they immediately start digging up everything."

I had never even heard a hint that Travolta was gay, although everybody has heard the rumors about another Hollywood A-list Scientologist. But not so long ago the *National Enquirer* published a photo of Travolta kissing another man on the lips while he was coming down the airstair of a private jet at an airport in Hamilton, Ontario, while he was in Toronto filming *Hairspray*, in which ironically he plays a woman.

Travolta's lawyer, Martin Singer, was quick to respond to the media uproar that resulted from the seemingly damning *Enquirer* photo. "As a manner of customary greeting and saying farewell, Mr. Travolta kisses both women and men whom he considers to be extremely close friends," said Singer. "People who are close to Mr. Travolta are aware of his customary, non-romantic gesture."

Not long after reading the *Time* article, I tracked down and met with a former high-ranking member of Scientology, a Beverly Hills artist named Michael Pattinson. In 1998, Pattinson had filed a lawsuit in a US district court against Scientology and many of its top officials and adherents, including Travolta. In his suit, Pattinson charged the church with a number of offenses, including fraud and false imprisonment. Chief among his allegations was that the church had promised to "cure" his homosexuality but that, after twenty-five years and more than $500,000 shelled out in fees, he was still gay.

When I talked to him, Pattinson, a British expatriate, was still bitter about his long ordeal. He told me he first encountered Scientology in 1973, when he was living in Paris, and his doctor recommended a book called *Dianetics* by L. Ron Hubbard.

"I had a stomach ulcer and the doctor actually thought Scientology might help me," he explained. "So I went to one of their centers in Paris and tried the auditing. Soon I was hooked."

The appeal for him, he said, was something he read by Hubbard where Hubbard promised he could cure people of their homosexuality by auditing.

"You have to understand that back then, where I came from—England—being gay was still very taboo," he said. "It was probably like the American South is now. So, along comes this religion that can supposedly make me straight. Of course that appealed to me."

He said he kept taking the courses, which required paying higher and higher fees, anticipating that if he reached a high-enough level, he would finally be offered the auditing process that Hubbard had said could cure homosexuality.

"Whenever I asked, they would tell me to be patient but that eventually I would be ready," he said. "The case supervisor is the one who decides these things, but he kept putting it off. Meanwhile, I was spending a fortune on these courses."

Pattinson said that nobody ever explicitly used Travolta as an example of a gay adherent who had been cured of his homosexuality by Scientology but that people inside the church would constantly refer to the movie star as one who had been cured. He said he traveled in the same circles as the star.

"I joined pretty much the same time as he did, knew all the same people. In fact, I was considered a celebrity, I think, even before he was, and was even once on the cover of the church's magazine, *Celebrity*. Everybody knew about him early on. It was pretty obvious. Travolta was a role model for the cure, especially after he got married. I thought, well, if he could get married, he must be cured, and I took even more courses and spent even more money, just waiting for the day when I would also be cured of what they called my 'ruin.' Well, that day never came and finally I'd had enough."

By the time he left the church, Pattinson says he had achieved a very high rank.

"I was treated by the same handlers, or Terminals as they're called, as any other celebrity, such as Travolta, such as Tom Cruise, such as Kirstie Alley. I know that it is very important for public relations that within the industry some of these people are seen to be straight while actually being gay and trying to handle it within Scientology. . . . All this, of course, would be in their 'pre-clear' folders under an assumed name, a code name because all their innermost secrets are there. But it's very important to have that paradox going on. Maybe they have something in the industry that would seen to be terrible and yet they have to be shown to be straight. They would probably be very inclined to go into an arranged marriage."

Pattinson eventually dropped the suit after he ran out of money, claiming that the church's deep pockets made it impossible to fight the case any longer. "They spent more than $2.5 million fighting it, and it was obvious they were going to keep fighting it till I couldn't afford to pursue it any longer," he claims.

What had Travolta done to personally incur Pattinson's wrath, I wondered. A clue, perhaps, can be found in his district court filing:

> *Defendant Travolta has knowingly participated in the intentional violation of the Establishment Clause of the First Amendment to the United States Constitution, thus instigating the "excessive entanglement of church and state." Defendant Travolta has known of Scientology's "gulags" and "concentration camps," otherwise known as RPFs, through both personal observation and information received from a certain former Scientologist, but has deliberately chosen to turn a blind eye to their existence and to refrain from disclosing his knowledge to people such as Plaintiff who trusted and relied upon him as a principal spokesperson on behalf of the Defendants. Indeed, when the movie* Saturday Night Fever *was first released, he knowingly arranged for a hard copy of the movie to be shown to members of the Sea Org sentenced to armed confinement in the RPF, or "gulag" in Scientology's buildings in Hollywood, California. Defendant Travolta's public statements, "handling" and subsequent marriage were material statements Plaintiff reasonably relied upon, as Commodore Hubbard intended when he taught Defendants how to "use" celebrities, such as Defendant Travolta, for the recruitment, brainwashing and retention of the Plaintiff and others.*

I was damned if I could figure out what all that meant, or if I wanted to be delving too deeply into anything associated with gulags and concentration camps. But I figured those terms were probably a little hyperbole used for dramatic effect. At least I hoped so.

With Pattinson's nightmare ordeal fresh in my mind, I decided it might be time to join Scientology and experience the religion for myself. But first I paid a visit to a veteran reporter for the *Hollywood*

Reporter named Barbara Sternig, who has written a lot about Scientology and celebrities over the years.

"I can only assume the idea is to get them while they're young," she tells me. "Get them before they're successful and there will be a loyalty base there that will stand you in good stead forever. If you get another Tom Cruise coming out of that, another Lisa Marie Presley coming out of that, you have your income guaranteed for the future; you have a generation of money. I'm sure it is based on money, though the church would probably deny that."

According to Sternig, Hollywood is terrified by the rise of Scientology, so much so that it has skewed the results of Oscar voting on more than one occasion.

"There's allegedly a good reason why neither Travolta nor Cruise have won an Oscar," she reveals. "For example, look at Cruise's performance in *Born on the Fourth of July*. It was brilliant, tailor-made for an Oscar, but he was shut out. Then he was also denied for both *Jerry Maguire* and *Magnolia*. And, of course, Travolta was the odds-on favorite for *Pulp Fiction* and he should have won, but again he was shut out. It's fairly obvious that the Hollywood establishment doesn't want to see a Scientologist win an Oscar for fear that it will just help them recruit more celebrities and everyday members. Can you imagine the speech that one of them might make to a billion viewers if they actually won?"

She points to Cruise's ex-wife, Nicole Kidman, as a perfect example of this phenomenon. "If you remember back to Nicole's brilliant performance in *To Die For*. All the reviewers were predicting she was a shoo-in for an Academy Award. That, of course, was when she was still married to Cruise and she was a practicing Scientologist. She wasn't even nominated. Then a few years ago, only after she divorced Cruise and renounced Scientology, she won her Oscar. That's probably not a coincidence."

I really had no idea what to expect when I set out to invade Scientology's castle headquarters on Hollywood Boulevard. From what I had been reading, most of the world's anticult organizations regarded the religion as a sinister sect. I had heard countless stories of journalists attempting to invade other religious cults, such as the Moonies. These journalists, the story goes, were quite knowledgeable in the particular church's practices before "joining" and were certain they could withstand the cult's sophisticated brainwashing methods, which include sleep and protein deprivation. But before they knew it, they had been brainwashed into joining the church. I didn't really think Scientology employed those kinds of methods, but I packed a case of protein bars before I journeyed in just in case.

I also insisted that my publicist, Melanie, accompany me for some extra protection. And I brought along my cameraman, Miles, as well, though I was fairly sure he would be turned away when they saw his video camera.

On the day in question, the three of us swept up the steps and through the entrance. The receptionist seemed a little taken aback to see me in the garish green outfit that I had employed as part of my undercover quest and asked what she could do for us.

Melanie quickly introduced me. She explained that I was think-ing of joining Scientology and wanted to take their personality test. A church official immediately approached us and said, "No cameras." I tell her (truthfully) that my uncle invented the credit-card key and that he had long been fascinated by Scientology. As an actor, I explained, I was also quite interested because of the church's track record in producing celebrities. At this point, I can almost see the dollar signs light up in her eyes, calculating just how many tens of millions my uncle must have made from such an invention.

Melanie explained that we were documenting my quest to become an actor on video, at which point the official finally relents and agrees to let the camera in. She insisted on processing my mem-bership and overseeing my test personally.

We walked through what can only be described as a shrine to L. Ron Hubbard. His photo and writings are everywhere, and it reminded me of a trip I once took to Soviet Russia, where Lenin was omnipresent. The only difference is that his little social experiment eventually ended up in the crapper, while Hubbard's seems to be thriving.

She brought me over to a table and produced a written test. "Read the front page," she said to me, "fill out the top, open the booklet, and start answering the questions. The front page will explain how to answer. When you're done, you'll get a computerized graph showing the strong points, weak points, and from the viewpoint of improving something about your life, and it will give you a good bird's-eye view of what's going well and what can be improved."

I signed my name and my address then started to fill out the lengthy test.

The questions themselves seem rather innocuous. Among them:

- Is it easy for you to relax?
- Do you have little regret on past misfortunes and failures?
- Does the idea of fear or apprehension give you a physical reaction?
- Could you take the necessary action to kill an animal in order to put it out of pain?

I decided to answer each question the opposite of how I really feel, just to see what would happen.

While I was waiting for the results, I asked my Scientology handler whether the church could really help my acting career take off. "Obviously I'm not at the level of Travolta or Cruise," I tell her, "but are there any classes for me to take to help me become a star?"

"Absolutely," she replies. "I mean, that's what we do. We have courses that people can take where they learn how to, on the one hand, handle certain things in life that are causing trouble. It could be marriage, money, or any other problem you might be having."

Bobby Brown and Whitney Houston pose with baby Bobbi Kristina.

Bobbi Kristina joins mom Whitney onstage during a New York City concert on July 16, 1999. *L. Busacca/Larry Busacca/WireImage/Getty Images*

Four-year-old Bobbi with grandmother Cissy backstage at Madison Square Garden. *Richard Corkery/NY Daily News Archive/Getty Images*

A young Bobbi Kristina, Whitney Houston, and Bobby Brown at the *Princess Diaries 2* premiere. *Lee Celano/ WireImage/Getty Images*

From left to right: Whitney Houston, Michael Jackson, Whitney's rumored lesbian lover Robyn Crawford, and a friend. *inf-00/INFphoto.com/CORBIS*

From left to right: Bobby Brown, Cissy Houston, Whitney Houston, and Clive Davis attending a pre-Grammy party in 1998, at the Plaza Hotel in Manhattan. *Steve Azzara/ CORBIS*

Whitney and Bobbi take the *Good Morning America* stage in 2009. *Ida Mae Astute/ABC/Getty Images*

Cissy and Bobbi at *The Houston's: On Our Own series* premiere party.
Dave Kotinsky/Getty Images

Bobbi Kristina and Nick Gordon in happier times. *Shareif Ziyadat/FilmMagic/Getty Images*

Whitney Houston and Bobbi Kristina together on the red carpet during the 2011 Clive Davis Pre-Grammy Party. *Jeffrey Mayer/WireImage/Getty Images*

Arriving at the funeral home for a private viewing of Whitney's body. *Paul Zimmerman/Getty Images*

Bobbi Kristina and Pat Houston emotionally accept the Billboard Millenium Award on behalf of Whitney Houston in May 2012. *Ethan Miller/Billboards2012/ Getty Images*

Pallbearers carrying Whitney's casket.
Noah K. Murray/Star Ledger/CORBIS

Left to right: Nick Gordon's engagement ring; the Neil Lane engagement ring Nick Gordon bought Bobbi Kristina in 2014. *Courtesy of Author's Collection*

Jason LaVeris/FilmMagic/Getty Images

Courtesy of Author's Collection

The entrance to the Houston's private gated community.
BRANDEN CAMP/epa/CORBIS

Emory University Hospital, where Bobbi Kristina stayed for two months in a medically induced coma.
John E. Davidson/Getty Images

Nick Gordon and Bobbi Kristina with Max Lomas (center), one of the people at Bobbi's house when she was discovered in the bathtub. *Splash News/Corbis*

Cissy Houston arriving at Emory University Hospital to visit Bobbi. *John E. Davidson/ Getty Images*

Bobby Brown and friends stand outside Emory University Hospital after visiting with Bobbi Kristina. *AP Photo/Ron Harris*

"And you'll be able to tell with this test?" I asked.

"Yeah, it's actually very accurate," she asserted.

I then proceeded to tell her that I am actually having a big problem. I'm gay, and I'm worried that it might hurt my acting career.

Melanie jumps in. "He needs this because he's so hung up about being gay," she told the handler. "It's affecting his overall confidence. As an actor, he needs confidence to make it."

"Do you think it makes any sense?" I asked.

"Sure. Absolutely," she responded.

"Well, that's why I'm here, because I think my homosexuality is ruining my career. Is there any way to get over that?"

"Possibly," she replied matter-of-factly.

I asked her how.

"Through auditing," she replied.

"What's auditing?" I asked.

"Auditing is spiritual counseling."

Then the other shoe dropped. She suggested that I was ready for the "E-meter" test. I had come across this bizarre device during my research and was somewhat apprehensive. The E-meter, otherwise known as the electroencephaloneuromentimograph, was introduced by Hubbard in the 1950s as a supposedly simplified lie detector, designed to measure electrical changes in the skin while subjects discussed private and intimate moments from their past. Hubbard argued that unhappiness sprang from mental aberrations (or "engrams") caused by early traumas. Counseling sessions with the E-meter, he claimed, could knock out the engrams, cure blindness, and even improve a person's intelligence and appearance. The US Food and Drug Administration actually stepped in at one point and sued the church because of its claims concerning the effectiveness of the device.

In his 1973 ruling on the matter, U.S. District Judge Gerhard Gesell called Scientology a "pseudo-science that has been adopted and adapted for religious purposes" and that Hubbard's "quackery flourished throughout the United States and in various parts of the world." Gesell declared:

> *Hubbard and his fellow Scientologists developed the notion of using an E-meter to aid auditing. Substantial fees were charged for the meter. They repeatedly and explicitly represented that such auditing effectuated cures of many physical and mental illnesses. An individual processed with the aid of the E-meter was said to reach the intended goal of "clear" and was led to believe there was reliable scientific proof that once cleared many, indeed most, illnesses would automatically be cured. Auditing was guaranteed to be successful. All this was and is false—in short, a fraud. Contrary to representations made, there is absolutely no scientific or medical basis in fact for the claimed cures attributed to E-meter auditing.*

The judge ruled that (1) the church could no longer advertise its services as a scientific cure for disease, (2) must label the E-meters as ineffective in treating illnesses, and (3) could only use the E-meter in "bona fide religious counseling."

But even more controversially, the E-meter is often used for something Scientology allegedly calls the "sexual and criminal security check." Given to members at different phases of their Scientology career, they are asked to hold on to the E-meter while they are asked questions about past criminal acts, crimes against Scientology, and sexual deeds or misdeeds. It is through this exercise, according to stories that have circulated for years from Scientology defectors, that the church garners embarrassing and incriminating information that can be used against members if they try to leave the church or reveal its secrets.

Among the questions supposedly given to new members, known as preclears, are:

- Have you ever raped anyone?
- Have you ever been raped?
- Have you ever been involved in an abortion?
- Have you ever assisted in an abortion?
- Have you ever committed bigamy?
- Have you ever practiced cannibalism?
- Have you ever practiced homosexuality?
- Have you ever practiced or assisted intercourse between women?
- Have you ever had intercourse with a member of your family?
- Have you ever practiced sex with animals?
- Have you ever killed or crippled animals for pleasure?
- Have you ever practiced sodomy?
- Do you collect sexual objects?
- Have you ever had anything to do with pornography?
- Have you practiced sex with children?
- Have you ever used hypnotism to procure sex or money?
- Have you ever used hypnotism to practice sex with children?
- Have you ever been a prostitute?
- Have you ever slept with a member of a race of another color?
- Have you ever been a voyeur?
- Have you ever had intercourse after placing another under alcohol or drugs?
- Do you have any bastards?
- Have you ever masturbated?

Needless to say, I did not relish the idea of being hooked up to this device and possibly revealing my true intentions toward Scientology. But what was the worst they could do to me at this point?

I'm not exactly sure what I was expecting as I was hooked up to the E-meter, but I definitely was not expecting anything as innocuous as the questions they asked me. My handler explained that if the needle on the device moves, it shows stress points, and that if it moves far enough to the right, it's a "fail," which indicates just how much I need Scientology.

Then she asked the first question: "Is anything bothering you today?"

Other than the prospect of being discovered as an undercover filmmaker and sent for "reeducation" by being forced to watch the John Travolta Scientology epic *Battlefield Earth* for hours with my eyeballs propped open, I didn't have a care in the world. This became obvious when the needle on the E-meter failed to move. It just sat there, as if the machine were broken. The handler looked nervous as she waited and waited for something to happen, appearing to will the needle to go haywire. I suspected the lack of movement was unusual. We both just sat there, staring at the needle for what seemed like three minutes, until finally it moved a teensy bit to the right.

"You see," she practically shouts with glee, "that demonstrates a problem."

Then she asked the next question: "Are you nervous about something coming up in your life?" Again, we both waited as nothing happened. Again, she looked nervous, as though she was calculating how much money I wouldn't be shelling out to them to fix my problems. Perhaps it was she who feared having to watch the Travolta film, supposedly based on one of Hubbard's novels and on many critics' lists as the worst movie ever made. Or perhaps there is an even worse punishment (though I couldn't imagine how that's possible); maybe some weird Hubbardian science-fiction torture meted out to Scientology tour guides who fail to meet their sucker quota.

Again, the needle just barely moved. Again, she appeared gleeful, nodding her head in sympathy, as if she had just seen test results showing that I had terminal cancer.

Then she asked me to "Think about something, anything in your life, and focus on it."

My mother had died not long before, so that was the obvious thing to focus on. And naturally, the needle jumped to the right, about an inch. This time the handler could barely contain her excitement; in fact, I think she may have had a tiny orgasm as she watched the needle jump.

I told her I was focusing on my homosexuality and how much it was screwing up my acting career. I asked if their courses could help me overcome my "problem."

"Absolutely," she declared. "We can definitely help you with that. You need auditing." By this time, the results of my personality test had come back in the form of a computerized graph. Not surprisingly, considering that I answered most of the questions the opposite of how I really felt, they revealed that I had a few issues. She announced that I was stressed, depressed, insecure, emotionally fragile, and slightly unstable.

"As I expected," she said, "you are under severe emotional turmoil, but you do have potential. I think Scientology can definitely help you with that. We have courses that you will benefit from greatly. It will turn your life around."

Remembering Michael Pattinson and how much money he had doled out for these courses—at least $500,000 over twenty-five years—I tried to press her about how much it would cost and how long the courses usually take, but she was noncommittal. I was still waiting for her to ask me more questions—perhaps to determine whether I was telling the truth about my sexuality—but, to my disappointment, and relief, she told me the test was over.

I was actually somewhat surprised after all I had read that they didn't probe into anything of a remotely personal nature while I was hooked up to the E-meter, but I supposed they save that for when you're already reeled in.

At least I assumed so, before I returned home and did a little further research.

The origin of the idea that Scientology could "cure" homosexuality actually dates back to a 1951 booklet, published by the Hubbard Dianetic Research Foundation, entitled *Dianetic Processing: A Brief Survey of Research Projects and Preliminary Results*, providing the results of psychometric tests conducted on eighty-eight people undergoing Dianetics therapy. It presents case histories and a number of X-ray plates to support claims that Dianetics had cured "aberrations" including manic depression, asthma, arthritis, colitis, and "overt homosexuality."

The same year, in Hubbard's *Handbook for Preclears*, he set out instructions for Dianeticists to "cure" homosexuality. After claiming that the cause of homosexuality was a fixation on a dominant parent of the opposite sex, he advised, "Break this life continuum concept by running sympathy and grief for the dominant parent and then run off the desires to be an effect and their failures and the homosexual is rehabilitated."

He also wrote *Science of Survival*, in which he called for drastic action to be taken against sexual perverts, whom he rated as "1.1 individuals." Such people, he wrote, should be "taken from society as rapidly as possible and uniformly institutionalized." One of the most effective measures a society threatened by war could take, he argued, would be "rounding up and placing in a cantonment, away from society, any 1.1 individual who might be connected to the government, the military or essential industry." For such people, he reasoned, are "potential traitors, the very mode of operation of their insanity being betrayal." On this level, he continued, are the "slime of society" such as sex criminals, political subversives, and people whose activities are merely the "devious writhings of secret hate."

It is pretty gruesome stuff, but I discovered that Hubbard had actually issued an edict in 1967 altering his previous extreme positions.

"It has never been any part of my plans to regulate or to attempt to regulate the private lives of individuals," he wrote. "Whenever this has occurred, it has not resulted in any improved condition . . . Therefore all former rules, regulations and policies relating to the sexual activities of Scientologists are cancelled."

Whether the edict was disingenuous is anybody's guess, but, five years later, the church published *How to Choose Your People*, a book by Scientologist Ruth Minshull, which was copyrighted to Hubbard and given "issue authority" by the Scientology hierarchy, meaning it had all the weight and credibility of a papal edict. Scientology churches were selling the book alongside Hubbard's own works until 1983. In the book, Minshull described "the gentle-mannered homosexual" as a classic example of the "subversive 1.1 personality." She claimed gays were social misfits. Homosexuals, she wrote, don't practice love because 1.1s can't love. Their relationships, she explains, consist of "brief, sordid and impractical meetings" as well as longer "arrangements" punctuated by dramatic "tirades, discords, jealousies, and frequent infidelity." Their love, she concludes, eventually turns to deep contempt.

Minshull, however, did caution that homosexuals should not be abused or ridiculed. "But a society bent on survival must recognize any aberration as such and seek to raise people out of the low emotion that produces it."

It has actually long been rumored that the homophobic writings of Hubbard might have come from his own embarrassment over Quentin Hubbard, his gay son, who committed suicide in 1976.

A few years ago, a Scientologist wrote a pamphlet entitled *Straight Dope: About Gays and Scientology*. The pamphlet claims that Hubbard abandoned whatever homophobia he once had and that the church's dedication to human rights and clinics designed to fight drug and alcohol addiction should be supported by the gay, lesbian, bisexual, and transgender communities. The pamphlet calls the accusations that the church is a homophobic cult the work of "hate groups" spreading lies. It also argues that the church's refusal to take a position on gay rights issues is not a contradiction in its support of human rights.

In 2002, the American Church of Scientology published a press release on its website quoting gay activist Keith Relkin as saying: "Over the years I have worked with the Church of Scientology for greater inclusion of gay people like me, and today represents a milestone in that progress."

In 2005, an article in *Source* (an official magazine published by the Church of Scientology) featured a gay man and his partner in a success story about their WISE consulting business.

Is all this merely window dressing to disguise what really goes on behind the scenes with the church and gays? I still had no idea. I suppose that I could have taken a bunch of courses and eventually determined for myself whether they were trying to convert me, but I had neither the time, the money, nor the necessary dedication to my craft for the task.

What I did conclude is that the Church of Scientology is no more homophobic than fundamentalist Christianity or Orthodox Judaism, both of which still regard homosexuality as an aberration. Like Scientology, elements of each of these religions have endorsed so-called conversion therapy, although Scientology appears unique in its apparent mission to focus on celebrities.

But I digress.

Although my experiences in Hollywood convinced me beyond any doubt that actors will go to extreme lengths to remain closeted and preserve their bankability, some have argued that those same constraints didn't apply to Whitney to the same degree, because she was merely a singer.

However, the cautionary tale of Clay Aiken convincingly demonstrates that the vinyl closet may be as pervasive as the celluloid variety.

In 2003, the then twenty-four-year-old freckle-faced redhead burst onto the scene during the second season of *American Idol*, the hugely popular singing competition. Aiken ended up coming in second by a whisker to Ruben Studdard in the finale—a result that shocked many observers, because, by that point, he had already secured an enormous fan base that had taken to calling themselves "Clay Nation." In the days before social media took off, Internet fan forums set the trends and Aiken had a massive following—an eclectic mix of Middle American tweens, grandmothers, and Christians who gushed at his boyish good looks and aw-shucks wholesome image.

Even before the results were announced, Internet trolls regularly popped up in these forums to speculate on Aiken's sexuality. Many were convinced that his slightly effeminate manner and singing style were signs that he was unmistakably gay. But as he professed his devotion to God and leaned hard on his bio of how he developed his mellifluous voice in the Baptist church choir where he sang every Sunday, Clay Nation savaged any such possibility.

Gradually as the drumbeat of speculation grew louder, these fans would protest that it was none of anybody's business and that they would love Clay even if he were gay. What does his sexuality have to do with his music? they trumpeted.

Although Clay had placed second in the competition, his first recording efforts far surpassed Studdard's own sales. His first album, *Measure of a Man*, debuted at number one on the *Billboard* charts in 2003, selling an astonishing 613,000 copies in its first week. It was the highest-selling debut album for a solo artist in more than a decade. His Clay Nation, in fact, was vaguely reminiscent of the "Belieber" phenomenon that made Justin Bieber a monster pop idol not long afterward.

A year later, Aiken's Christmas album, *Merry Christmas with Love*, became the best-selling holiday album ever released since Soundscan began tracking these numbers.

When his album *A Thousand Different Ways* debuted at number two on the *Billboard* chart in September 2006, it made Aiken only the fourth recording artist in history ever to have his first three albums debut in the top five and sell more than 200,000 copies in the first week.

He was a genuine megastar even as the gay whispers intensified. As far back as July 2003, *Rolling Stone* featured the singer in a cover story in which he says, "One thing I've found of people in the public eye, either you're a womanizer or you've got to be gay. Since I'm neither one of those, people are completely concerned about me." As speculation grew, he was forced to repeatedly deny the rumors.

"It doesn't matter what I say. People are going to believe what they want," he told *People* in 2006.

Meanwhile, the whispers about his sexuality grew louder, especially after a Boston teacher revealed in 2006 that he had an exchange with Aiken on the gay chat site Manhunt.net. Blogger Perez Hilton posted the exchange between Aiken and the teacher on his popular website along with actual webcam photos. Suddenly Aiken's secret was out.

Soon after, while Aiken appeared on the talk show *Live with Regis and Kelly*, he was chastised by Kelly Ripa when he put his hand over her mouth, causing her to recoil and protest, "I don't know where those hands have been, honey." Rosie O'Donnell, by then out of the closet herself, accused Ripa of homophobia—an accusation that was seconded by another *American Idol* contestant, Katharine McPhee, who told *People* she believed that Ripa's gesture was responding to Aiken's perceived homosexuality. "She did. She kind of outed Clay," McPhee said. "That's his personal business that no one really knows."

Kelly then called in to Rosie on *The View* and protested that she was the only talk show host who didn't question his sexuality. She merely didn't want his hand over her mouth because it was "cold and flu season." Rosie wasn't buying the disingenuous explanation and stood by her accusation.

In 2008, Aiken finally confirmed what just about everybody on the planet already knew when he appeared on the cover of *People* to confirm that he is indeed gay and had just had a baby through in vitro fertilization with his friend, producer Jaymes Foster.

"I cannot raise a child to lie or to hide things," he said, ignoring the fact that he had been lying to the public for five years. "I wasn't raised that way, and I'm not going to raise a child to do that."

And how did Clay Nation—which long professed they would love Clay whether he was gay or straight—react to the news? A few months later, *People* reported that his record label was dropping him because his recent album, *On My Way Here*, sold only 159,000 copies in the U.S. compared to his debut album, which had sold 2.78 million copies. A greatest hits album was released a month later and sold only a paltry three thousand copies in the U.S. in its first week.

And, although Clay went on to carve out a new niche as a Broadway performer and a gay rights activist, he has long been abandoned by his once-huge fan base.

Given his career trajectory, it is difficult to question why Whitney or any other huge star would risk the career-killing decision to come out to their fans. But even though the bigotry of his largely Christian fan base undeniably contributed to Aiken's fall, homophobia alone might not be the only reason Whitney chose to remain in the closet. After all, she barely tried to disguise her relationship with Robyn during her initial rise to stardom, and her fan base was undeniably more diverse than Aiken's had been.

But singing wasn't Whitney's only ambition. For years, she had harbored ambitions to act on the big screen. As far back as 1989, in fact, she had been lobbying for the role of Deena in *Dreamgirls*, but that fell through when Whitney's people demanded she be allowed to sing more songs than had been contemplated for that role. Beyoncé was eventually tapped to play Deena, a performance that earned her a Golden Globe nomination. At one point, when Whitney heard a rumor that Diana Ross wanted to star in the film, she said of the then forty-four-year-old star, "Then they'd have to retitle it *Dreamgrannies*. How old is she anyways, fifty?"

She would eventually get her chance to be a film star and would make the most of it, being the highlight of her career. But the odds of landing a role as a romantic interest in a Hollywood film would have been undeniably nil, had she chosen to reveal herself as anything but a heterosexual woman that audiences could picture Kevin Costner falling for.

From a career standpoint, she likely made the right decision. On a personal level, it may have been a whole other matter.

And whether she was thinking of her fallen standing in the black community or a new career in Hollywood, Whitney's life definitely changed forever on the night she was booed at the Soul Train Music Awards on April 13, 1989. That happened to be the night she met a man named Bobby Brown.

CHAPTER **FOURTEEN**

The credits had hardly rolled on the *Dr. Phil* show when the critics started to pile on. Kevin Fallon of *The Daily Beast* fired the first volley, calling the intervention "despicable and exploitative."

"It is already clear that this episode of *Dr. Phil* may be the most despicable thing that has aired on television," he wrote.

Already on the ground in Atlanta, I barely had time to process the show and gauge whether Gordon's breakdown was simply playing for the cameras or legitimate evidence of a distraught young man's sincere grieving for his girlfriend's life-threatening condition.

I asked my Miami psychiatrist neighbor, Dr. Eva Ritvo, for her thoughts.

"It was difficult to watch the show. It is very uncomfortable to watch someone's personal health crisis unfold on national TV. Nick had consented to be interviewed but it was immediately apparent that he was in no condition to be speaking rationally to anyone and certainly not to such a large audience. It was clear almost immediately that he was quite impaired. His slurred speech, rapidly shifting emotions, inability to sit still, and his rambling conversational style all indicate acute mental illness.

Nick's use of alcohol combined with Xanax is clearly threatening his life. He mentioned wanting to die on many occasions to his mother and to viewers. I agree completely with Dr. Phil that inpatient detoxification followed by rehabilitation is the right treatment. I also agree that an involuntary hospitalization would have been warranted if Nick refused to enter treatment on his own.

Dr. Phil was very effective in engaging and using his mother. I liked his calm tone. I felt he was a bit too challenging and perhaps could have shortened his explanations after Nick agreed to enter treatment. Explaining anything to someone intoxicated is a not a good use of time or energy. Once Nick agreed, the right move was to end the conversation and begin the process of getting to treatment as quickly as possible.

Nick has many hurdles to overcome. Mixed substance abuse combined with the ongoing stress of Bobbi Kristina's illness and the trauma of finding her in the bathtub. It seems he has not successfully grieved the loss of Whitney and is carrying a lot of guilt. He will need extensive therapy to resolve these issues once his brain has recovered from the effects of the drugs and alcohol. Long-term treatment will be key if he is to successfully recover. Family support is essential alongside the medical and psychological treatments. It seems there is a strong religious faith in the family that can also help in his recovery.

It appeared to me that Dr. Ritvo had been swayed just as effectively as the other lay viewers who came away sympathizing with Gordon rather than vilifying him. None appeared to pick up on his frequent admission that he feels "guilty" for what happened to her. Was I the only one who wondered whether this could be significant, rather than simply taking it at face value that his guilt concerned his inability to save her? It was obviously a smart move for his handlers to let him on the show, but it brought us no closer to the truth about what had happened that morning.

At the same time, some observers believed they had actually discovered damning evidence of Nick's guilt in the broadcast.

Michelle Gordon's revelation that Bobbi and Nick had argued after returning from a night of partying was an important clue, believes a website called *Celebrity Dirty Laundry*.

"It seems rather odd that Nick's mom would be spewing out such intimate details on national television," observed the entertainment blog. "Whether she means to or not, Michelle Gordon is making her son look extremely guilty. When you consider the fact that Bobbi Kristina had bruises and a bloodied mouth when she was discovered, it certainly sounds like their verbal spat led to physical violence."

Such was the nature of the quality and tone of the reporting on this case by mid-March. I was hoping my own investigation could add a loftier analysis and maybe even some salient facts to counter the increasingly absurd speculation and innuendo in this case, akin to that which had made the initial O. J. Simpson media frenzy worthy of a Pulitzer by comparison.

When I arrived in Atlanta at the beginning of March, my first goal was to get to the bottom of an enduring mystery that has all but gotten lost in the ongoing saga.

Was Nick Gordon actually married to Bobbi Kristina?

On July 10, 2013, Bobbi had posted on her Facebook page, "Yes, me and Nick are engaged." A year earlier, they had also announced an engagement on their short-lived reality show but then apparently later called it off, on the grounds that her family "disapproved." On January 9, 2014, Bobbi then tweeted,

> "@nickgordon! #HappilyMarried.SO #Inlove. If you didn't get it the first time that is."

She posted a photo of her hand resting on his with their weddings bands on display. When Max Lomas called 911 on January 31 to report that Bobbi had been discovered in the bathtub, he reported that her "husband" was performing CPR.

For weeks, the media referred to Nick as Bobbi's husband. If that was the case, I wondered, how could he be barred from the hospital? Under Georgia law, the spouse has a number of rights that would trump even the victim's parent. Yet Bobby Brown has been by his daughter's bedside for weeks, while Nick has been completely shut out.

But visitation isn't the only issue impacted by whether the two are married. I expect that if Bobbi fails to pull through, there will be a ferocious legal battle over her estate as the sole beneficiary of Whitney Houston's estimated $20 million fortune.

The fate of that money, in fact, may come down to whether Nick and Bobbi ever tied the knot, especially since common-law marriages have not been recognized by the state of Georgia since 1997. Nick, therefore, will have to produce a piece of paper to establish any bona fide claim.

A quick trip to the Fulton County Probate Court failed to produce any record of a marriage between Nicholas Gordon and Bobbi Kristina Brown. Neither did a search of the State Office of Vital Records. It's possible, of course, the two jetted over to Vegas for a quickie wedding—maybe even presided over by an Elvis impersonator—but all indications are that the two are not husband and wife.

That still leaves a potentially complex battle over who's entitled to Whitney's fortune and one that I intend to delve into later, but it looks like that fight will involve Bobby Brown and Whitney's family, while Nick will be forced to watch from the sidelines.

Although my first investigation hardly required rocket science, I quickly realized that I would need someone who is familiar with Atlanta and could help get me answers in a hurry. I had already been in contact with a number of private investigators, most of whom sounded like they came out of a Dashiell Hammett novel or had read too much Philip Marlowe. They all promised to get to the bottom of the case fast for a rather hefty fee. But I had an unsettled feeling about all of them. I sensed this wasn't a case that called for a heavy hand or intimidation of key witnesses. This was a case where I needed to locate friends and friends of friends of the key players. And I needed to locate them right away.

That's when I was referred to a woman named Sheila McPhilamy of the Complete Investigations agency, who I was told specializes in searching for exactly that. Her credentials are definitely impressive, having collaborated on cases with the FBI and the Georgia Bureau of Investigation. The moment I heard her Southern accent and concise no-nonsense analysis of what needed to be done, I knew I had found my woman.

Of course, I wasn't used to having other people do my sleuthing. I had established something of a reputation for undercover investigations over the years that saw me assuming the identity of a male model, a gay actor, a junkie, a male prostitute, a mental patient, and an array of other identities in my journalistic endeavors. It turned out that Sheila was happy to cooperate with helping me transform into yet another undercover persona—private investigator. I would accompany her as her "assistant" as we cruised Atlanta looking to establish what happened on the morning of January 31, 2015, that left Bobbi Kristina in a coma.

CHAPTER **FIFTEEN**

It's difficult to remember, given subsequent events, but Bobby Brown—more often known in later years as Mr. Whitney Houston—was once a force to be reckoned with in the music industry and had made a name for himself as an artist and a commercial powerhouse before the world had ever heard of Whitney.

Bobby was a genuine man of the streets. He was born in the hardscrabble Orchard Park projects in Boston's working-class Roxbury neighborhood, where prostitutes, gang members, and drug dealers circulated in the dense, low-rise housing development that was built as part of the failed well-intentioned housing experiments that came to destroy the fabric of many American inner cities. The area was known as "Beirut" because of the frequent murders and violence that had plagued the projects for years.

His parents—a substitute teacher and a construction worker—did their best to shelter their eight kids from the social turmoil around them. Music became the glue that kept them together.

His father, who looked a little like Chuck Berry, would pull out his guitar and lay down some Berry riffs or classic soul while the kids gathered around the living room.

At age four his mother took him to see James Brown at Boston's

Sugar Shack. During intermission, she plopped him onstage and he started entertaining the crowd with his James Brown impressions. They ate it up, and Bobby knew this was what he wanted to do.

"He was never shy," his brother and manager, Tommy, later recalled. "Not Bobby."

Whenever his parents had guests over, he'd put on the costume he'd constructed for his new persona, "Flash B," and entertain any chance he got. When he was eleven, his friend Jimbo Flint was killed by gang violence, which left him itching to escape the projects and never return.

"That was the turning point in my life," he later recalled. "That's when I realized that running the streets can't last forever. You don't always have good luck."

When he was twelve, he had his own near miss, when he was shot in his right knee.

"I had been at a party dancing with some guy's girlfriend," he later recalled in his memoir, "when all of a sudden she said, 'You better run! That's my boyfriend.' I was like, 'It's too late.'"

Brown had discovered a knack for choreography when he was only seven years old, orchestrating complicated break-dancing moves to the music that permeated the projects night and day.

When he was nine, he put together his first group, Bobby and the Angels. Three years later he put together the group with his friends Michael Bivins and Ricky Bell—along with Travis Pettus and Corey Rackley a little while later—that would help launch him to stardom. Soon, they added another kid from the projects, Ralph Tresvant, and called themselves the Intruders.

Bobby started as the lead singer but soon ceded the microphone to Ralph, whose tenor voice was reminiscent of a young Michael Jackson, and instead focused on the dancing and choreography that he would soon be famous for.

In 1982, the four boys performed at a show at Boston's Strand Theatre, Hollywood Talent Night, put on by producer Maurice Starr, for a prize of $500 and a record contract. Although the boys failed to win, Starr was so impressed that he offered them a deal on his independent label, Streetwise Records. Soon after, they added a fifth member, and New Edition was born—so named by Starr because he believed they were like a new version of the Jackson Five.

Before long, he brought them into the studio to record an album comprised of material they had written—including a Bobby Brown composition, "Jealous Girl," and a song written by Starr, "Candy Girl," which would be released as a single and top both the American R&B charts and the UK singles chart. It would also be the name of their first album.

As they hit the road on a nationwide tour, the quintet and their music soon established them in a new niche that would transform the industry during the eighties—the era of the boy band. The boys were on top of the world at the excitement of touring and dreams of stardom. But when they returned to Orchard Park, they were stunned to receive a check for $1.87 as compensation for their efforts.

Starr explained the vagaries of the business and the expenses of touring, but the streetwise teenage musicians weren't buying it. They believed they were being ripped off and hired lawyers to get out of their contract with Starr in 1984.

But having perfected the boy band formula with New Edition, he wasted no time assembling another group of boys that he would transform into a phenomenon known as New Kids on the Block.

Bobby was only fifteen when New Edition signed to MCA Records to record their second album, *New Edition*, which would go on to sell two million records and vault the boys to stardom.

Despite their success, not all was rosy within the group, which had no natural leader. As the lead singer, Ralph got much of the attention but the other members fought hard for their share of the limelight. None more so than Bobby, whose dance moves had gained him a steady following, especially among the older women who came out to the shows to join the young girls whose piercing screams could be heard throughout the performances.

"While Ralph had the teenyboppers, I had their mothers," Bobby recalled.

Bobby's penchant for partying and his growing ego were causing considerable animosity among his bandmates. Bickering and backstage arguments caused significant tension. Bobby would claim the others resented that he would constantly question management about their meager paychecks—$120 a week on the road—while they played in sold-out venues.

"It was almost like we were whores getting pimped," Bobby recalled in his memoir. "Coming off the road, the tour bus would drop us back in the projects and we were back to our reality—poor, struggling project kids. I had a serious problem with this, but the other guys didn't see it."

Meanwhile, MCA—recognizing a maturity in his voice and style that belied his age and the boy band sound—had quietly offered Bobby his own deal, estimated at $250,000, to record a solo album.

Between tours with New Edition, he was already laying down tracks for the new album. On the road, he was increasingly belligerent toward the other members, to the point where he threw a microphone that struck Bivins one night, then stormed off to his dressing room and changed into a robe. Returning to the stage, he delivered a number that he claimed blew the roof off and had the crowd on their feet.

"Bobby was a purist," MCA executive Ernie Singleton later recalled. "There was a tremendous amount of friction between Bobby and the rest of the guys."

In late 1985, his showboating antics had finally become too much for the other members, who took a vote and decided to throw Bobby out of the band. He claims he didn't actually learn of their decision until two years later, when he saw a piece on VH1. He claims he believed he had already left the band on his own to embark on a new career now that his solo album was finished and on the verge of release. By the time he left, he later claimed, "All I got out of New Edition was $500 and a VCR."

Regardless, his first solo album, *King of Stage*—released in 1986—went gold, and its single, "Girlfriend," hit number one on the R&B charts. It was considered something of a success. Still, many observers wondered if he had made a mistake leaving the group that had launched him from a life on the streets. Few predicted what would come next.

When *Don't Be Cruel* was released in June 1988, it exploded onto the charts almost immediately with a riveting style that almost overnight became the best-known example of the new jack swing sound, combining soul and hip-hop—pioneered by producers such as Babyface and Jimmy Jam—that would transform R&B during the late eighties.

The album, which was lauded by most reviewers, spent six weeks at the top of the *Billboard* charts and ended up as the best-selling album of 1989. It produced five top-ten singles, including the number one hit, "My Prerogative," which would become Bobby's signature song. It ended up selling more than eight million copies and turned him into a superstar. The choreography and dance moves that he had perfected during the New Edition days soon became an important part of his stage persona, and his live shows became a phenomenon.

Newsday called him "the most electrifying performer of his day." The *LA Times* called the album "a trailblazing collection that mixed traditional R&B with hip-hop energy: a brash, exciting, young urban sound." Michael Jackson, with whom Bobby was frequently compared, was so blown away that he hired the production team to work on his upcoming *Dangerous* album.

With the money from his MCA advance, he had finally moved his mother out of the projects—a feat he claims was one of his proudest accomplishments.

With the success of the album came the first reports of a hard-partying lifestyle that started to earn him the nickname the "Bad Boy" of R&B.

In concert, his performances became known for their racy content. At a 1989 performance in Columbus, Georgia, Bobby was arrested for violation of the municipal "lewd" act—prohibiting acts of "simulated sexual intercourse"—when he brought a female fan onstage to dance with him. It was the same offense a young Elvis the Pelvis was charged with decades earlier when he gyrated his hips a little too suggestively in Georgia.

Bobby later claimed he was dancing five feet away from the eighteen-year-old girl.

"I didn't even touch her," he protested.

But the officer who hauled him away during the break accused him of "hunching."

Calling it a "brush with ignorance," Bobby explained, "I'm a crowd-pleaser. I invite a fan onstage at all my shows. I just did a couple of pumps with my hips. There's nothing wrong or nasty about it. It's just a dance." He was released after posting $652 for bail. Such reports helped to fuel the subsequent Bad Boy image, and although Bobby later claimed the term itself was never used until later, he never really disowned it.

"The term to me doesn't necessarily mean that I have to rip your head off or do something illegal," he would tell his biographer, Derrick Handspike, about the moniker that would follow him for much of his career. "It does set the tone not to look at me as a pushover. I'm definitely going to stand my ground. I've always been a fighter in that sense. I'm a fighter by nature because I was raised in the projects where you had to fight for your life. . . . That doesn't mean that I go out looking for trouble or looking to be the aggressor. At the same time, I'm no punk. If trouble comes my way, I deal with it."

There were also reports of heavy drug use—one of the factors that had allegedly prompted the members of New Edition to vote him out of the band. He claims they were influenced by management who told them he was dealing and using drugs—an allegation he has denied. But in the biography on which he collaborated with Derrick Handspike, he acknowledges that he was often in a state of intoxication, though he would later claim he mostly smoked pot.

"There were nights when I'd get high out of my mind, and ghosts in the form of naked white women would come down from the ceiling and have sex with me," he recalled.

By most accounts, he liked to have sex—a lot of it, and although that hardly makes him unique in the music world, it was unusual to see a teenage boy being described as a "womanizer." At one point, he became known as the "Black Tom Jones," because frenzied female fans took to throwing their underwear onstage when he performed, a phenomenon that began in the New Edition days.

"There were little girls chasing us around," he later recalled. "Little panties onstage. Some of the girls were fast and it broke a lot of us down."

When he was seventeen, he had his first child, a son named Landon, with his teenage girlfriend Melika Williams. Like Whitney, there were also reports of bisexuality over the years, and a musician once told me that Bobby liked men, but I've never found any solid evidence to support that—and not for lack of trying, after I wondered whether his relationship with Whitney was merely one of convenience for both parties. Bobby, however, was unequivocal about his preferences.

"I think women are God's gift to this earth," he told *Vanity Fair*. "I *love* women."

With the success of *Don't Be Cruel* came a lot of money, and Bobby's penchant for spending it was legendary. He claims he would often spend $100,000 partying or a million on a "shopping spree." If he made $250,000 during a show, he noted, $50,000 would be set aside for expenses and the balance would be his "spending money." There were luxury cars and expensive gadgets and at least one practical purchase—a $2 million mansion in North Atlanta that he acquired from a man known as the "Porn King." The house came with an Olympic-size swimming pool, tennis courts, and a theater. He also bought a studio that he named "Bosstown."

But on the night Brown met Whitney in April 1989, all that was still ahead of him. He was still on top of the music world that night, having been nominated for three awards for his monster album of the year before. The twenty-year-old was also a featured performer, singing his best-known song, "My Prerogative." Whitney would later recall watching from the audience.

"He was kicking *Don't Be Cruel*—he was hot, he was on fire," she told *Rolling Stone*. "I and some friends of mine were sitting behind him. I was hugging them, we were laughing, and I kept hitting Bobby in the back of the head. Robyn said, 'Whitney, you keep hittin' Bobby, he's goin' to be mad at you." I leaned over and said, 'Bobby, I'm so sorry.' And he turned around and looked at me like 'Yeah, well just don't let it happen again.' And I was like 'Oooooh, this guy doesn't like me.'" Her friend the singer Cherrelle later claimed that Whitney told her the moment she saw him that night, "That is going to be my husband."

She claimed that she had always been curious when somebody didn't like her, so she decided to invite him to a party. When he accepted the invitation, she was surprised.

"He was the first male I met in the business that I could talk to and be real with," she recalled. "He was so down and so cool, I was like 'I like him.'"

Four months later, she saw Bobby again at a gospel show featuring her close friends BeBe and CeCe Winans. After the show, she went out to dinner with Bobby and the Winans.

"At the end of the dinner," she recalled, "Bobby walked up to me and said, 'If I asked you to go out with me, would you?' At the time I was dating someone, but it was kind of ehhhh. So I said, 'Yeah, I would.' And he said, 'You really would?'—he's so cool—'I'll pick you up tomorrow at eight.'"

While they were simply friends for a time after that, she claims that Bobby persisted in his romantic intentions.

For his part, Bobby claimed it was love at first sight. "All of a sudden, I felt someone poking me in the back of my head," he recalled in his memoir. "Startled, I turned around like, 'Who in fuck? What the fuck?' It was Whitney Houston. She said, 'Excuse me, was I hitting you?' I said, 'Yeah, you were hitting me, but it's ok as long as it was you.' At that moment, I thought, 'She's flirting with me.' I knew it was my chance to move in, so I went for the jugular. I said to her, 'If I asked you to go on a date, would you say yes?' She was like, 'Yea!'"

He claims that not long afterward they went shopping together on Rodeo Drive and had a great time. She was nothing like her "prim and proper conservative" TV persona, he recalled. Instead, he found her "down-to-earth."

Before long, he claims, they were dating. They'd meet between shows when one of them was on tour. They jetted off on "romantic vacations" on islands around the world or on private yachts.

And while many wondered what they had in common, he claims that he knows the secret. "I've always been known to be a pretty good lover," he tells Handspike. "The word on the street is that I'm well-endowed."

Over the years there have been many contradictory stories about when in fact their relationship turned romantic, including slightly differing accounts by both Bobby and Whitney. What is most striking is that he ended up purchasing his Atlanta mansion in 1990, more than a year after he first met Whitney.

This soon became known as Atlanta's version of the Playboy mansion, with parties held night and day featuring celebrities and VIPs cavorting with bikini models, though Bobby would later claim he stayed in the mansion only because he was afraid to go out, terrified that people would ask him when the next album would be released.

Partly because of the shenanigans during these parties, Bobby became known around town as quite the womanizer, and it was during this period—when he was supposedly dating Whitney—that he had two more children with a woman named Kim Ward. In 1990, his first daughter, LaPrincia was born. Another son, Bobby, came along in 1992. It is just one of the many anomalies in the story of their fairytale romance that would cause even the most mainstream media to express genuine surprise when the two eventually announced their engagement.

Meanwhile, Whitney's career was at something of a crossroads. In 1990, she finally headed back into the studio to record her third album, *I'm Your Baby Tonight*. It featured many of the same writers and producers as her first two efforts, along with some of the personnel, including Babyface and L.A. Reid, who had helped craft Bobby's album into a masterpiece. Perhaps stung by the criticism that she had been sounding "too white," Whitney seemed intent on adding a little bit more edge and more of a distinctive R&B sound than on *Whitney*.

The results appeared to pay off when the first reviews came in. *Rolling Stone* said the album displayed a "slick R&B edge." The *Baltimore Sun* wasn't impressed by the material but took note of Whitney's "sultry moans, note-bending asides and window-rattling shouts."

But aside from increased R&B credibility this time around, sales were abysmal, especially by the standards of her first two efforts. Despite the fact that the world had been waiting in eager anticipation for her next effort for more than three years, the album debuted at a disappointing twenty-two on the *Billboard* charts. It would eventually rise as high as number three—although it did hit number one on the R&B charts—and spent ten weeks in the top ten, but considering her previous monster success, it was considered something of a failure, at least in the United States. Steady international sales helped make up for its slow pace, but it was clear that Whitney had lost some of her luster.

The poor sales reignited media speculation of a backlash against the suddenly waning superstar. And while many believed the rumors about her sexuality were a contributing factor, Whitney chose to inexplicably blame Arista for failing to properly promote the album.

"I know a lot of folks who would like to sell as many records as *Baby Tonight* sold," she told *TV Guide* somewhat defensively. "What disappointed me was that my record company did not do what they should have done to make [the record] more of a success. They bungled."

Still, despite the slow start, she had been asked to perform "The Star Spangled Banner" at the Super Bowl in January shortly after the album's release—providing a massive platform and worldwide exposure.

By the time the big game came on January 27, events had conspired in her favor thanks to Saddam Hussein. Ten days earlier, the United States had launched Operation Desert Storm to repel Saddam's invasion of Kuwait. What better opportunity to capitalize on Americans' wartime fervor than delivering the most patriotic song of all. Whitney took full advantage of the opportunity. When NFL officials first heard the jazzy version she intended to sing, they were beside themselves and demanded a more mainstream rendering. They argued that her version was "too flamboyant for wartime."

Whitney's father told the league in no uncertain terms that his daughter would sing the song the way she wanted, causing considerable consternation among the conservative suits that ran the league.

They had no reason to worry. Wearing a white tracksuit, she stepped out on the field that afternoon in Tampa and delivered a stirring rendition surrounded by American flags scattered all over the field and various military personnel in uniform whom the cameras frequently focused on as she sang. It had the crowd in a frenzy and the TV audience of 115 million choked up.

"Every so often, a singer comes along and reclaims 'The Star-Spangled Banner,'" gushed *Entertainment Weekly*. "Now, with her stirring Super Bowl rendition, it's Whitney Houston's turn."

Within hours of the performance, the Arista phone lines were flooded with callers requesting a copy of her rendition. The company scrambled to rush out a single, which sold 750,000 copies in a week, the company's fastest-selling single of all time. Later, Clive Davis admitted they had intended all along to capitalize on the wartime patriotism and had planned the release in advance of the day, anticipating the reaction. All proceeds were donated to the American Red Cross Gulf Crisis Fund. Whitney was hot again, though she and Arista were forced on the defensive a month later when NFL official Bob Best revealed that the single had actually been taped in a recording studio the week before the game took place. Cissy would later claim the recording was necessary because a fighter-jet flyover above the stadium was planned and they needed to time the flyover to coincide with a particular point in the song. It turned out that Whitney had in fact sung into a dead microphone while the pretaped version was played, although her publicist unconvincingly told the media that Whitney had no knowledge of the plan and believed she was singing into a live mike. "This isn't lip-synch gate," she said.

Whitney's former bodyguard Kevin Ammons later reported another controversy around the time of her Super Bowl appearance. He claims there was an altercation between Whitney and Robyn at an event that started when MC Hammer flirted with her backstage.

After Hammer departed, Ammons claims, Robyn grabbed Whitney's arm and started screaming, "Don't ever disrespect me like that." Whitney jerked her arm away and told her assistant to "go to hell." Watching Robyn slap Whitney, Cissy allegedly yelled, "Don't you ever put your hands on my daughter," then started punching her and kicking her, yelling, "I'll kill you, you stupid bitch!"

———

Whitney had not given up her ambitions to appear on the big screen and had let her management team know that this was one of her top priorities as the new decade got under way. The stories about how she came to appear in *The Bodyguard* have nearly as many versions as the origin of her romance with Bobby Brown.

One story has it that Kevin Costner had first approached Whitney about appearing in his film as far back as 1989 but that she was initially reluctant.

It's the version she would tell *Entertainment Weekly* in 1993.

"I kept saying to him, 'What makes you think I can do this?' And he used to say to me—she launches into a playful imitation of Costner's flat Southern California drone—'Whitney, listen. Every once in a blue moon you get this person who just comes around and has this quaaality. When you thought about a movie that had music in it, you used to think about Barbra or Diana. But now it's you.' And I'm like, "That's what I want. I want it to be meeee!'"

To another interviewer, she claimed that Costner began wooing her for the part in early 1990, and when her agent confirmed she was up for the part, she was flabbergasted. "My God," she would tell her biographer Jeffery Bowman. "Can you imagine this! Kevin Costner calls me up out of the clear blue sky and asks me to be in a movie with him. Who would believe this?"

The idea for the film itself was making the rounds in Hollywood as far back as the seventies, when it was first envisioned as a starring vehicle for Diana Ross and Steve McQueen. But it reportedly fell through at the time when McQueen was unhappy that he would be overshadowed by Ross. A few years later, the idea was resurrected but with Ryan O'Neal as the lead male character and Ross as his love interest.

The writer, Lawrence Kasdan, had shopped his screenplay around Hollywood for a decade with no success before he finally interested Costner, who saw himself in the lead role as a white bodyguard who fell for his black protectee.

Meanwhile, poor record sales for Whitney's third album weren't the only signs of a career lull. Whitney had kicked off her 1991 tour with a concert to capitalize on the patriotic frenzy sparked by the

Gulf War. It was originally scheduled as an HBO special, with Whitney singing for the troops on Easter Sunday. But by the time of the scheduled concert, the war was over and instead it was billed as a "Welcome Home, Heroes" concert, with Whitney performing in a Virginia naval hangar to welcome home military personnel returning from Iraq.

In August 1991, the *New York Times* reported that she was playing to less than capacity crowds on her US tour. And, although the recession may have played a part in the poor sales, critics had noted that her performances left a lot to be desired.

"Onstage, Ms. Houston was actually shallow and bland with no trace of emotional depth," wrote the reviewer for the *Dallas News* about the Texas leg of the tour.

Apart from the rumors of her sexuality, to this point Whitney had always been portrayed as the good girl. It was all the more surprising, then, when headlines screamed in April 1991 that she had been arrested and charged with assault and threatening to kill a man in a Lexington Kentucky hotel lounge.

She and Robyn were still inseparable, sharing a room on the tour. On the night in question, Robyn, Whitney, and her brother Michael—surrounded by bodyguards—arrived at the Radisson hotel lounge around midnight to watch the Evander Holyfield bout with George Foreman following an evening watching horse racing at The Red Mile racetrack.

While they settled in, a group of drunken men started making loud racist and "sexual" comments, allegedly because bodyguards had stopped them when they approached Whitney for an autograph earlier. Finally, the three decided to leave the bar and watch the fight in their rooms on the seventeenth floor.

Three of the men followed them to their floor and insisted on an autograph. When Michael confronted them, one of the men punched him in the jaw, starting a brawl. One of the men reportedly called Whitney a "stuck-up nigger bitch," prompting Michael to jump him.

As the man pinned Michael on the floor, Whitney allegedly jumped on his back and punched him in the jaw. One of the hotel guests who emerged from his room to watch the melee claims that Whitney shouted, "You're going to die, you son of a bitch." Eventually, police arrived and broke up the brawl.

Ammon claims he heard Whitney telling her publicist, "I kicked ass, baby. I wasn't about to let those hillbilly motherfuckers hurt my brother."

Days later, Whitney was charged with assault and "terroristic threatening." The charges were eventually dropped, but the men filed a civil lawsuit against Whitney, prompting her to file a countersuit for defamation. She claimed they had demanded $425,000 to keep the story out of the press.

When the story hit the press, Whitney's camp was forced to acknowledge that she had indeed been involved in a fistfight, setting off a predictable tabloid frenzy.

Whitney's father, who was running his daughter's management company at the time, issued a statement praising the dignity and professionalism displayed by his son Michael during the incident.

"I am equally proud of my daughter, Whitney, who would not let any career concerns prevent her from protecting her brother," John Houston told *Jet*. "By exposing herself to potential physical harm, she risked career-threatening injuries."

The tour resumed, but ticket sales remained dismal. Eventually, Whitney canceled the tour altogether, claiming she had damaged her vocal cords, but some observers were skeptical, given the ticket sales. A number of acts had fared poorly that year, but not nearly as badly as Whitney, given her status as a superstar at the peak of her career. By year's end, it was revealed she had performed in the bottom ten of touring acts and had contributed to the $4 million in losses music promoters suffered that year.

Although publicity around the Kentucky melee revealed once

again that Robyn and Whitney were still as close as ever, it would prove to mark the last year that the two women were inseparable.

By the time of the hotel incident, when it was revealed they shared a room on the road, they were still evidently making little effort to hide the nature of their relationship even as Whitney continued to publicly deny they were anything more than friends.

Observing them together backstage at an event, *Vanity Fair*'s Lynn Hirschberg would observe, "It's easy to see why conclusions were drawn: Houston and Crawford have been best friends for 15 years and are virtually inseparable. Crawford counsels her on all aspects of her career—from what dress to wear at a photo shoot to how loud the vocal should sound on a particular track from *The Bodyguard*. They watch each other constantly. 'Doesn't Robyn look thin?' Houston will ask as she sees Crawford's reflection in the makeup mirror."

But the prominent British gay rights and environmental activist Peter Tatchell based his own assessment on more than just their close working relationship. He remembers when Robyn accompanied Whitney to a 1991 HIV benefit, the Reach Out and Touch rally, in London's Hyde Park.

"When I met them, it was obvious they were madly in love," he later recalled after Whitney's death.

"Their intimacy and affection was so sweet and romantic. They held hands in the back of the car like teenage sweethearts. Clearly more than just friends, they were a gorgeous couple and so happy together. To see their love was infectious and uplifting," recalled the former Labour Party parliamentary candidate.

His description echoes that of Frank Giles, a prominent member of the Miami hospitality industry, who recalls serving Whitney on two occasions when he was a waiter at LA's famed restaurant Chasen's, in the early nineties.

"She came in with another woman," Giles told me in March 2015. "They were in a good mood, smiling and showing lots of energy.

When I brought their order, I was taken by surprise when I found them kissing. They were jamming on those kisses. I pretended as if I didn't notice when I put their food down on the table. I'm sure they knew I saw them but it seemed as if they didn't care. I had no idea who the woman with Whitney was. She was a pretty black woman."

Many others have described to me similar encounters with Whitney and Robyn during the eighties and early nineties but chose not to talk on the record.

However, in late 1991, two significant milestones were about to change the nature of their relationship, at least in how they presented it to the public.

Although Whitney had allegedly been dating Bobby for months, perhaps more than a year, and they were supposedly gallivanting around the world on "romantic vacations," they somehow managed to keep it a secret from the media. Paparazzi dogged Whitney whenever she appeared in public but the tabloids were still peddling the fiction about her liaisons with another celebrity.

"Whitney Houston Pregnant with Eddie Murphy's baby," blared the headline of one breathless exclusive. "Whitney Houston and Eddie Murphy are getting married this spring. And if that isn't enough to quell the rumors of Houston's sexual preference for women, Murphy is tying the knot with her because she's pregnant with his child."

A friend of Whitney's later told her biographer Jeffery Bowman that she and her PR staff deliberately planted these stories to deflect the other rumors.

However, it wouldn't be long before the media had some genuine news to report about her personal life.

"The first time he asked me to marry him," Whitney later recalled, "I said, 'Forget about it, no way. It's just not in my plans.' After a year or so, I fell in love with Bobby. And when he asked to marry me the second time, I said yes."

To this day, nobody except Bobby himself really knows what's true about the timeline of their relationship, but by the time Whitney finalized negotiations to appear in Costner's film, the first reports started to leak that she was dating the legendary bad boy.

Film production began in Miami in February 1992, and it wasn't long before the publicity machine went into overdrive. For Arista and those handling Whitney's business affairs, the upcoming film was a chance to both reignite her flagging music career and reinvent her as a movie star.

First up, her people and Costner's production company entered into a deal to star Whitney in her first network TV special, an hour-long extravaganza on ABC featuring behind-the-scenes interviews with the stars of the upcoming film as well as live performances from her last album. And just when it looked like a fluff piece designed merely to hype a film, Whitney dropped a bombshell.

"I know what it's like to be in love these days," she tells the camera, displaying her ring finger. "This is my engagement ring to Bobby Brown. Bobby and I got engaged I think it was in August of last year."

After a shot of her talking on the phone to her new fiancé, she turns to the camera. "Are we going to have children? Yes, definitely."

The news of the engagement certainly took the world by surprise. But the most surprising aspect was how even the mainstream media questioned the optics of the engagement, especially given its proximity to Whitney's movie debut in a romantic role.

The respected *LA Times*—a newspaper hardly given to tabloid gossip—immediately took note of the disbelief that greeted the couple's engagement. The paper remarked that some observers were calling the union

Too good to be true, literally. Cynics suggested everything from a publicity ploy to a lifestyle convenience. For Brown, the marriage would soften the rebellious image that has grown out of the longstanding drug rumors and the admission that he has fathered three children out of wedlock. For Houston, 29, it would help combat tabloid stories questioning her lifestyle and asking

*whether the pin-up queen prefers the companionship of women
to men.*

The open skepticism, even from the mainstream press, was revealing. It brought to mind a conversation that I had had years ago with
a reporter who worked for the Hollywood trade papers. She told me
that the entertainment media know for the most part who is gay
and who is not but choose not to report on it because of an "unwrit-
ten code" and the knowledge that they would "lose access" if they
revealed the names. She also took issue with Joe Franklin's assertion
that most actors are gay. She told me that the true figure is "closer to
half."

I wondered if somehow Whitney had broken this code by so
openly flaunting her relationship with Robyn for so long. The only
parallels I can think of are two other female stars, Jodie Foster and
Lily Tomlin. Both lived openly with women for years and never bothered to hide their sexuality in public, but for many years neither for-
mally came out. As with Whitney, the mainstream media frequently
alluded to their sexuality as if they believed the stars had given tacit
permission by failing to close the closet door behind their open relationships the way the vast majority of closeted celebrities very deliberately choose to do. And while Foster is still often coy about her
sexuality, Tomlin was candid when she finally decided to open up
almost a decade ago about her four-decade relationship with screen-
writer Jane Wagner. In 2006, she explained her slow coming out to a
Washington weekly:

> *I certainly never called a press conference or anything like that.
> [Back in the seventies] people didn't write about it. Even if they
> knew, they would [refer to Jane as] "Lily's collaborator," things
> like that. Some journalists are just motivated by their own sense
> of what they want to say or what they feel comfortable saying or
> writing about. In '77, I was on the cover of* Time. *The same week*

I had a big story in Newsweek. *In one of the magazines it says I live alone, and the other magazine said I live with Jane Wagner. Unless you were so really adamantly out, and had made some declaration at some press conference, people back then didn't write about your relationship. . . . In '75 I was making the* Modern Scream *album, and Jane and I were in the studio. My publicist called me and said, "*Time *will give you the cover if you'll come out." I was more offended than anything that they thought we'd make a deal. But that was '75—it would have been a hard thing to do at that time.*

Two years later, Tomlin told *Just Out* magazine, "Everybody in the industry was certainly aware of my sexuality and of Jane . . . in interviews I always reference Jane and talk about Jane, but they don't always write about it."

As filming got under way on *The Bodyguard*, Whitney had suddenly announced to her family that she was pregnant. None of them even had an inkling that she was dating Bobby Brown. But in March, only a month into shooting, she had a miscarriage that she later said left her "desolate."

Bobby revealed that he had asked Whitney to marry him in the back of a car a few months earlier.

"She came to pick me up at the airport," he later recalled. "I asked her, 'Do you wanna marry me?' And she went crazy—'Yes, yes, yes!' She told the car to pull over."

When she was thirteen, Whitney later recalled, she was not like the other girls who dreamed of marrying their Prince Charming one day. On the contrary, she had vowed to avoid that scenario.

"I just knew that whatever I wanted to do with my life, marriage wasn't going to be a part of that for a long time," she said.

Now that the news was out about the engagement, a date was set for July 1992. Whitney's parents were said to be unhappy about whom she had chosen to marry. Cissy in particular was scandalized that Bobby had three children out of wedlock, though she confessed that she found Bobby "charming."

Although Robyn was about to be officially supplanted as the most important person in Whitney's life, her public statements revealed no resentment.

"Whitney is precious," she told *USA Today* in May. "I think once she's married she'll feel a lot more complete. I think that'll be a self phase where she'll be doing something for her life, not just for her public image."

But behind the scenes, Robyn was said to be apoplectic at the thought of the marriage, even though she had already agreed to act as Whitney's maid of honor at the ceremony. Things came to a head one day a few weeks before the planned nuptials when Bobby sent Whitney four hundred roses. When Robyn next saw him, according to Whitney's former bodyguard Kevin Ammons, she allegedly got into a violent confrontation with him.

Again, reports of the feud reached the mainstream press, putting Whitney on the defensive. "I read that Bobby and Robyn got into this fight in front of a hotel," she told the *Philadelphia Inquirer*. "First of all, if that were true, Robyn would have been knocked out, but my husband is a gentleman who would never fight a woman."

She told the reporter that Robyn was her best friend and knew her better than any other woman.

"But by the time I met Bobby," she explained, "Robyn and I had had enough time together and our relationship had changed from friendship to more of an employer-employee arrangement."

She revealed that Robyn no longer lived with her "but in her own place, which is about 30 minutes from me."

CHAPTER **SIXTEEN**

The logical first stop when I embarked on a quest for the truth with my PI was a trip to the Roswell town house where Bobbi Kristina was found on January 31. It is here that the first wave of media had descended after the incident. Within days, however, almost everybody had packed up and left when they hit a brick wall in getting past the imposing security gate that protects the upscale residents from the riff-raff. It is something you see all over Atlanta's suburbs even though the city is actually remarkably safe and ranks only thirty-first in the nation for violent crime. In fact, Atlanta's crime rate is lower than Salt Lake City's, best known for its Mormons and Donny and Marie. But unlike Salt Lake City and Tacoma, Washington—which also boasts a higher crime rate—a majority of Atlanta's population is African American.

There is a whiff of racism in seeing how the affluent residents of this city choose to protect themselves from the supposed menace of black crime. What's even more interesting is that many of the people who live in these gated communities are black themselves.

Whitney Houston, then, wasn't an anomaly when she chose to live here, although her celebrity status arguably warranted more pro-tection than your average wealthy Atlantan.

When I meet Sheila for the first time and take in her petite frame, it's hard to believe she is a private investigator until I spot the exposed handgun tucked in her holster. She explained that she doesn't take any chances, especially after a mother and daughter PI team were killed during an investigation. Sheila told me she was once held at gunpoint.

As we pull up to the security gate at the Ellard Village complex, Sheila flashes a badge and identifies herself to the security guard as a private investigator looking into the circumstances of the Bobbi Kristina case. "You're going to have to get clearance from the Roswell police, ma'am," the guard informs her politely. We were expecting as much.

A U-turn brings us almost immediately into a strip mall adjacent to the property. But this isn't like any strip mall I've visited before. Instead, the stores are tucked into an elegant brick façade of shops and cafés.

This is where the police headed first when they began their own investigation into Bobbi's near drowning. In early February, E! reported that Roswell detectives were investigating reports that another person or persons had been present on the morning that Bobbi was found but had fled the scene, allegedly over the wall behind her house, before police and paramedics showed up.

Each of the storeowners in this mall as well as at a nearby bank were asked to turn over footage from their surveillance cameras, but so far, the police were staying mum on their findings.

Our first stop is the Quest Women's Spa and Fitness Center, an upscale facility in the center of the mall. A woman named Mojgan Shamar greets us and identifies herself as the VP of Operations. She tells us that Bobbi occasionally came in to do "beginner yoga" and once came in for a pedicure.

"There was a woman who used to look after her like a mommy, Debbie Brooks. She brought her here twice. [Brooks] comes in here frequently for yoga so she was trying to help Krissi when she was going through stuff," she recalled. "The last time I saw her was a few months ago walking around the parking lot with Nick. She looked like she was on drugs; she looked very thin, very weak. They both looked out of it."

"How did they interact with each other?" I asked. That's when she reveals something neither of us were expecting from a routine question.

"To tell you the truth," she says, "I was working part-time in Kay Jewelers last year during the holidays and they came and they bought the ring. He purchased the ring for her, the engagement ring. It was a Princess cut from the collection; I forget what it's called. They spent something like eight thousand. He came back another time and he bought her a charm with an open heart with a diamond. They seemed very happy like they were pretty much in love. I saw them always together and there didn't seem to be any tension," she said. "I didn't see anything strange. But things happen. It's very sad; she's so young. And now she's going through the same thing her mom had. I hope she gets a second chance."

She gives us the location of the jewelry store. As we're about to leave, her husband tells us that he witnessed the aftermath of an accident when Nick flipped his SUV nearby the previous summer and was arrested for DUI.

"I got there when the car was upside down. One of the ladies who does yoga here knows them well and said it wasn't the first time and that Nick had several car mishaps. This particular car flip occurred at the corner of Barnwell and Holcomb Bridge Road. Nick was known to drive at very high speeds recklessly in the neighborhood."

Next, we made our way to the nearby Starbucks, where we were determined to find acquaintances of the couple. On our way in, we quickly found a patron of the spa complex named Jessie, who said she took yoga with Bobbi.

"We were in the same class together a couple of times," she recalls. "It's a basic intro class. One time after the class we came here and started to chat. About two minutes into the conversation, she answered her cell. She told me she had to leave because her boyfriend needed her at home. She looked fine and happy until she got that call. After that she looked worried, her whole mind-set changed. It was strange."

The Starbucks staff told us both Nick and Bobbi were "regulars." None of them had ever witnessed anything out of the ordinary. A twenty-something black customer, Trevor, overheard the conversation. He said he saw them there frequently.

"They were always high on something," he recalled. "I saw them in here a few days before the accident and they looked like they were on heroin, they both looked thin and frail. I was afraid Bobbi would end up like her mother, that's the thought that went through my mind."

Another customer, Steve Toney, jumps in and informs us that he had seen them a few weeks earlier and witnessed what he described as a "verbal war" in the parking lot.

"They came in, got their coffee, and on the way to their car started yelling and screaming at each other. It was ugly. Bobbi yelled at the top of her lungs at Nick, and then Nick yelled back at her with very abusive language. They both got in the car and slammed their doors before driving off."

Our last stop is Hooligans bar, also located in the mall. The manager tells us he saw them frequently. "They'd have the munchies at night and come in here," he says. "But it was usually for take-out."

Outside, we run into a twenty-one-year-old girl named Ella who claims she knew Bobbi for years. She last saw her about a week before the incident.

"Sad to say when I heard about it I wasn't surprised," Ella said. "The crowd she hung out with was out of control. Krissi used to hang out with a good crowd. The past couple years she hung out with a bunch of crazies, they were very wild and reckless. I used to meet her at parties; we had mutual friends. She was nice a few years ago. When I saw her before her accident she looked like she was on something. She looked like she got much thinner, looked like she was into heavy drugs. I felt sad because I don't think Nick had her best interests at heart. Face it, if she didn't have all that money from her mom I betcha

Nick would have had nothing to do with her. He's an opportunist, and he tried to manipulate Krissi. A girlfriend of mine hung out at their house with them a few times and said Nick would interrupt Krissi during conversations and twist it his way. He tried to not let her have her own voice. I hope and pray she gets better. And if she does I hope her family takes her far away from Nick and that gang."

So far, we haven't learned much that we don't already know, but Sheila has tracked down what she thinks is a significant lead. Nobody had been able to locate Max Lomas since the accident. But she located an address in her database, and it was only a few minutes away. We decide to head there and try our luck before the jeweler.

When we arrive at the location, it turns out to be a gated community even more luxurious than the one where Bobbi lives. "That can't be right," she says. "There's no way he could afford that." Parked across the street, it's like a TV stakeout, except we don't know what we're looking for, and there's little chance we'll have any better luck getting through these gates than the first ones that morning.

As we wait, we notice the complex has two gates, one marked for visitors and one for residents. We notice a black SUV pull up at the visitor gate. Twenty minutes later, it is still there; the driver is speaking to a female security guard.

I told Sheila I had an idea. "Drive up to the resident gate while the guard is distracted," I suggested. She did. The guard turned away from the SUV and peered in our vehicle. Sheila flashed her badge. The guard smiled and said, "Good to see you," as if she recognized Sheila, then raised the gate and let us in. It took us a while to find the address and we could see the guard looking at us suspiciously as we made a U-turn. Finally, we found the place: a huge detached house, almost a mansion.

An elderly woman answered the door. When Sheila flashes her badge, asks to see Max, and tells her why we're there, she stammers and looks around as if wondering how we got through while searching for security to toss us out. "He's not talking to anybody," she informs us. At that moment, I can see a tall fellow standing around the corner of the vestibule. Before I can shout out, she slams the door in our faces.

"That's where he's hiding out," Sheila concludes, guessing the woman is his grandmother.

We then headed for the Kay Jewelers at the North Point Mall where the fitness center VP told us Nick had bought the engagement ring when she worked there last year. When we got there, we spoke to an employee behind the counter, Kau Hawkers, who remembered Bobbi coming in with Nick in January, not long before the incident.

"He had put the ring in for repair in January," she recalled. "The center stone was falling out. They brought it in together actually in January. She was in the store as well. And then last month [February] he came to pick it up. He was nice. He was always nice."

Then the store manager approached and introduced herself as Alisha Williams. Sheila flashed her badge and told her why we were there. She said she remembered when the couple came in earlier in the winter.

"I spoke to them a couple of times and the last time they brought their ring in," she recalled. "Actually he just came in and picked it up a couple of weeks ago because it was in here when she went to the hospital. It was in two pieces like the stone was actually out. It's weird how that happened. The last two times before that they were both in here together."

Sheila asked how they seemed.

"They seemed a little all over the place," she recalled. "Kind of like they were on something. She was talkative, but they were kind of moving fast. They had a younger guy with them who they said was like their bodyguard. It was the guy we seen on TV after she was found, the young guy with the blond hair."

"Was it Max?"

"Yeah, I think so. They were like, 'This is our bodyguard.' They were all over the place. Real fast talking. They were bubbly, probably on something. She looked real frail every time I seen her. The last time they both had sunglasses on and didn't take them off the whole time. I remember because they had a Sunglass Hut bag and had probably just bought the glasses. There's one here in the mall, up the elevators."

I wondered who paid for it, but she told me the ring was under warranty and it was under [Nick's name]. "He always filled out the ticket," she remembered. "That's why he was able to pick it up without her."

Sheila asked about the heart-shaped charm necklace that the fitness woman told us about. "We can look up Nick Gordon's name and see if he bought something," she offered.

A few minutes later, she came back and informed us of a discovery. "Actually, we still have a ring that he bought that's in our repair room that has 'Nick Gordon' on there. It's like sterling silver, kind of a guy's ring with a diamond in it. He never picked it up. He probably forgot about it."

She assumed that it was his engagement ring "because that's what we usually use them for."

"The first time I ever met him he came in by himself," she recalled. "He said, 'Oh, my wife is going to kill me if she knew I lost the ring. I think he was looking for this ring, he just probably didn't know where it was and he didn't realize we had it here and I guess we didn't realize it either. Other than that, the very next time he came in he came in with her.

"It was under Nick's name, the claim slip. It was always under his name. He always paid cash. When he bought it he paid cash. He carried lots of cash. The designer of the ring was Neil Lane. The last time he was in here was a couple weeks ago when he picked up the ring. He was in here with his mother. They came in to pick up the ring.

"She acted just like her mom. You know how you see on TV. Happy, bubbly, all over the place, and then watching her on her reality show. She looked like her dad but acted just like her mom. It was eerie, weird to see her like that. And this was after she died but I said, 'I just met Whitney Houston, but it was Bobbi Kristina.' I just treated her regular; I never let her know that I knew who she was. He never had any attitude. He was nice."

We were more interested in Nick's most recent visit when he came to pick up the ring. She looked up the details for us.

"We received it in the store on December 13, 2014," she said. "He picked it up February something, I can't make it out. Here, it says we called on January 6 to tell them to come get it but he only picked it up after she was in the hospital."

She sent an assistant to retrieve the pickup slip from the February box. While we waited, Alisha told us that she always wanted to be a private investigator and asked Sheila questions about her job. Sheila told her it's not as glamorous as it's made out to be on TV. The manager said she is always able to figure out who did it in the movies before they reveal the killer.

"Let me keep your card," she said. "One day I might want to make a career change." Then, as if to show us that she would make a good gumshoe, she offered her opinions on the case.

"What I think happened, and this is what I tell my husband: They probably got into a fight before and I think she probably tried to commit suicide. It seemed like he left, they had a fight right before he left with his friends and she said, 'I'm done. I'm tired.' The anniversary was coming up so she was probably depressed. And then he just happened to come in and all the things happened so it kind of seemed like he had something to do with it. He wouldn't benefit in trying to kill her. They weren't married. He was benefiting more from her being alive because he could spend her money that way. Now he doesn't have anything so why would he try to kill her? She could have been on drugs and had a lapse or something. But I don't think he intentionally killed her. He was living the life, spending, shopping sprees, now he's out in the cold."

She noted that Nick always paid with cash, including the nearly $9,000 he paid for Bobbi's engagement ring. "And you know whose money that was. So why would he kill her?"

She told us a store clerk named Claire Graham served them the first time they came in. And she also served Nick the last time he came in to pick up his ring when he was there with his mom. It was Graham's day off, but Alisha offered to call her at home and let us talk to her. When we reached Graham, she confirmed that Nick came in with his mother a couple weeks earlier to pick up the ring.

"I thought it was strange that he picked up the ring so soon after the accident," recalled Graham. "He said he wanted her to have it when she wakes up. He was with his mom. He didn't really look distraught or anything out of the ordinary. When I saw [Bobbi and Nick] together previously, they always looked like they were on something. He was always loving and affectionate with her. She was affectionate back. My true feeling was that they were in love."

Although it didn't seem significant at the time, Graham's revelation that Nick was with his mom when he picked up the ring would come back to me after I watched the *Dr. Phil* episode a couple of days later.

The way the show presented it, they had flown in Michelle Gordon from Orlando unbeknownst to Nick for a surprise intervention. When he saw her and threw his arms around her, the producers implied that they hadn't seen each other in a very long time. Michelle herself repeatedly talked only about her phone conversations with her son since the incident. Never once did she mention she had actually seen him since Bobbi was hospitalized, though she did tell Dr. Phil at one point, "I have Krissi's engagement ring. He wants me to hold it," without furnishing any explanation.

Now the revelation that she was with him in Atlanta a few days before the show was taped—and that he didn't seem at all distraught—makes me wonder whether the entire broadcast was simply an elaborate PR stunt designed to drum up sympathy for him. To be fair, nobody actually lied, but I felt misled and wondered what else we weren't being told.

CHAPTER SEVENTEEN

As the wedding approached, the media couldn't seem to decide what to make of the unlikely pairing. Aside from the note of skepticism sounded by countless publications because of Whitney's long-rumored lesbianism, other media suggested that wasn't the image she sought to clean up. Rather, it was her credibility in the black community that needed burnishing.

"Whitney's gone through a real rough spot with her black base," the president of MCA's 'Black Division' told *Vanity Fair*. "She wants to 'cross-black.' Being married to Bobby Brown might help her with that." For his part, Brown assured the black press, "Whitney is a real Black woman."

The bride-to-be did a round of press interviews seemingly designed to convince the skeptical public and press that their love was genuine. Many wondered why she had never before showed any interest in a serious romantic relationship.

"I just never wanted to be married," she told one reporter. "I had an independence that didn't include marriage. I always thought men were full of shit. I did. For the most part, they used to talk shit to me all the time. They always had a rap. And I had two brothers, so they all told me what the deal was. They would tell me about the girls they did and they used to say, 'Do you want to be a whore?' 'Do you want to be a slut?' 'Do you want to be treated like shit?' They made me feel guilty for being a girl."

Whitney was worth considerably more than her husband-to-be at the time of the engagement. Jeffery Bowman pegs her net worth in 1992 as more than $30 million, while Brown was worth around $5 million. And despite the boundless skepticism about the marriage, the couple assured anybody who would listen that their love was so sincere that they weren't going to sign the prenuptial agreement that most celebrities enter into to protect their assets in case of divorce.

"If I can't trust my own husband, then who can I trust?" Bowman quotes a friend of Whitney's. But Bobby later let the cat out of the bag, revealing to *Jet* in August 1992 that they had indeed signed a prenup.

"If anything ever happens in this relationship, we both want to be protected," he explained. But he was certain they wouldn't need it. "I'm going to be with this woman for the rest of my life." According to her biographer Mark Bego, the agreement was signed "at the insistence of Whitney's lawyer and her family."

According to Whitney's former bodyguard Kevin Ammons, who at the time was dating her publicist Regina Brown, Robyn had not come to terms with her friend's new liaison. "If Whitney goes through with the marriage," she allegedly told Ammons along with Brown and her father, "I'll hold a press conference and tell everyone I'm Whitney's lover, that we've been lovers for years, then I'll kill myself."

Nevertheless, despite any supposed lingering resentment, Robyn was front and center as maid of honor when the reported wedding took place at Whitney's New Jersey estate on July 18, 1992, attended by eight hundred family members and celebrity friends, including Aretha Franklin, Dick Clark, and Donald Trump.

Unconfirmed reports circulated that Brown burst into tears during the ceremony and kept interrupting the reverend with shouts of "Yes, yes, yes."

Stevie Wonder and Luther Vandross provided the entertainment at the lavish $1 million reception after the bride and groom tied the knot both dressed in white. Whitney's gown was said to have cost $50,000. As the minister pronounced them husband and wife, seven doves were released overhead in a ceremony *Jet* likened to the first wedding of Elizabeth Taylor and Richard Burton. In lieu of gifts, guests were asked to donate to Whitney's foundation, which raised more than $250,000 that day.

At the conclusion of the ceremony, Robyn left the estate in a black Porsche given to her that day by Whitney as a token of their friendship. Ammons claims the gift was "to ensure she would be in a good mood and not cause a scene or embarass her at the wedding." The bride and groom jetted off to a European honeymoon given to them as a wedding present by Clive Davis, which included a week aboard a $10,000-a-day yacht cruising the French Riviera.

After photos of the honeymoon were leaked, Robyn suspected Whitney's publicist Regina Brown was the source and let her suspicions be known to Whitney, who refused to believe her longtime employee would betray her like that. Years later, Ammons claimed that Brown had indeed been the source of the leaked photos, and had sold a tabloid the location of the honeymoon. Not long afterward, Brown was fired from Nippy Inc.

Meanwhile, whatever the skeptics believed about the new union, the honeymoon appeared to be a romantic one, because it wasn't long after they returned to New York that the couple revealed that Whitney was once again pregnant, though the dates would later suggest that she was already with child at the time of the wedding.

Although filming of *The Bodyguard* had concluded before the wedding, Whitney headed into the studio to record the music that would be an integral part of the film. Whitney was no actress. Her previous roles had been confined to a couple of soft drink commercials and small guest spots on the sitcoms *Gimme a Break* and *Silver Spoons*. From the outset, the studio worried about her lack of acting experience and had brought in a coach to provide instruction. But it was Whitney's musical abilities that they knew would make the film, and the screenplay had been altered to let her character deliver several musical numbers onscreen.

As the film's co-producer, Clive Davis was once again heavily involved in the musical selections, which he hoped would help reignite Whitney's career as a singer at the same time as it transformed her into a full-fledged movie star.

But when he heard that Costner had chosen as the film's closing number the Dolly Parton song "I Will Always Love You," his reaction was less than enthusiastic. Seven years earlier, Davis had almost vetoed the choice of "Greatest Love of All," which would end up being one of the most successful songs of Whitney's career. Now he questioned the choice of a country ballad that had already been used once before in the soundtrack of Parton's film *The Best Little Whorehouse in Texas*. If Whitney was going to reestablish her credibility in the black community, was a white-bread country tune really the way to achieve that goal?

Later, Costner would describe Davis's reaction when he informed them of his choice. "When I said to Whitney, 'You're gonna sing "I Will Always Love You,'" the ground shook," he recalled. "Clive Davis and those guys were going, 'What?!'"

The film was scheduled to premiere in November. The producers were a little concerned at the interracial theme that saw Costner's white bodyguard character fall in love with a black woman. Although America had come a long way, this was still controversial territory. Would Middle America and the South accept the premise? Costner would later admit that Warner Bros. had initially balked at the commercial risk but that they had changed their minds after watching Whitney's screen test, which finally persuaded them to green-light the project.

The studio insisted on including scenes that directly addressed the interracial aspect of the relationship if producers wanted to keep the final scene in which the lead characters kissed. But Costner stead-fastly refused.

"I said 'Absolutely not,'" he revealed to ABC after the film's release. "This is not race. This is a man and a woman. This is chemistry, romance. That's what that kiss was all about. It was two people thanking each other. I kissed her once for all of America, and I kissed her once for myself."

In advance of the film's release, it was essential to ready filmgoers for the romantic premise. To that end, the publicity machine sent Whitney on an endless round of press interviews in which she gushed about her marriage to Brown and professed happiness with what was being described as a fairy-tale romance.

"I love being married," she told *Ebony*. "I want to spend my whole life with him, to give to him and to take from him." To the *LA Times* on the eve of her film premiere, she couldn't quite muster up the word "love" to describe why she had married Bobby. "Women are supposed to have husbands," she explained. "We are validated by that, and we validate ourselves that way."

Brown was a little more reticent in his own press interviews. "Our personal life is our personal life," he told a reporter. "We don't like talking about it." But he revealed that dating in the age of AIDS was treacherous and that single life wasn't what it used to be.

"There's too much going on in the world today to be alone," he said.

For the most part, the marriage had succeeded in silencing the incessant questions about Robyn. The tabloids, not to mention the mainstream media, had finally changed their focus from questions about lesbian trysts to stories about Bobby's reputed drug use and reports that he was a "crackhead," a rumor reported in *Vanity Fair* as early as 1992.

Yet FBI files released under the Freedom of Information Act reveal that on the eve of the *Bodyguard* premiere, Whitney's camp scrambled to contain information that could have done tremendous damage to the carefully crafted image that she and her publicity machine had constructed for months to ensure the film's success and revive her career.

The official pre-premiere gala was scheduled for November 24 with a star-studded red carpet Hollywood screening. But only a day earlier, an FBI file was received at the bureau's Newark office, reporting that both Whitney Houston and her company, Nippy Inc., had been the "victim" of "extortion." The heavily redacted version reveals some key details.

The initial letter from a Chicago attorney—sent to the singer's New Jersey business office a week earlier on November 16—had revealed that her client possessed damaging information about Whitney but would be willing to sign a "confidentiality agreement" in exchange for a financial settlement.

When John Houston eventually brought the extortion attempt to the bureau's attention on November 23, a special agent was assigned to question the attorney about the demand.

The woman informed the agent that her client had "knowledge of intimate details regarding Whitney Houston's romantic relationships and will go public with the information unless _____ is paid $250,000."

The bureau twice interviewed John Houston, who headed Nippy Inc., about what they had initially deemed the "extortion" attempt. Both times they asked to interview Whitney but was told she was unavailable. John informed them he had tape-recorded his conversations with the alleged extortionist and offered to make a transcript. By that time, the film had premiered and Whitney was on a promotional tour. John informed them that his daughter was very busy.

On December 15, the bureau advised that there would be "no further investigation conducted by the FBI until Whitney Houston has been interviewed and a determination has been made as to whether or not a violation has occurred."

Subsequently, the bureau spoke to John via speakerphone about

Memorandum

To   :   SAC, NEWARK (9A-NK-77369)   Date   12/15/92

From   :   ⓙ/USA ☐   b6
                                                                b7C

Subject: ☐
           WHITNEY ☐
           NIPPY INCORPORATED,
           FORT LEE, NEW JERSEY - VICTIM;
           EXTORTION;
           OO: NEWARK

    On December 3, 1992, Special Agent (SA) ☐
☐ spoke with ☐ on the telephone.
☐ advised he called ☐ on December 2, 1992
and discussed the letter she sent to JOHN HOUSTON and WHITNEY
HOUSTON, dated November 16, 1992, on behalf of her client, ☐
☐ said that in the course of their conversation,
☐ admitted her client had no claim for wrongful ☐
but ☐ goes on to say that ☐

    ☐ said ☐ told him that ☐ has
knowledge of intimate details regarding WHITNEY HOUSTON's
romantic relationships, and will go public with the information
unless ☐ is paid $250,000. ☐ told ☐ her client
will sign a confidentiality agreement if ☐ is paid the
$250,000.

    ☐ advised SA ☐ he tape recorded his
conversation with ☐ and would have transcripts of the tape
made up as soon as possible. ☐ said he would also make
copies of the tape and preserve the original recording.

    SA ☐ advised ☐ that if he wished to
send copies of the tape and the transcripts to the FEDERAL BUREAU
OF INVESTIGATION (FBI) and the U.S. Attorney's Office, we would
review them but there would be no further investigation conducted
by the FBI until WHITNEY HOUSTON has been interviewed and a
determination has been made as to whether or not a violation has
occurred.

    9A-NK-77369-3

2-Newark
JMM/gya
(2)

SEARCHED_____ INDEXED_____
SERIALIZED__✗✗__ FILED__✗✗__
DEC 15 1992
FBI — NEWARK

the matter at the New Jersey offices of Nippy Inc. with two of Whitney's attorneys present.

Not long afterward, an FBI special agent interviewed Whitney
at the office. A heavily redacted file from the interview reveals that
Whitney acknowledged the extortionist to have been a "friend" and
assures the agents that _____ "would never do anything to
embarrass her."

She revealed that she had discussed "personal things" with the
purported friend that the person "could possibly write about."

On January 12, 1993, a special agent sent a memo to the FBI's
Newark office informing them that John Houston had mailed a confidentiality agreement to the alleged extortionist in November almost
immediately upon receiving the threat. The bureau had obtained a
copy of the agreement, which is attached to the file but redacted in
full.

As a result of the subsequent investigation, and the settlement,
the memo reveals that the assistant US attorney general concluded
the original letter "is not a violation of federal law." However, he did
request "further investigation."

Attached to the file is a redacted version of the original letter
from the attorney, dated November 16, addressed to both John and
Whitney at the offices of Nippy Inc.

It reveals that her client had "already turned down several offers
for _____ rights which are in the six figure range."

The wording of the letter suggests that it was crafted in such a
way that it could not be interpreted as blackmail or extortion per se.
Instead, it gives Whitney the opportunity to purchase the "exclusive
rights" to the friend's story—including damaging personal information
about her own romantic relationships. In exchange for $250,000, the
former friend offered to sell the rights to the story to Whitney instead
of a publisher and sign a confidentiality agreement to ensure the
potentially damaging information never sees the light of day.

The letter goes on to reveal that the friend had "suffered emotional stress" which possibly "constitutes a separate cause of action against the individuals in your company as well as the corporation itself."

The client, added the attorney, "would like to avoid negative publicity out of respect for Ms. Houston's position in the worldwide entertainment industry." Should a lawsuit be necessary to enforce the client's rights, the letter adds, "the fall-out will undoubtedly be negative."

It demands a "speedy resolution" within seven days of any offer to settle.

Although the file confirms that John settled the matter by sending a confidentiality agreement almost immediately, it is unclear how much money was paid to silence the person and whether he met the initial demand for $250,000.

On January 12, 1993, FBI agent James Esposito sent a memo informing US Attorney for the District of New Jersey Michael Chertoff of the investigation.

"Since no evidence that a federal criminal law had been violated was presented, prosecution of this matter would not be pursued," he wrote.

We may never know what the information was about Whitney's love life that was evidently so damaging it caused John Houston to settle the so-called extortion attempt even before reporting the threat to federal authorities. It may be a secret that both Whitney and John took with them to their graves.

The premise of *The Bodyguard* focuses on a famous singer who is victimized by threats from an anonymous stalker. Ironically, a large section of Whitney's FBI files unrelated to the extortion attempt concerns a Vermont man who claims he fell in love with Whitney from afar and is angry that she will not return his love.

He begins his first letter with a declaration of his love. "Miss Whitney, you are a beautiful lady and a beautiful person. I really and truly am in love with you." In scores of subsequent correspondence, he escalates his obsession to the point that he would write to John, declaring, "I might hurt someone with some crazy idea and not realize how stupid an idea it was until after it was done."

He informs Whitney that he is so in love with her that if she doesn't respond, he is considering going on *The Phil Donahue Show* or turning to the *National Enquirer* to force a response. But when the FBI interviewed him, he revealed that he changed his mind about this "crazy idea" because it would have hurt Whitney's reputation, so he decided not to follow through.

A different stalker, residing in Holland, enclosed countless audiotapes declaring his love and revealing his long-standing obsession. The tapes proved so disturbing that the FBI requested that Dutch officials interview the man.

During the interview, the stalker claimed to be the "President of Europe" and to have purchased Brazil for $66 billion. He also claimed credit for the downfall of the South African apartheid regime and for the election of Nelson Mandela.

———

The Bodyguard had its pre-premiere gala on November 24 at Mann's Chinese Theatre as a benefit for Magic Johnson's Pediatric AIDS Foundation. The evening kicked off with a prescreening party hosted by *People* magazine for one hundred of the foundation's major donors at Hollywood's Old Masonic Hall. The post-screening party took place under a huge tent set up in a parking lot adjacent to the hall.

The *LA Times* reported that among the star-studded guest list was a "very pregnant" Whitney.

The film hit theaters the next day, and the first reviews were savage. *Entertainment Weekly* called the film "an outrageous piece of saccharine kitsch—or, at least, it might have been, had the movie seemed fully awake. Instead, it's glossy yet slack; it's like *Flashdance* without the hyperkinetic musical numbers and with the romance padded out to a disastrously languid 2 hours and 10 minutes."

TV Guide called it a "dreary turgid melodrama."

Many of the poor reviews focused on the lack of romantic chemistry between Whitney and Costner.

The *New York Times* singled out this aspect in particular in its own negative review. "Two long hours and 10 minutes after this tale begins, Rachel and Frank seem no closer than seatmates on a long bus trip. It takes a dizzying 360-degree shot of them embracing, plus the swelling of the hit-bound soundtrack, to suggest any passion."

Entertainment Weekly agreed with this assessment. "To say that Houston and Costner fail to strike sparks would be putting it mildly." The *Austin Chronicle* also struck a similar note: "The only chemistry that Costner and Houston are able to generate with one another is something akin to the tension between two pieces of plywood propped together in a soggy drizzle."

Roger Ebert was one of the few who singled out Whitney's performance for praise.

"This is Houston's screen debut," he wrote in the *Chicago Sun-Times*, "and she is at home in the role; she photographs wonderfully, and has a warm smile, and yet is able to suggest selfish and egotistical dimensions in the character."

The film received a total of seven Golden Raspberry nominations, including a Razzie for Worst Picture, and two nominations for Whitney, Worst Actress and Worst New Star.

And yet despite the generally negative reviews that might have sank Whitney's film career almost before it began, an interesting phenomenon occurred.

First, the Dolly Parton song that had been added over the objections of Clive Davis started to be played everywhere. It soared to the top of the *Billboard* singles charts and stayed there for an amazing fourteen consecutive weeks. And all the more remarkable, every single other song on the soundtrack except one also became a hit.

The album ended up as the most successful soundtrack of all time and one of the most successful albums in history, with more than forty-five million copies sold.

Variety called the film "a soundtrack in search of a movie." Indeed, the monster success of the musical numbers appears to have propelled a mediocre film into a box office hit. The film would end up as the second-highest-grossing Hollywood film of 1992.

Whitney Houston was not only once again a superstar singer, but she was also a bona fide movie star. For the moment, however, none of that mattered to Whitney as she realized the accomplishment she said she had dreamed of all her life.

The baby was almost named Tekatia. That's the name Bobby had chosen for his new daughter. But when Cissy heard the choice, she exploded.

"That child will have to carry that name through her whole life," she told the parents-to-be when she learned of their choice. "You are not giving my grandbaby that name. Just name her Christina or something like that."

And so Bobbi Kristina Brown was born on March 4, 1993.

CHAPTER **EIGHTEEN**

The Roswell Police Department has been keeping the results of their investigation very tightly guarded. I was both impressed by their tight ship—unusual, in my experience, with cases involving celebrities—and frustrated by their lack of cooperation.

So far, they have refused to release any information about the events of January 31, because the investigation is ongoing. There had been a number of purported leaks but none that I considered reliable.

When I arrived at the Roswell police headquarters with Sheila to see what we could turn up, we were told by a desk officer that we couldn't enter the premises with cell phones. Sheila had left her weapon in the car but not her phone. None of the other police stations had denied us entry with phones. Handing me her phone and flashing her badge, Sheila was waved through the metal detector. It flashed, but the policewoman said, "It's just your badge. You're good."

Left behind, I asked the officer why cells aren't allowed.

"If we let people in with cells they could take pictures of our facility and come back and bomb us," she explained. "We need to take precautions."

Sheila came back a few minutes later, complaining about how uncooperative and rude the clerk was when she attempted to access information. "She didn't want to give me the reports. I told her I'm a private investigator and that I'm entitled to that information. She finally shoved some papers at me and told me it will cost fourteen dollars an hour for their search time." As she left to fill out the paperwork, I tried small talk with the desk officer.

"It's really quiet here," I told her. "You must get bored sitting here all day."

"Yes, sometimes it's very boring," she said. "Sometimes I fall asleep."

I asked her how she stays awake. "Simple, I play Candy Crush on my iPad. It keeps me going." She shows me the screen, and sure enough, she's been playing all this time.

Noticing an officer smoking out front, I stepped outside and tried quizzing him about the case.

"I can't comment on it," he said. "It's been intense here. They're taking their time to make sure they get it right. It's a high-profile case."

We had collected a series of names of assorted friends and hangers-on of the three people known to have been with Bobbi on the morning she was found.

We had been frantically calling each of these people in hopes that somebody would want to talk. Most hung up immediately.

I had been told repeatedly that I needed to talk to a woman named Debbie Brooks who was Bobbi's "caregiver," even as an adult. She had been described to me as "like a mommy" to her and a "sort of nanny." I was assured Brooks would know what went on behind closed doors. We tracked down a number but had so far been unsuccessful in reaching her. When she finally answered her phone, she gave a predictable response.

"Bobbi Kristina was a personal friend of mine but I don't feel comfortable talking about her. You should contact the family."

I was more successful when I reached a twenty-year-old woman who I'm told knew the couple well. She confirmed that she was close to Bobbi and that she had plans to come over on the afternoon Bobbi was found.

"I was supposed to help Krissi shop online for some new clothes," she told me. "I heard the news from a friend who called me crying. It's so sad. Krissi was messed up but she's an amazing person with a huge heart. I never trusted Nick. He was a Svengali figure to Krissi. He didn't have her best interests at heart."

When I asked her what she thought happened, she referenced Whitney's death three years earlier.

> When Whitney was found dead it was in very hot water, which explains that she probably drowned accidentally. When they found Krissi it was in cold water. It just doesn't make sense. Why would she jump into a cold bath of water? I know Krissi and she would never do something like that. Somebody put her in there; there was foul play. Somebody is behind it. Krissi was found there, facedown.

She told me that Bobbi was in "good spirits" and that she doesn't for a minute believe it was a suicide attempt.

Next, I got through to a friend of Max Lomas and his brother, Nick. He suggested we meet that night at an Atlanta strip club called the Pink Pony. He told me it's where a lot of musicians and athletes hang out.

When we met that evening at the establishment, which bills itself as a "Southern Gentlemen's Club," the friend pointed to the strippers onstage and told me that this is where Max and Nick often hung out.

"They've partied with a lot of the young, pretty things you see in here tonight," he said. He told me he last spoke to Max in early February.

"When I spoke to Max a couple days after the accident he seemed very worried. He said he was told not to say a word to anybody. I never heard his voice sound so weak. He was nervous, and he sounded like he was at the end himself. I told him I was worried about him, he said he'd be okay. The thing that struck me most is when he said it wasn't him who committed a crime. He used the word *crime*; that concerned me. He said it wasn't him but he insinuated it was some-one else."

The friend asked me if I wanted to do a couple of lines with him. He seemed put off by my refusal.

"Atlanta is Hollywood South, man. Loosen up, brother. Tonight's a new night."

He told me he was going to go into a back room with one of the strippers and have "a few shots and do a couple lines." When he hadn't returned a half hour later, I left.

So far, the only thing we know for sure about the incident is that shopkeepers in the Ellard mall and a nearby bank were asked by the police about a person or persons who had possibly been in the house the morning that Bobbi was found but may have left before authori-ties arrived. During Sharon Churcher's interview with Danyela Bradley's mother, Marlene, she suggested the fifth person was a man named Duane Tyrone Hall.

Duane was the man who we know was in the car with Nick on February 2, two days after Bobbi was found, when police stopped them for a lane violation and found marijuana residue in the center console.

I discover that Duane also happens to be the man who appears in one of the two Instagram photos posted by Bobbi on January 31. The photo shows a young man with his arm around her as she displays a fierce expression for the camera.

The caption reads:

YAYYYY :) finally my famBAM!!!

and links to the page of an "Edwin DeMarco."

I can't make any sense of the cryptic caption nor why Hall goes under the name Edwin DeMarco, so we decided to track him down, hoping to get some answers.

When we arrived at the address listed on the police report of the traffic incident, his father, Delroy, answered. When we told him why we were there, he said his son wasn't at home, that he was "at school." Eyeing Sheila's badge, he appeared concerned and refused to answer any questions. "You have to talk to my son about that," he insisted. Nervously, he asked us what the police had told us.

When we returned to the car across the street, we waited for a few minutes. Suddenly the garage door opened and a white car sped out. Sheila snapped a photo as it pulled away. We didn't get a good glance at the driver, but Sheila thought it might be Duane's sister. We phoned the next day, asking to speak to Duane. When Delroy answered, he angrily demanded to know why we followed his son, who he said was driving the white car. When we asked him why he lied to us, he hung up.

More than one person told us we needed to talk to Mason Whita-ker. A number of hangers-on described themselves as Bobbi's BFF or best friend after the incident. Danyela Bradley, for example, had tweeted in February:

> *"I don't care about anything else, I just want my best friend back."*

But we had been told that Danyela was actually just a "groupie" or "hanger-on" who knew Bobbi through her boyfriend, Max, but wasn't very close to Bobbi. Her actual best friend was a man named Mason Whitaker, a twenty-four-year-old lacrosse coach and security guard who is almost certainly the person the jewelry store manager was referring to when she recalled that Nick and Bobbi were with a "young blond kid" that they referred to as her "bodyguard" when they brought their ring in to be repaired.

On his Facebook page, Whitaker describes Nick as a "family

member." It was he who was with Nick in the BMW sedan that struck a curb while changing lanes and hit a fire hydrant, ending up upside down.

After the accident, police had charged Nick with a DUI and driving with a suspended license. Both men were unhurt. But seven months earlier, Whitaker posted on Facebook about another incident involving Nick: "All I can say is thank you to the best man alive, Nick Gordon, for saving my life after I wrecked my car. Love you bro!"

In another post, he describes Nick's involvement after a friend expressed concern for his welfare:

"Yeah I made it home, some nice guy pulled my car out of the ditch and towed it up the street then my brother Nick Gordon saved me, and I was only stranded for like 13 hours by myself."

Over the last year, Whitaker tweeted a number of selfies taken with Bobbi in various poses. One is captioned "Best sister and best friend." In another, he refers to her as "little sis."

It is clear they are close. One photo of the two friends in particular stands out: a selfie with Bobbi in which Whitaker is holding a huge hunting knife. He also frequently posts photos of shotguns and hunting rifles. Bobbi and Nick appear to have shared his passion for guns.

In a photo Bobbi posted last year, Nick is aiming a shotgun in a room filled with animal head trophies and gun racks. She captioned it: "We are gun collectors. We live in the south. We have the right to bare [*sic*] arms."

In February, at the height of Nick's Twitter feud with Bobby Brown, Whitaker tweeted:

"I personally know if it wasn't for @nickgordon Krissi wouldn't even have seen her Dad in the past 5 years. Show the same respect Bobby!"

One person told us, "If anybody knows what happened to Bobbi, Mason knows. He knows where all the bodies are buried, so to speak." Needless to say, we were anxious to talk to him.

But we ran into the same roadblocks as we had with other key figures. His mother and grandmother abruptly hung up on us. When we finally located a former neighbor who knows him, he told us, "I think he's laying low."

It is clear that Bobbi and Nick's friends were circling the wagons. So far, my trip to Atlanta had been a waste of time. Although it had been fun posing as a private detective, I realized that I should probably keep my day job.

CHAPTER **NINETEEN**

Although Robyn continued as Whitney's assistant for some time after the marriage, she would spend noticeably less time with her old friend. Eventually, her official title changed from executive assistant to creative director at Nippy Inc., Whitney's management company, where she would eventually found Whitney's record label, Better Place Records—a venture that would occupy much of her time.

Although the media focus had largely shifted from rumors about a lesbian relationship to stories about Bobby's bad-boy reputation, the subject of Robyn would still occasionally surface, and Whitney was noticeably less patient when doubts continued to persist about her sexuality despite marrying Bobby.

"Once someone gets to be a success, there are a number of things that are going to be said about you automatically," she complained to *Entertainment Weekly* in 1993.

> *One is that you're gay. One is that you've got a drug problem [a rumor that has circulated about Brown and that he has denied]. The other one is that you have no idea what the hell you're doing. At one point it hurt me to have to dignify what I wasn't with an answer. It used to fuck me up, to be honest with you. I used to go*

*to my mother and say, 'Why, why, why is this happening? I can't
be friends with women?' The [media has] to have some sort of
tag on you, especially if you're private. That's the only thing I can
come up with. You got any other theories?*

Cissy, who happened to be present during the interview, offered
her own theory. "It's because Whitney doesn't wear clothes up to her
behind with her tits out, excuse my French. Either you're the biggest
whore or you're a lesbian."

Observing what she described as the "intensity" of the relationship between Whitney and Robyn, *Vanity Fair*'s Lynn Hirschberg
had opined in a profile that "it's difficult to imagine anything—even
Houston's marriage—coming between them." But it was soon clear
that something had.

According to Kevin Ammons, Robyn was not as accepting of the
marriage as she had professed to be. Nor was John Houston pleased
that Whitney's old friend had been reassigned to work under him at
the New Jersey management office, especially since she was allegedly
still threatening to go public about her relationship with Whitney.
Ammons also said Robyn purported to have secret information about
a drug deal involving Bobby Brown.

Ammons, still working as one of the singer's bodyguards, claims
that around this time, John offered him a large sum of money to contain this threat.

"We've got to do something about that motherfucking bitch," he
claims John Houston told him. "She's ruining my family and driving
everybody nuts. She's lost her grip on reality. I'll pay you $6,000 if
you put the fear of God in her."

Ammons claims that he refused the offer but that subsequently
John warned the bodyguards to "keep an eye" on Robyn.

For a newly married couple who professed their love for each
other at every turn, Whitney and Bobby spent remarkably little time
together during the initial stages of their marriage.

Following her daughter's birth, Whitney had professed no hurry to return to professional pursuits. Asked what her immediate plans were, she was adamant that her new domestic life came first.

"Really, it has nothing to do with business whatsoever," she told *Rolling Stone.* "It's my family. To raise children, to raise decent human beings. To keep my husband happy. To keep him strong. Things of that nature. They are very simple things. There's nothing I want to do individually at the moment that I can think of. I'm a mother, and that's my concern for the most part right now. . . . Right now that little girl is my focus, and that's it."

She even hinted not long after Bobbi Kristina was born that they were already thinking of adding another to the brood.

"Bobby and I were talking the other day," she told a reporter. "He cracks me up. He goes: 'You think you're so fine now'—because I dropped the weight—'but you know what? Bam, I'm gonna pop you again.' I said: 'What! You got to be kidding, I just dropped a baby!' He said, 'Nah, we're gonna have some more kids, honey.' We were joking about it—we were talking about having more children."

In reality, she and Arista were already making plans to capitalize on the monster success of *The Bodyguard* soundtrack, which was still tearing up the charts. Less than four months after giving birth, she embarked on what would be known as the "*Bodyguard* World Tour," which spanned almost two years. Meanwhile, Bobby was on a year-long tour of his own.

For Whitney, however, being a new mother and a megastar were not incompatible in the least. Bobbi would simply come on the road with her while nannies and friends cared for the baby during concerts and rehearsals. Still, there is no question that she doted on the little girl. Asked shortly into the tour whether she wanted more children, she was all too eager to share her joy at being a mother.

"Oh, yeah. Definitely," she told a reporter. "Having Bobbi Kristina . . . I could never do anything that could top that. There's been nothing more incredible in my life than having her. God knows, I have been in front of millions and millions of people, and that has been incredible, to feel that give-take thing. But, man, when I gave birth to her and when they put her in my arms, I thought: 'This has got to be it. This is the ultimate.' I haven't experienced anything greater."

Cissy recalls how there was a constant entourage looking after the baby on tour.

"Oh, how we loved that baby girl," she wrote in her memoir. "Everybody, from Nippy's friends to family to people who worked for her, just couldn't get enough of that child. She was so pretty, and such a sweet baby, laughing and smiling all the time, that people always wanted to see her and hold her."

Occasionally when their schedules permitted, Bobby would join Whitney on the road, or vice versa. But it wasn't long before stories began to circulate about his erratic behavior on tour, which included reports of excessive drinking, drugs, and womanizing.

Pamela Howell, a journalist for an Atlanta magazine, revealed that when she tried to interview Bobby after a local music awards show, the encounter was disturbing. "He started hugging and kissing me," she reported. "He had me in a headlock at one point. He never answered one of my questions. He just wanted to grope me. He acted like a thug."

MCA Records executive Ernie Singleton was forced to deny rumors of drug use. "I have heard stuff like this over the years on numerous occasions, but I can tell you, I have never had an experience with Bobby that painted a drug picture to me and I think I am pretty streetwise. You don't have to be around me when you do it. I can tell when you are whacked. I've also confronted Bobby . . . and he said no."

Bobby's longtime friend Jamie Foster Brown, publisher of *Sister 2 Sister* magazine, later revealed that "There were bets being made at the wedding as to how long this would last." Now the media were wondering the same thing aloud.

People took particular note of a habit that Whitney had developed whenever Bobby infrequently joined her on tour, where she would bring him onstage and leap into his arms while wrapping her legs around his waist and shouting, "I'm a woman in love and the man I'm in love with is very much in love with me."

The reporter described this over-the-top display of affection as "weird" and noticed that Bobby didn't seem too pleased to be used as a prop.

"Bobby having served his purpose, would then walk off silently, and sullenly, into the wings," the magazine reported.

Meanwhile, the tabloids had lately changed their focus from alleged lesbian trysts to stories about Bobby's behavior. "Whitney catches hubby with sexy beauty in hotel room," blared one headline. Scores of others hinted at marital discord.

"I know that [the media] are trying to make my husband out to be this man who has no respect for his wife and family, who has no respect for his marriage, who has no respect for much of anything—but they're very wrong," she insisted in *Ebony*.

For his part, Bobby assured reporters the relationship was sound and that the new baby was helping them bond as a couple.

"Bobbi Kris is the cement that holds our relationship together," he told one reporter. "When we're going through changes, when we're arguing or whatever, all it takes is for Bobbi Kristina to go waaaahhhhhhhh. And we crack up."

Whitney repeatedly talked of her domestic bliss, painting Bobby as a "protective and respectful" husband who is "very very romantic," often sending her flowers and cards just to say he missed her.

"I love him more than I thought I could ever love anyone in my life," she told a reporter after downplaying any rumors of conflict.

Still, many had noticed a change in her demeanor. Known as the "once-perfect Prom Queen of Soul," as one profile described her, Whitney was for the first time in her career being called a "diva" with regularity and many wondered if it was her marriage that had changed her.

The first signs of trouble emerged almost immediately as she kicked off a national tour at Miami's Knight Center in July 1993. First, fans were locked out of the concert hall until ten minutes before the show was scheduled to begin, forcing thousands to wilt in the blistering heat. Once inside, they had to endure a seventy-minute delay due to technical issues. Then, after two warm-up acts, there was another forty-five-minute delay before Whitney finally took the stage with no apology.

When a fan approached the stage after the opening medley with an autograph pad, security quickly whisked her away as Whitney hissed, "I do believe your ticket says seat." That prompted the first of a smattering of boos throughout the evening from the unimpressed crowd.

In his review the next day, *Miami Herald* writer Leonard Pitts complained that "Houston took the stage with an attitude that smelled like rotting fish." The *Orlando Sun-Sentinel* pop critic was even harsher, addressing an open letter to Whitney about her demeanor:

> *Whitney, your attitude is indicative of the perennial blame-passing and so much of what else is wrong with the entertainment business. Now that you're a movie star and your pop career is back on track, you've never been more famous. From a person of your stature, fans have a right to expect a little class. I can only wonder how many of them will be silly enough to line up for albums and tickets next time. I wouldn't.*

It was an inauspicious start to the tour and just an omen of things to come. In June, the *New York Post* reported that Whitney had overdosed on diet pills, the first time her name was ever publicly associated with drugs. When she threatened to sue, the paper retracted the story, but Barbara Walters would twice reference the purported overdose in an interview later that year, and Whitney remained silent.

Still, as awards season dawned, it was clear that Whitney was back on top. The success of *The Bodyguard* and her marriage to Bobby had clearly reestablished her credibility in the black community: She won the award for Outstanding Female Artist at the NAACP Image

Awards and Best R&B/Soul song at the Soul Train Music Awards for "I Will Always Love You." At the American Music Awards she swept all eight categories for which she was nominated and then took three more awards home at the most prestigious music event of the year, the Grammys.

It was an incident that took place while she was in Los Angeles for the Grammys, in fact, which appeared to indicate that Robyn had not made her peace with Whitney's marriage after all.

Shortly after midnight, security guards were summoned to Whitney's room about an altercation at the Peninsula Hotel where Robyn was staying along with Whitney, Bobby, and the entourage.

According to Jeffery Bowman, one of the security guards reported:

When we arrived at the hotel room, Robyn Crawford answered the door. She had a scratch on her hand and red marks on her arms and neck. Although she played down any incident that may have happened, something was clearly wrong. We asked Ms. Houston if she would like us to stay until the police—who had also been summoned—arrived. But she said she could handle the situation from here. We noticed by his behavior that Mr. Brown had apparently been drinking. It seemed that Brown, Houston, and Crawford had all been involved in some sort of physical altercation.

And, although this altercation stayed out of the press, it was an incident in the fall of 1994 that would prompt the first open questions about Whitney's erratic behavior. In October, South African president Nelson Mandela was to be honored by President Clinton with a state dinner at the White House. Whitney, who was a lifelong opponent of apartheid, had been invited to perform for Mandela, whom she had described as one of her heroes. But as the dignitaries arrived to honor the ANC leader, there was no sign of Whitney. When nobody could reach her, protocol officials were scrambling to find a replacement, when Whitney finally appeared with Bobby a full two hours late.

"I just got off tour," she explained. In fact, she had finished her most recent engagement at Radio City Music Hall four days earlier.

The diva-like behavior was starting to attract attention. A month earlier, in Las Vegas, she had dismissed fans' anger at yet another lengthy delay by haughtily observing, "Stuff happens."

At a concert in Anaheim at the height of the OJ trial, Whitney interrupted her performance to request a spotlight be turned onto Simpson's two children who were in the audience. The following day, a newspaper critic described the request as "weird" and "mortifying."

Her bodyguards kept fans at arm's length and she frequently refused to sign autographs, though it seemed she had delighted in interacting with fans early in her career, at a time when she was often praised as refreshing and down-to-earth for her humble attitude. Now she was said to throw tantrums if she didn't get what she wanted.

"Everyone was afraid to say no to her," a member of her entourage would later tell *People* about this period. "For stars like Whitney, when it comes to getting their way, it's almost like arrested development. They never emotionally mature past the age where they become famous. They're like children, ranting and raving until they get what they want. It's like, 'I want my coke, and if you say no, you can find yourself another job.'"

Meanwhile, Bobby's career had noticeably stalled. His follow-up to *Don't Be Cruel*, the 1992 release *Bobby*, was a let down after the monster success of his groundbreaking album. *Rolling Stone* was not impressed by the effort, noting that the new album "lacks the one ingredient that made 'Don't Be Cruel' so exciting: daring. Put bluntly, 'Bobby' hews so closely to the sound and structure of (the previous album) that you half expect there to be a *II* in the title."

The *LA Times* called sales "sluggish" after the album debuted at number two but quickly dipped to number five and kept falling. Now, with his new superstar wife outselling him and hogging the spotlight, it appeared Bobby wasn't handling the comedown very gracefully.

In December, *People* took note of Bobby's conspicuous absence when Whitney was honored in New York for her achievements in music and film.

"In her speech accepting her award," the magazine reported, "Houston didn't mention his name once. Instead, addressing little Bobbi Kristina, who was sitting wide-eyed in the front row, the superstar said, as she choked back tears, 'You are my reason to be.'"

Four months later, while Whitney was in Singapore, touring, Bobby was involved in the most serious incident yet of an increasingly troubling pattern. He and two bodyguards were arrested at a Disney World nightclub after Bobby got into an altercation with a tourist who interrupted him when he was flirting with a female patron.

Bobby and his handlers reportedly started to punch and kick the thirty-seven-year-old man as he lay on the floor. One of the trio also smashed him over the head with a bottle. The victim was rushed to the hospital, where he needed six surgical staples to close a gash in his head and eight stitches to reattach his ear.

According to police, they placed Bobby in the back of a squad car where he proceeded to bang his head repeatedly against the window.

Describing the incident, an Orlando police spokesman reported, "When the deputy came back a couple of minutes later, Bobby Brown had peed on the seat, on the floor, and all over the cage, which separates the good guys from bad guys. He'd also taken a pen and written on the seat: 'Fuck.'"

The three men were charged with aggravated battery and disorderly conduct and eventually released on a $5,000 bond.

Suddenly, instead of describing Bobby as the "Bad Boy," the media frequently made references to his bad behavior.

In August 1993, he was once again arrested for assault after he kicked a security guard who responded to a noise complaint at a West Hollywood hotel room where Bobby was hosting a private party.

Rumors had already been circulating of trouble in the couple's year-old marriage after Bobby was frequently seen partying at nightclubs without his wife. But Whitney denied any problems and insisted her marriage was strong.

"Marriage is a beautiful institution," she told *Ebony*.

People don't know Bobby because there hasn't been much on Bobby except that Bobby is this sexy man who does all this bumping and grinding. But Bobby is a family man. Bobby loves his mother, loves his family. He goes out when he wants to hear music, when he wants to know what's happening. He comes home. I know where my husband is; I know what my husband does. There are certain things that I don't go for, and Bobby knows that. And there's stuff that he doesn't go for. That's why we can be together, because we both have the same standards.

To *Essence* magazine she again denied that her marriage was simply designed to burnish her public image. "This ain't about publicity," she said.

I wouldn't do it if it were about publicity. I don't want to spend the rest of my life with somebody I thought was just gonna give me publicity. I've got enough of that on my own. And so does he. You don't have a baby based on that madness. People don't live like that. Especially Black people who were raised in families with morals and standards and integrity. But the press isn't gonna sell a paper if they're saying 'Well, Whitney and Bobby are doing great!'

Finally, in September, the couple was forced to acknowledge their domestic troubles when they issued a press release announcing that they were separating because of "marital difficulties." Three months later, Whitney acknowledged the separation in an interview with the *Chicago Tribune* but insisted, "I am still married."

During this period, Bobby's street-thug image was bolstered when his sister's fiancé—his occasional bodyguard—was shot and killed in a hail of bullets after driving away from a Roxbury bar with Bobby in a $295,0000 Bentley registered to Whitney. As he watched the man be gunned down, Bobby was reported to have shouted, "They shot my boy!"

When a twenty-two-year-old Boston woman named Lacresha Robinson saw news reports of the shooting, she immediately contacted authorities to have Bobby hauled in for a paternity suit he had been avoiding for months because his lawyers said he was in Atlanta and unavailable. Robinson claimed she had an affair with the singer shortly before he married Whitney in 1992—and that he was the father of her daughter, Zipporah.

Shortly afterward, Bobby quietly checked into the Betty Ford clinic to treat "alcohol abuse." The stint in rehab appeared to be a precondition for Whitney to take him back because soon after he checked out in December, they were once again together, much to the chagrin of her fans and the media, who appeared to blame Bobby for Whitney's own increasingly diva-like and erratic behavior.

The cover of the December 18 edition of *People*, in fact, posed the question many were asking, "So why is she back with bad boy Bobby Brown?" That same week, Whitney poured out her growing frustration at the increasing media scrutiny of her private life.

"We all have our problems and troubles," she told *Entertainment Weekly*. "All I want to do is to be able to work them out in private. They say he cheats on me. I haven't caught him yet. If I had, I'd break his fucking neck. I got projects coming up for kids that are incredible, for child abuse and things of that nature, and all these people want to write about is who we're fucking and who we ain't fucking and all this other bullshit and I'm tired of it. I know who he comes home to."

She was especially upset when she discovered that *People* had once again alluded to her relationship with Robyn. *EW* describes her as nearly in tears as she peruses the article: "Oh my God, oh my God, oh my God. I am not a lesbian, I wish they'd stop saying it. I have a daughter, for God's sake. What do they mean by this? They write this shit and one day I'm gonna have to talk to my daughter. Please, I'm so pissed off right now. Excuse me."

By 1995, it was common for Whitney to bring up the subject of Bobbi, now almost three years old, whenever the media brought up information that she perceived was damaging to her heavily crafted public image.

In an interview with *Entertainment Tonight*, she explained that she had a "hands off" rule when it came to the press.

"I find that I am now more defensive because I'm very very protective of her and I will fight you and I will tear your house down brick by brick about her." In the same interview, she once again raised the old canard about Eddie Murphy after the interviewer asked her to describe her worst date. She recalled an incident where she had cooked dinner for Murphy and he never showed up.

If her personal life was something of a mess during this period, her professional career was still strong. With the success of *The Bodyguard*, Whitney was now a hot commodity in Hollywood.

As the scripts poured in, the one that jumped out at Whitney was an adaptation of the 1992 best-selling novel *Waiting to Exhale*, about four black women looking for love in Phoenix, Arizona. Although she could likely have had her pick of roles after the box office success of her first film, she was attracted to the character of Savannah Jackson, a successful television producer who falls for a married man. Joining a stellar all-black cast that included Oscar-nominated actress Angela Bassett, she reported for filming in the spring of 1995. Forest Whitaker had signed on to direct.

Like her previous effort, the film received decidedly mixed reviews but once again Whitney proved to be box office gold, with the film debuting at number one when it was released in December 1995. And critics noted that her acting had noticeably improved since her big-screen debut three years earlier. Still, this film wouldn't come close to the success of the blockbuster that had made her a movie star.

Back home in Mendham Township, Whitney was a familiar figure to the townspeople who had watched her arrival in their sleepy
community with trepidation but were pleasantly surprised by her
attitude, never experiencing the diva-like behavior that would be
described in later years.

"The experience we all had was very positive," her next-door
neighbor Claire Kaplan recalled. "There were lots of workmen reno-
vating her house for close to a year after she moved in. To thank us for
putting up with that, she sent us all red roses."

The townspeople often saw her on walks or out and about in
town. According to Bobby Spiropolous, the owner of her favorite
diner, she liked to order Greek salads with grilled chicken. At the
Black Horse Tavern and Pub, where she would come with Bobbi, she
would order the pot pie. The manager, Michael Horty, said Whitney
"had a beautiful air about herself" and recalled that "One time she
was humming a tune and I had to stop by and say, 'Oh, that sounds
so beautiful.' The same song was playing on the Muzak system." But
her favorite local eatery, as she later told a radio interviewer, was the
China Gourmet.

Former police chief Steven Crawford said he once stopped her
for a moving violation.

"She jumped out of the car," he recalled. "Obviously, I recognized
her from music videos. She was very down-to-earth and genuine,
especially considering her stature with regard to fame."

He was surprised by her short stature and the fact that she had
no chauffeur.

"For a woman who had number one hits, she was, first, driving
herself around," he said. "Second, she was extremely personable and a
pleasure to deal with."

He let it slide.

According to local councilman Rich Krieg, Bobbi attended the
local Montessori school when she was little. "Bobby and Whitney
were very clear that they wanted their daughter to be mainstreamed

and not singled out," he recalled. "Their daughter showed up the next day in a chauffeured Rolls-Royce."

She was also a generous contributor to local causes, according to the local county freeholder Jim O'Brien, whose daughter Deirdre was murdered by a serial killer—inspiring the creation of Deirdre's House, for children who are victims of abuse or neglect.

"We were running low on money and didn't have enough to establish a medical room where doctors would give treatment to victims," recalled O'Brien. "Word got around and we got a call from Houston, who said she'd like to donate $60,000 for the room."

Denzel Washington had for more than a year been been talking to Whitney's people about his planned remake of the 1947 Cary Grant film *The Bishop's Wife*, about an angel who comes to the aid of a bishop. The remake would take the original premise and involve the clergyman of a struggling Baptist church in the inner cities of New York at Christmas. The role of Julia had been written with Whitney in mind to play the preacher's neglected wife. A former nightclub singer, the character is the mainstay of the church choir, providing an opportunity for some rousing musical numbers. The role would give Whitney a chance to return to her gospel roots. Penny Marshall had signed on to direct but Whitney was slow to commit. Only when the producers came back with an offer she couldn't refuse—$10 million—did she finally sign on. Less than two weeks after *Waiting to Exhale* premiered in December, she reported to her new set.

But no sooner had filming wrapped up on her latest movie in the spring than Bobby got himself into trouble again. Only four months after he checked out of Betty Ford, he was pulled over with an unidentified woman at three in the morning after an officer saw him speeding and swerving in his Mercedes. So intoxicated that he couldn't recite the alphabet as a sobriety test, he refused to take a Breathalyzer and was hauled into the station where he was booked and released on $1,260 bail.

In August, he was arrested once again in Hollywood, Florida, when he lost control of a Porsche registered to Whitney and crashed it into a condominium complex. His blood alcohol level was almost three times the state's legal limit, but his urine test also tested positive for cocaine and marijuana—the first confirmation that the singer's problems went beyond alcohol. He suffered four broken ribs in the accident.

So far, none of Bobby's public scrapes had involved his wife. Although each incident had received more than its share of publicity, they tended to feed the existing public perception of musicians as wild and immature. And because Bobby was already perceived as the Bad Boy, they served more than anything to give Whitney some added street cred with segments of the public that may have found her a little too saccharine in the past.

That all changed in June 1997, when reports emerged that Bobby slapped Whitney in a Honolulu parking lot. Whitney had performed at the city's Aloha Stadium the night before and the couple had arrived to do some Sunday morning shopping at the Kahala Mall.

Witnesses said they saw Whitney exit her limo, followed by Bobby in an agitated state. Holding a beer in one hand, he used the other to slap her across the face.

"It looked like somebody—probably her—was trying to get out of the limousine and she was either pulled back or yanked back," one witness told *USA Today*. "There was a lot more noise and perhaps 10 minutes later they left."

When security guards came out to investigate the altercation, the couple said they had it "under control." Whitney's publicist later insisted it had been a case of "mistaken identity."

It was the first public report of domestic violence during their tumultuous marriage but it wouldn't be the last. It also helped fuel rumors that had been swirling since the spring that the couple had become habitual drug users. The first whispers began after Whitney failed to show up to the televised Essence Awards ceremony at Madison Square Garden in April, where she was scheduled to receive the

Triumphant Spirit Award at a star-studded gala that also included the Living Legend Award for Muhammad Ali. But when Whitney's name was called out, she was nowhere to be found and Cissy had to accept the award on her daughter's behalf. "They said she was in Florida but they couldn't find her," a production source later revealed to *People*. "It was terribly weird and devastating."

In July, the couple was vacationing in the Mediterranean on a 120-foot yacht with her brother Michael and his wife, when Whitney was brought to Capri's Capilupi Hospital with a two-inch gash on her left cheek. Police were called in when the hospital reported that there were conflicting accounts of how she received her wound. Whitney told doctors she was injured when she hit a rock while swimming. But a member of the yacht's crew reported that she got the cut aboard the yacht.

Before police had a chance to investigate further, Whitney and her party departed the island by helicopter.

Needless to say, the tabloids had a field day. Forced on the defensive, Whitney would repeatedly deny that Bobby ever hit her.

"Contrary to belief, I do the hitting; he doesn't," she told *Redbook*. "He has never put his hands on me. He is not a woman-beater. We are crazy for one another. I mean crazy in love, love, love, love, love. When we're fighting, it's like that's love for us. We're fighting for our love."

The Preacher's Wife was released in December 1996, and although it wasn't a blockbuster at the box office like her previous two efforts, it garnered generally positive reviews, including a number of critics who, for the first time, singled out Whitney's acting as well as her singing. "Whitney Houston is rather angelic herself, displaying a divine talent for being virtuous and flirtatious at the same time," the *San Francisco Chronicle* praised. Her thespian efforts, in fact, would garner her her first and only acting trophy when she won the NAACP's Image Award for Best Actress. The soundtrack, though hardly comparable in sales to *The Bodyguard*, would become the highest-selling gospel soundtrack of all time. Sadly, the positive publicity around the film and its accompanying album would be the last glory for an artist who was about to begin a tragic descent.

Whitney had signed on with Disney in 1996 to produce and costar in an adaptation of Rodgers & Hammerstein's version of *Cinderella*, a musical fantasy. Whitney had originally planned to play Cinderella but decided that, at thirty-three, she was too old to pull it off. She approached Brandy to play the part, and she agreed, on the condition that Whitney, her "idol," play the fairy godmother. The new role allowed Whitney to deliver some tour de force musical numbers, including two duets with the rising young star in the title role.

When the TV movie aired on television in November 1997, it once again proved the drawing power of the superstar singer turned actress, attracting a massive audience, the most watched program of the week.

A month earlier, however, another TV production in which she was involved had proved something less of a success. In October, HBO had aired a live concert special of Whitney from Washington DC's Constitution Hall as a benefit for the Children's Defense Fund. A number of onlookers had observed that she appeared stoned throughout the concert.

Reviewing the special, *Entertainment Weekly* observed, "Clearly *something* was wrong during Houston's Oct. 5 live HBO concert, in which she strained to sing her tunes, reeled off a random, bewildering medley of tributes to dead celebrities—including the Notorious B.I.G. and Princess Diana—and dripped more flop sweat than Nixon." Another reviewer called the performance "a tape-delayed near-death experience."

Reports had started to surface that Whitney was showing up late nearly every day to the set of *Cinderella* and was displaying erratic behavior.

"She shows up on her own time, she's rude, she doesn't come to rehearsal," a producer revealed. "It saddens me that a person who has everything in the world going for her is screwing it up." And then a week before the TV musical aired, Whitney went on the talk show circuit to promote the upcoming broadcast.

On October 30—the first day of the crucial November sweeps period—she had been scheduled to guest on Rosie O'Donnell's popular daytime show, a heavily anticipated appearance that O'Donnell had been hyping all week. But forty-five minutes before the show's scheduled taping time, a rep called to inform the producers that Whitney would not appear, citing "stomach flu." Said to be apoplectic, the host proceeded to inform her audience, "Whitney's not here. She's ill. I hope she's *very* ill." To make matters worse, Whitney appeared to have made a miraculous recovery, because she was seen that afternoon tagging along with Bobby to his taped appearance on the *Late Show with David Letterman*.

By this time, Bobby's own career was in a tailspin. His latest album, *Forever*, had tanked commercially, and Whitney had been repeatedly forced to bail him out; first, when the bank foreclosed on his Atlanta mansion, and then when the IRS froze his assets because he owed millions in back taxes. Like his wife, Bobby had his sights set on a film career and had appeared in a small role in 1989's *Ghostbusters 2*. He had signed on in the role of Powerline in Disney's *The Goofy Movie* and had already laid down some numbers for the soundtrack. But the studio couldn't get insurance because of the singer's increasingly evident drug problems and he was quietly dropped from the cast.

At the beginning of 1998, Bobby was sentenced to five days in county jail stemming from the 1996 DUI incident in Hollywood, Florida, which he had appealed. In addition to the jail sentence, his driver's license was suspended, he was placed on a year's probation, and forced to spend thirty days in a residential drug and alcohol treatment center.

A few months later, he was taken into custody at the Beverly Hills Hotel and charged with sexual battery—defined as "unlawful touching for the purpose of sexual arousal"—following a complaint by an unidentified woman about an incident that happened at the hotel swimming pool. He posted a bond of $2,778 and was released, but the charge was later dropped.

"I wouldn't hurt nobody. I wouldn't touch nobody," Bobby told the Associated Press following his release.

Whitney's movie offers had slowed to a snail's pace after the lackluster box office performance of *The Preacher's Wife*. Other than a duet with Mariah Carey for the soundtrack of *Prince of Egypt*, her once-promising film career had stalled, so it was back to the studio to record her long-anticipated fourth album and her first in almost eight years that wasn't a soundtrack. Once again, Whitney and Clive Davis were at the helm. When *My Love Is Your Love* was released in November 1998, however, the commercial reception proved less than enthusiastic. It entered the *Billboard* charts at number thirteen and never went any higher, although it did enjoy more success in Europe than in the United States and its single, "Heartbreak Hotel," became a monster hit on the R&B charts. Still, the disappointing sales were conspicuous and not a good career harbinger.

The critics, however, were impressed and lavished praise on an effort that many found harder-edged and more authentic than her previous recordings. *Rolling Stone* called it "easily her most consistent album ever—in fact, it's her first consistent album." Many critics took note of her maturing voice, which may have lost an octave or so since the peak of her career but was more "fully developed," according to the *New York Times* review.

Looking back, the most poignant moment on the album was at the top of the title track when the voice of five-year-old Bobbi Kristina is heard interjecting, "Sing, Mommy." Whitney would later describe how her daughter's voice came to be included on the track.

"We were in the studio with [producer Wyclef Jean], and she just said, 'Mommy, I want to sing,'" she told a reporter. "Wyclef was quiet for a minute, and then nodded his head and said, 'That can work.'"

Bobbi would later join her mother onstage during some of the tour dates singing some of the lyrics.

Asked by the *Los Angeles Times* whether she was grooming her young daughter to follow in her footsteps, Whitney proudly replied, "She wants to do it. I would love to say to you that it looks like she's gonna be a lawyer or a pediatrician or a ballet dancer. But it's none of those. You can always tell a singer by the way they hold a microphone, and she holds that mike with confidence. She's a little diva-in-training. If there's ever gonna be another me, it's gonna be Bobbi Kris. There ain't gonna be no more after that."

From what the world learned later, growing up in the household of Whitney and Bobby during this period must have been very confusing for the young child, although she was usually looked after by nannies and by Whitney's Auntie Bae, so she was sheltered from both parents' increasingly erratic lifestyles. Publicly, both parents still professed domestic bliss at every opportunity and indicated that their first priority was their young daughter.

In an interview with the women's magazine *Redbook*, Whitney seemed particularly spirited when talking about her life as a mother, although she expressed frustration about periods of long separation from Bobbi while on the road.

> *Being away from my child for weeks at a time is the tough part for me—unlike other professions where it might be a couple of days. That kills me. It just kills me. I was just at a meeting with her teacher because I had taken Krissi out of school so much. I missed her when I was away. And the teacher said, 'She can't be taken out anymore. She has to catch up to the other children. And if you keep taking her out of school she won't be able to.' But she and I need each other. Krissi will call me and say, 'Mama, I miss you.' And that does it. That does me in. I say, 'Okay, I am going to send for you tomorrow.' I am weak like that.*

Asked whether she considered herself a protective mother, she was unequivocal. "Yes. I would kill for Krissi. I know that I could really kill for my daughter. I know because I'm living for her, so I'm fierce when it comes down to it. And I feel the same about my husband."

On the subject of Bobby, she was forced to address the increasingly loud media speculation about the state of their marriage, which included multiple reports about screaming matches and other flare-ups.

> I don't know anybody who hasn't gone through ups and downs in a marriage. It just so happens that Bobby and I have done it in public. The first five years of marriage are rough—if you can get past them you're doing good. But during those years it was rough. We are two very famous people. I had my own money and my own career. It can be tough on a very strong male who has his own success to be with a woman who has hers, too.

In contrast to the liner notes of her first albums, which contained lavish praise for her friend Robyn, including a declaration on *Whitney* that "I love you," her new album simply listed Robyn as part of the "production coordination" team. In contrast, she gushes thanks to Bobby. "You were meant for me. Nothing can come between this love."

Observers noticed that Whitney's old friend—once inseparable from her—was spending less and less time by her side. Yet Robyn still played an active role in the singer's career and was an integral part of each artistic project, including day-to-day involvement as a producer of *Cinderella*. But since Bobby entered the picture, her interaction with Whitney appeared to shift from the personal to the political. Her title was no longer executive assistant but "creative director" at Nippy inc. Among her projects was founding Whitney's music label, Better Place Records, which saw her taking an active role in the career of musicians other than Whitney, including the short-lived all-female quintet Sunday.

As I reviewed behind-the-scenes footage of the two friends working together in the early days and the ease with which Robyn could calm Whitney and keep her grounded while focusing on the task at hand, I can't help but think Robyn's steadying influence was just what Whitney could have used as she began her personal descent during this period.

In a rare interview with a European magazine, Robyn described the shift in their long-standing relationship and hinted that they were no longer even friends, explaining,

> The foundation that we had years ago, the friendship that we shared, is pretty much back there in the past. Now it's business. Those of us who work with her have to change to accommodate what happens. I would say that, as a person, Whitney has pretty much stayed the same. I think that it's the people around her, myself included, who have had to make the change to adjust to the fact that she is now so famous, so in demand . . . A lot of times you get your feelings hurt. I may look at her in a room and think, 'That was my best friend.' None of us around her, not her mother or father or me, could be to her what a husband can be. In a marriage it seems to me that it is always the woman who has to do more—commit herself more, devote herself, always be there. And Whitney is going to be that kind of wife: she's very traditional. She is not high-handed or temperamental or arrogant, but although she walks softly, she carries an invisible stick. If you back her up against a wall, you will be sorry. In the nicest way, she will make you feel (very small).

As the new millennium dawned, Whitney was at a very different crossroads than she had been a decade earlier when her life and career were on an upward spiral. Now it appeared to both the public and those around her that she was heading straight down.

No sooner had the world dodged the long-feared Y2K virus than the couple faced a catastrophe of their own. After a Hawaiian vacation on the Big Island in early January, Whitney was passing through security with Bobby at Kona International Airport, when a search of her carry-on luggage found two Baggies of marijuana and three half-smoked joints—more than fifteen grams in all. The guards had no authority to detain passengers, but they immediately confiscated her bag and called the local law enforcement authorities.

Rather than wait, the couple simply boarded the plane. By the time police arrived, they were taxiing down the runway and were allowed to take off. Authorities later filed a petty misdemeanor charge against Whitney, which could have carried a thirty-day jail sentence, but the charges were eventually dropped amid accusations of favoritism and VIP treatment.

"There was no way in hell I was going to hang around and let those rent-a-cops put me in jail over this bullshit," she was reported to have said.

Still, it was one more headline linking the couple to drug use. Before long, her antics were the fodder for comedians and late-night talk show hosts.

At the Grammy Awards ceremony in Los Angeles the following month, Rosie O'Donnell was the host and Whitney was scheduled to perform. Introducing Whitney, she made a veiled reference to the Hawaiian bust when she referenced the Doobie Brothers, then said, "Our next performer is a huge fan of the doobies. What can I say but Maui Wowie."

In early March, Whitney pulled out of performing at the Rock and Roll Hall of Fame induction ceremony, citing "throat problems." Three weeks later, she had been scheduled to perform at the Oscars in a medley with Garth Brooks, Ray Charles, Isaac Hayes, Queen Latifah, and her cousin Dionne Warwick. But only forty-eight hours before the telecast, she was quietly removed from the number. The official excuse was again "throat trouble," the same reason she had given several times the previous year when she canceled tour performances. It later emerged that during rehearsals, she kept flubbing the lines to the song she was supposed to sing, "Over the Rainbow." Somebody who attended auditions told *People*, "She just kind of moved her mouth a little bit." Another revealed, "She missed her entire cue." A TV producer told the magazine the fiasco was indicative of Whitney's growing reputation in the industry. "When this Oscar thing happened, it did not surprise me," he told the magazine. "She has a reputation for being a flake and no-showing, and it's dangerous to book her because until she walks on that stage, there's no guarantee she's going to show up." *New York Post* columnist Liz Smith described her performance at rehearsals as "discombobulated." The legendary songwriter Burt Bacharach, who served as Oscar music director that year and reportedly fired her from the broadcast, observed, "Whitney's chronic condition is very sad."

A week later, Nathan Lane was hosting a Broadway Cares benefit tribute to Elton John, when he turned to his cohost Christine Baranski and said, "Thanks so much for filling in at the last minute for Whitney Houston." Baranski grabbed the mike and mimed snorting cocaine.

It was clear that at least one of Whitney's secrets was out, although she and her handlers went to great lengths to deny she had a problem. Her mother in particular was now often front and center defending her daughter from the growing accusations.

"It's not easy," Cissy told a reporter. "Everyone is innocent until proven guilty. It's difficult for a mother as visible as I am. With God, I've learned to handle most things. They build you up to tear you down. You really have to hold on to God. That's the only thing that gets me through and the only thing that will get her through."

For her part, Whitney was still portraying herself and her husband as a normal couple who were trying to maintain a regular family life. In the spring, they took Bobbi on a Disney cruise. "I don't hang out," Whitney told *BET Weekend* magazine. "I don't go to clubs. I like to go shopping. I'm a homebody. I like to stay home. I play with my daughter. She's my best friend. I'm a hands-on mother. Krissi knows I have the final word. I try to help Krissi to understand if the response was no, why the answer was no. I'm a mother who knows how to say no."

Bobbi was now seven years old and was attending an exclusive private school, Wardlaw-Hartridge, in Edison, New Jersey, under an assumed name so as not to receive any unwanted attention.

With the whispers growing into full-fledged media accusations about her mother's drug use, Whitney appeared especially concerned with sheltering Bobbi from the fallout.

"I have to protect my daughter, so it's not funny," she told *Redbook*. "She has to go to school with kids whose parents read those magazines. I am sure the children hear about it and I have to deal with what she hears."

Asked if Bobbi had ever brought up the rumors, she responded, "Krissi knows the truth. She knows what happens in this household. If she hears anything she can say, 'This is not my daddy, this is not my mommy.' We are very straight up with her, saying, 'You are going to hear a lot of stuff in your life about Mom and Dad. Anything you have any doubts about, anything you want to know, ask us, we will tell you.' "

But it was getting increasingly difficult for Whitney to deny she had a problem, especially since it was the mainstream media rather than the tabloids that was feasting on her difficulties.

In May, *Jane* magazine ran a cover story about the singer that revealed she showed up for a photo shoot four hours late. The writer revealed that observers present at the shoot noted that when she did show up, she exhibited bizarre behavior, and that she was "extremely unfocused, had trouble keeping her eyes open and kept singing and playing an imaginary piano." Whitney's excuse for her lateness was a trip to the dentist to repair a cracked tooth.

There had been a lot of excuses lately.

CHAPTER **TWENTY**

On January 29, two days before she was found in the bathtub, Bobbi took to social media, as was her habit. She started the day by tweeting a photo to a page called "Bitch Problems," where females like to complain about problems in their love life. The photo showed a man lying on top of a smiling woman, kissing her in a sensuous pose. She added the caption, directed to Nick's Twitter account: "This would be perfect right now."

A little while later, she retweeted a post from one of her favorite sites, Fitness Motivator.

> *"I get hit, I get up. I get hit, I get up. I get hit, I get up. Get knocked down seven times, get up 8."*

Later that day, she posted a tweet with just three words in large letters:

> *"On My Own."*

Whatever that meant, she didn't appear to be in any distress, because a little while later she posted two shots of the actor Jake

Gyllenhaal to a site called "Pictures for Girls," on which women often post beefcake shots of men they fantasize about.

One of her last tweets of the day followed an increasingly common theme for Bobbi, who was very much concerned with pursuing her longtime dream of stardom, so far with not much success:

> *"Let's start this career up && moving OUT to YOU ALLLL*
> *quick shall we!?"*

Although the third anniversary of her mother's death was still two weeks away, it was clearly on her mind three days earlier when she directed a tweet to the generic hashtag #Anniversary:

> *"Littlelady&your growing young man @Nickgordon miss you*
> *mommy..:') SO much . . . loving you more every sec."*

Her last tweet of the day—also her last tweet before the incident two days later—was posted to the hashtag #Can'tbelieveit. It was a retweet of a fan's observation that Bobbi would be turning twenty-two in little more than a month:

> *"I can't wait for the music and much more."*

But what did her cryptic tweet earlier in the day—"On My Own"—signify? Had she split up with Nick?

The answer is hazy, but I obtained a copy of a 911 call made by a security guard on January 23, a week earlier, that may contain some clues:

Identifying the exact address—9046 Riverbend Manor, where Bobbi lived with Nick—he identified himself as "Rick" from Ellard Security:

"I've got a domestic dispute. I just had a neighbor call and report that there are people hitting each other, swinging, outside of their town house in Ellard Village." The 911 dispatcher then advises the guard to tell the neighbors to phone 911.

So far, during my travels in Atlanta, virtually everybody whom I've talked to who knew Bobbi and/or Nick told me they believed Bobbi likely attempted suicide or overdosed because she was distraught at the impending anniversary of her mother's death. The eerily similar circumstances—found unconscious in a bathtub—only bolstered the theory.

Now here were some clues, from the days leading up to the incident that indicated Bobbi was ruminating about the anniversary and that she may have broken up with her fiancé only two days earlier.

Still, this was circumstantial at best and left a number of important unanswered questions.

When I met up with a DJ who knew the couple from the club circuit, I asked him to describe their relationship. Did he think that a breakup could cause Bobbi to attempt suicide?

"Nick is bad news, bad news brother," he said. "He's heavy into drinking, heavy into drugs. I know Nick for a few years. That brother got worse by the day. All that money Krissi came into went to buy drugs. They thought they were higher than life. So sad what happened to Krissi. I assure you it was Nick who took her down a dark path. He controlled her. He put her in very bad, very dangerous circles. And now look where they are—she's in a hospital fighting for her life and he's in some rehab center. So sad, but anyone who knew them knew that they were heading for trouble. I used to hang out in Atlanta's meanest clubs with Nick. But the last couple years he ditched all his friends to be with Krissi. He didn't remember where he came from, who his friends were when he was a nobody. All that money and celebrity shit got to his head, Nick has a huge ego; he's very insecure especially when it comes to Krissi. He wants her all to himself. He usually doesn't let her walk out of the house alone because he's afraid to lose her, he's afraid somebody might tell her what kind of a dude he really is, which might make her leave him."

He declined to answer my initial question because of what he called the "drug thing." Their immersion in drugs, he explained, makes it difficult to analyze their state of mind or what he called their "volatile" relationship.

"The last time I saw them was at Publix a couple months ago. I barely recognized Krissi; she looked like she became a junkie. Nick looked out of it, very stoned. I didn't say anything to them but they looked like they needed help, both of them looked like they needed to enter rehab."

I also met a guy named Rasheed, who claims to have been friends with Nick until June 2014. He told me he was disturbed by what he observed of Nick's relationship with Bobbi.

"He used to be a homie," Rasheed said. "But in the last year he acted like a total jackass. All the fame and money was getting to his head. He was living the life, living in a fancy house and driving pimped-out cars. He forgot where he came from. I didn't like the way he treated his girl. He acted as if he owned Bobbi. He had her brainwashed. I know that for a fact because I was with them a few months ago and she mentioned she might move to LA for a bit to do some acting. She said she had offers. Nick interrupted right away and said the offers were too small for someone of Krissi's stature and that unless the offers were serious and would put her in a big, starring role Krissi was going nowhere. He looked at her and she nodded her head like a puppet. For some reason it seemed she was afraid to go against him. I've heard them argue. Their voices would escalate. But Nick always got his way. She was afraid of him. She always backed down."

One of the people I was told who would be better able to tell me about the state of their relationship is Bobbi's ex-boyfriend Zach Jafarzadeh, who also knew Nick. Zach happens to be the same person who leaked photos of Bobbi snorting cocaine to the *National Enquirer* in 2011—the first indication that she might be following the same disturbing path as her mother.

When I tried to track Zach down, I discovered that he was lying low and making plans to move to San Francisco. But two weeks after Bobbi was found, he talked to the London *Daily Mail* in which he posited his own theory about what had happened. Zach claimed that Bobbi had long since given up coke, explaining it was just a "small phase" of her life. He says that she smoked cigarettes but not marijuana, because she didn't like the way it made her feel.

In fact, he claimed that Bobbi did a fair amount of drugs before Whitney's death, but when she saw what happened to her mom, she "wanted to learn from that."

Since 2012, he claimed, she had limited her drug use to Xanax, which she took every morning and often more than she was prescribed. He believes the Xanax may have played a role in her near drowning. He revealed that the relationship between Bobbi and Nick had been on the rocks.

"I know they got into a fight a few days before and she was really depressed about that, and probably took a few Xanax and bathed and fell asleep." Taking more than two or three with alcohol, he explained, is a "deadly combo."

After putting this theory foward, he came up with another.

"Some of it makes me feel like it could be a possible suicide," he told the British tabloid. "Not even just a mistake. Something symbolic like: 'This is the way my mom died, this is the way I want to kill myself too.' It's eerie how similar that is. It sent chills down my spine and it made me sick to my stomach when I heard about it."

Like the DJ I met with, he admitted that the couple's relationship was volatile. "Nick has a short temper," he reveals. "And Bobbi can be difficult. It was a tug of war, because they are both very stubborn people. Bobbi is very sweet, giving and caring, but she wants all of you, everything. And Nick likes space, that's where a lot of the tension between them came from. Nick was getting a little wild. He was getting into car accidents. He's been in about three or four accidents over the last couple of years. He's got a need for speed."

Despite what he knows about Nick's temper, however, Zach was quick to rule out foul play.

"Everybody's trying to make it all 'Nick Gordon beat her up' but I don't believe that. I don't believe he beat her up and threw her in the bathtub. That's kind of stupid. Why would you put her in a bath if her mom just died in a bathtub?"

His theories about a Xanax-related blackout or suicide attempt are plausible and although he is far from the first to raise the possibility, they bear a little more weight, coming from an insider who knew the couple well. However, after reading his "exclusive account," I can't help but wonder whether Zach really knows as much as he claims. Why would Bobbi have anything to do with the man who betrayed her years earlier by selling damaging photos to the *Enquirer*? I'm especially suspicious that he chose to tell his story to the *Daily Mail*, another publication known to pay its sources. Having freelanced for the paper for years, I'm especially well versed in how they operate.

Moreover, as I met friends of Bobbi who definitely knew her in the more recent past, I discover that Zach's downplaying of her drug use doesn't match the hard-partying girl they knew.

Alas, Zach's revelations likely bring us no closer to the truth about what happened on the morning of January 31.

CHAPTER **TWENTY-ONE**

Describing the controversies swirling around Whitney in a profile of the singer, *Us Weekly* delivered a surprising revelation in their June 2000 issue.

> *And now she's a woman without a trusted advisor. In May, Crawford resigned from Houston's New Jersey–based company, Nippy Inc., and moved to Los Angeles. Houston watchers, who know that Crawford and Brown were often at loggerheads, were stunned by this once unimaginable fissure. 'It's hard to imagine [Whitney] functioning without her,' says a former associate."*

The same week, *People* confirmed the story:

> *The office manager at Nippy Inc., the New Jersey management company owned by Whitney Houston, has quit. Robyn Crawford, 35, who was also the dulcet diva's best friend and confidante since they were teenagers, has reportedly relocated to California. Houston's spokeswoman would not comment on the reason for Crawford's departure."*

The writing appeared to be on the wall as early as April, when Whitney appeared for her first public performance since the no-shows at the Oscars and the Hall of Fame induction ceremony. Clive Davis was due to be ousted from the company he founded, and his stable of stars were gathering for a televised tribute to his legacy to commemorate Arista's twenty-fifth anniversary at Los Angeles's Shrine Auditorium.

Whitney's performance was anticipated as the evening's highlight, although there was much public speculation beforehand about whether she would even show after her previous high-profile cancellations.

When she did strut onstage, the audience rose to their feet in excitement. But almost from the first note, it was clear something was wrong. As the *New York Times* later described the performance, "Ms. Houston began on a troubled note: she had difficulty focusing, tripped on the stage and forgot the lyrics to her hit, 'How Will I Know.'"

There were certainly flashes of brilliance during her twenty-minute appearance that reminded the star-studded audience why she was once considered music royalty, but it wasn't long before the whispers began anew. There was no longer denying that there was a serious problem.

A few days before the appearance, *Newsweek* had revealed that there was growing concern among her friends and family about Whitney's behavior. An executive revealed that Clive Davis had recently approached the singer's family to do an "intervention."

Backstage after the Arista show, a reporter from MTV asked Whitney's cousin Dionne Warwick whether there was any truth to the report. But the singer denied there was a problem. "I read it like you did; I don't know where that came from," she said. "There's no need for intervention."

In her 2013 memoir, however, Cissy admits that Davis had suggested an intervention months earlier and had recommended a rehab center in Connecticut where Whitney could be treated. Cissy reveals that John, who had recently retired from Nippy Inc. for health reasons, actually traveled to Connecticut with Robyn to check out the facility recommended by Davis. Cissy claims she was "livid" that Robyn had taken such action without "the courtesy to let me know."

Whitney, she revealed, didn't end up going to rehab at that point, but her film agent, Nicole David, later asked Cissy to fly to LA to stage an intervention along with Robyn, Whitney's close friend CeCe Winans, and Michael's wife, Donna Houston.

"We're here to get you the help you need, baby," Cissy told her daughter, who started crying and pleaded not to be sent to rehab.

"Mommy, please don't let them do this to me," she reports Whitney as pleading. "I can take care of it." Instead, Whitney asked Cissy to move in with her for a few weeks to look after her. She promised to quit doing drugs, but her mother was skeptical now that she knew the extent of her daughter's problem.

Around the same time, a media report quoted a source close to the Houston family who revealed that Robyn had yelled at Whitney, "I can't just sit by and watch you kill yourself."

In April, *Out* magazine—America's preeminent gay publication—revealed that Whitney would be the subject of a cover story in their May issue. Rumors circulated that the diva was finally going to come out. Why else would she agree to an interview with the magazine after she had always gone to such great lengths to distance herself from the rumors? But anybody expecting such a bold move was to be disappointed. Instead, Whitney took the opportunity to issue her most vehement denial to date.

"I ain't 'ho'-in. I ain't suckin' no dick," she told the magazine. "I ain't getting on my knees. Something must be wrong: I can't just really sing. I can't just be a really talented, gifted person. She's gotta be gay. Listen, I took a lot of grief for shit that wasn't me, OK, 'cause

I had friends, 'cause I was close to people. But that ain't me. I know what I am. I'm a mother. I'm a woman. I'm heterosexual. Period."

Whether it was because of her friend's dishonesty or Whitney's failure to get the help she needed or some other reason, Robyn tendered her resignation that same month. The relationship that had begun on a New Jersey playground twenty-one years earlier—one that Whitney had described as "unbreakable"—had now come to an end.

The same month, Arista released a two-disc CD of Whitney's greatest hits that reached number five on the *Billboard* charts, another disappointing performance. Unusual for a greatest hits album, the release also garnered some scathing reviews because of the decision to include remixes of some of her best-known songs instead of the original versions. The *Entertainment Weekly* review was especially harsh: "To listen to the two discs is to hear the sound of a gift being squandered," it complained. "Continually pursuing mega record sales at the expense of invention, Houston needs to exhale—to loosen up and put more shoop-shoop R&B into her creative life."

To add to the growing litany of troubles plaguing the couple, May 2000 also saw another arrest for Bobby when the couple returned from a Bahamas vacation, to be greeted by customs agents in New Jersey who handcuffed him and transported him to Florida on an outstanding warrant for a probation violation after the Florida DUI four years earlier when he failed to submit to a mandatory drug test before the deadline. Ruling him a "flight risk," the judge denied him bail and Bobby ended up spending sixty-five days of a seventy-five-day sentence in a jail cell.

In August 2001, Arista announced that they had signed Whitney to a staggering $100 million six-album deal to remain with the label. Although she was Arista's best-selling artist ever, with almost 140 million records sold, her career was on a downward trajectory, and observers wondered aloud how the label could ever recoup that kind of advance. With Davis no longer around—having founded his own label, J Records, after his ouster the year before—it was speculated that the new parent company, BMG, couldn't afford to lose its signature artist. Still, her life was melting down before everybody's eyes and her career wasn't faring much better.

By the time Whitney appeared at Michael Jackson's thirtieth anniversary celebration at Madison Square Garden on September 7, 2001, her deterioration was evident to everybody around her and had been openly speculated about in the press for more than a year as reports of erratic and diva-like behavior circulated widely.

Whitney and Michael weren't all that close, but they both talked in admiring tones about the other whenever asked. Whitney would later profess to be his "close friend," but there is no indication that the two saw each other outside the many events and awards ceremonies at which they both appeared. Michael, whose favorite pet was famously Bubbles the Chimp, had given Whitney a monkey for her twenty-sixth birthday—a present that she found bizarre and promptly donated to a zoo. By the time she appeared for his anniversary concert, rumors had been circulating about MJ's own drug abuse for years—stories later confirmed after his death. Whitney had spoken publicly in his defense after he was accused of molesting a thirteen-year-old boy in 1993, and had long described MJ as her "idol." Now, the King of Pop was looking nearly as frail as she was.

No sooner had she appeared onstage that night than it was immediately evident to the millions who tuned in and to the audience of eighteen thousand who packed the arena that the icon was in a bad state. ABC News would later describe Whitney's appearance as "scarily skinny." Others described her as "gaunt" or "emaciated." Nearly everybody came to the conclusion that only drugs could have caused this state.

Nobody was more concerned than her longtime friend and mentor Clive Davis, who would reveal in his memoir that he sent a letter to Whitney with a personal plea following the concert:

Dearest Whitney,

When I saw you Friday night at the Michael Jackson concert I gasped. When I got home, I cried. My dear, dear Whitney, the time has come. Of course I know you don't want to hear this. Of course I know that you're saying that Clive is being foolishly dramatic. Of course I know that your power of denial is in overdrive dismissing everything I and everyone else is saying to you. . . . I will stand by you with love and caring to see you through it to new found peace and happiness in every way as a woman, as a mother, as a role model to inspire the rest of the world.

Love,

Clive

But still Whitney denied she had a problem. On September 10, she performed at a second Jackson tribute concert, which once again had the crowd whispering about her appearance. The day after the show, her publicist, Nancy Seltzer, issued a statement denying that her skeletal appearance was related to drug abuse.

"Whitney has been under stress due to family matters, and when she is under stress, she doesn't eat," she told the *New York Post*. A day later, Seltzer was forced to issue another statement when a number of radio stations reported that Whitney had died of a drug overdose. It didn't get a lot of attention at the time, because the nation was reeling from the attack on the Twin Towers two days earlier.

"I've just spoken to Whitney," reads Seltzer's statement. "She is perfectly fine and does not understand why, with everything going on in the world right now, they have to find new rumors to dig up. She is home in New Jersey with her family."

It would be another year before she would finally go public to admit she had a problem when she appeared alongside Bobby in a riveting hour-long ABC *Primetime Live* special with Diane Sawyer.

Sawyer started the interview by telling Whitney that her audience is going to be watching at home and "staring at you physically," asking, "How many bones can we see? Is she sick?"

She steers around the question until Sawyer calls her appearance "scary thin" and speculates that the singer may have anorexia or bulimia, as some of the media had reported. Whitney denied she had an eating disorder, and when Sawyer asked about reports that it's "because of drugs," she partially concedes the point. "Now, I'll grant you, I partied," she said.

Persisting, Sawyer noted the tabloid headlines: "Whitney dying, crack rehab fails."

Suddenly animated, the singer said, "First of all, let's get one thing straight. Crack is cheap. I make too much money to ever smoke crack. Let's get that straight, okay. We don't do crack. We don't do that. Crack is whack!"

Having ruled out crack, Sawyer asked whether the problem had been caused by other substances.

"Is it alcohol? Is it marijuana? Is it cocaine? Is it pills?" she demanded.

Whitney hesitated. "It has been at times."

"All?" Sawyer asked, incredulous.

"At times," she sheepishly replied.

Whitney goes on to complain that "I love to sing, but it's just not fun anymore."

Sawyer asked her, "If you had to name the biggest devil, the biggest devil among you."

Whitney's response was remarkably self-aware.

"That would be me. No one makes me do anything I don't want to do."

Yet despite her semi-acknowledgment that she has abused drugs over the years, she never admitted the extent of the problem. When Sawyer asked her whether she thought of herself as an addict, she coyly stated that she was addicted to "making love." For years, Whitney liked to boast in interviews about the quantity and quality of the sex she and Bobby were having, as if to answer the doubters, so this revelation wasn't all that unusual.

When Bobby joins the interview, he appears to have a different agenda, insisting that his reputed drug use was limited to smoking pot for his bipolar disorder. "Every now and then, you know, I smoke a joint," he said. "Every now and then, you know. It's not an everyday thing. It's maybe every other day. But it's not an everyday thing. But it, it, it keeps, it keeps, it keeps me calm."

Sawyer then asked about other drugs.

"No. No. I never have," he replied. "Never have and never will. That's, that's another thing that used to get me so mad."

Sawyer concluded the interview by asking Whitney where she would like to be ten years from that time. "Retired, looking at my daughter grow up, become a great woman of God. Grandchildren."

At this point, nine-year-old Bobbi joins her and Sawyer asked her if she liked to sing. "Yes, and I want to be like my mommy and daddy," the girl replied with an impish grin. Then Whitney interjected, "Early in the morning, she and I would have private time together when nobody's around. And I'll sneak up to her room, about six, and I'll get in the bed with her and I'll say, 'OK, we gotta get up in a little while.' And I'll rub her stomach, wake the stomach up, wake up your back, wake up the mind, wake up the, you know, body. And talk." Bobby brightens up. "You know, the perfect thing is like, on, like, a Sunday or something like that, when we like, like, sit and, you know, we get to watch TV or like, listen to gospel music or have breakfast together," she said.

Mother and daughter then sing a brief duet and hug each other playfully.

The night after the interview, the controversial Fox News host Bill O'Reilly interviewed Dr. Ira Kramer, the director of substance abuse from the New York Center for Addiction Treatment Services on his show *The O'Reilly Factor*. He started by asking Kramer what he saw when he watched Whitney's admission.

"Well, I saw somebody who's in trouble," the doctor replied. "There's no question about that. She's very sad. It really moved me, and it reminded me more than anything of Billie Holiday, the great talent."

Kramer also took note of something that Whitney had said during the broadcast, "It's not an everyday thing." He took that to mean that she was still using.

O'Reilly then launched into a tirade against the singer, saying she had a "sense of entitlement" and had squandered her talents. He seemed especially disgusted by the appearance of Bobbi on the broadcast.

"You're a degenerate if you're talking drugs and you have a little daughter in your house. That's what you are. You can get out of it, you can become not degenerate but there's no denial. These people know what they are."

When Kramer interrupted to note that she had a "disease," the belligerent host observed that she could afford any clinic in the world but refused to seek help. When the subject shifted to Bobby and his own addictions, Kramer speculated that Whitney was "codependent on her husband."

O'Reilly was unmoved. "So that's her fault for marrying an idiot."

They conclude the interview by agreeing that she needed to seek help, which was also the general consensus of the media, which weighed in over the next week. But still she declined to seek treatment.

By 2003, the couple had moved to a home in the Atlanta suburb of Alpharetta. It was from this address that Whitney called 911 just after eight thirty PM on the evening of Sunday December 7, to report a domestic dispute. She did not identify herself.

When police arrived, she informed them that she and Bobby had an argument that had escalated into a physical altercation in which he hit her face with his open hand.

The police report notes a "bruise" on Whitney's cheek and a cut on the inside of her upper lip. "She wasn't hysterical or anything, she was very calm," Corporal Kurtis Young told the media about her demeanor.

Three months later, in March 2004, Whitney's publicist, Nancy Seltzer, issued a brief statement, "Whitney Houston has chosen to enter a facility for rehabilitation. She thanks everyone for their support and prayers." It was her first rehab stint, but it wouldn't be her last.

Dick Clark told *Access Hollywood* that he had once tried to persuade Whitney to seek help but to no avail. "Finally, she's addressed it; she's taking care of it and thank God," he told the show. But after only five days, Whitney checked out to seek "private care" and most doubted she had overcome the problem.

Meanwhile, Arista's $100 million bet was looking like a catastrophe. Her first studio album under the deal, *Just Whitney*, sold a miserable 717,000 copies—the worst of her career—and was savaged by critics. Without Clive Davis to guide her, Bobby joined her to oversee the production, but they couldn't capture the old magic. *Billboard* complained that she was "simply going through the motions and her voice lacked emotion and verve." The album's first single, "Whatchulookinat," peaked at a miserable ninety-six on the charts. "If the jittery, bonethin Houston still needs to ask, 'Whatchulookinat,' she obviously hasn't gazed into the mirror lately," wrote the *Atlanta Journal Constitution*. It was now quite evident that her personal and professional lives were in disarray.

Her finances weren't faring much better. In 2002, her father's company had sued her for $100 million, although it was later revealed that John's business partner, Kevin Skinner, engineered the suit, and that John had little to do with it. Still, there is no question that John Houston was instrumental in helping guide the business side of the company for years and helped engineer the $100 million Arista deal. Many felt he deserved to be compensated and were bewildered that Whitney didn't quietly settle the suit.

Despite the $100 million Arista deal—which called for the money to be paid out in phases—it appeared that Whitney's finances were in disorder. Between legal bills, drugs, and lavish spending on "management expenses," there wasn't as much in the kitty as people believed.

This was made obvious when Whitney announced to her entourage, including numerous family members, that she was cutting their salaries in half. The exception was her sister-in-law, Pat Houston—Gary's wife—who had taken over for John at Nippy Inc., and was struggling to keep Whitney's flagging career afloat.

It was Bobby's brother and manager, Tommy, who negotiated a reality TV series in 2004 that would have cameras following the couple around as they went about their lives. It would be called *Being Bobby Brown*. With Bobby's musical career virtually evaporated, it had been a long time since he had been a reliable cash cow for his family members and assorted hangers-on. It's easy to understand why Bobby agreed to such a venture. As for Whitney, she would later explain that she did it because she "loved him" and "did whatever he asked because I was his wife."

By then, Whitney and Bobby had distanced themselves from much of the family, including Cissy, by moving from New Jersey to Atlanta, along with Bobbi Kristina and a few of Bobby's children. The one constant in Whitney's life, apart from Robyn—who had left years earlier—had been her Auntie Bae, who had looked after Bobbi from birth. But in 2005, Bae was suddenly let go and returned to New Jersey, leaving both Whitney and twelve-year-old Bobbi rudderless.

"After Bae came back to New Jersey," Cissy recalled in her memoir, "that's when things really started to go to hell."

In the winter of 2005, after the reality show had been shot but before it aired, Gary Garland called Cissy to tell her he believed his sister was "in trouble." He and his wife, Pat—who managed her day-to-day affairs—lived close by, so they were well aware that things had gotten worse.

Cissy flew down to Atlanta and visited the house with Gary, but when they arrived, Bobby's sister Tina answered the door and yelled upstairs to Whitney that her mama had arrived. Whitney refused to come down. Cissy later revealed that the house's walls had been spray-painted with "big glaring eyes and strange faces." She said it sent a "chill" through her. When she saw Whitney standing at the top of the stairs, she barely recognized her.

Cissy and Gary consulted an Atlanta attorney who advised them of their legal options. They proceeded to draw up a petition for the courts to have Whitney treated "involuntarily." They returned to the house with two sheriff's deputies who dragged Whitney to a hospital, where she was treated for a week. Describing the incident, Cissy never uses the word but it's clear the facility was a mental hospital. She reveals that "Nippy was telling everybody who came to see her that I'd had her locked up."

When she was released, Whitney flew to Antigua to be treated at the Crossroads Treatment Center, where she ended up staying for a month. For part of the treatment, Bobbi was allowed to join her mother at the rehab. Cissy explains the unusual arrangement by theorizing that Whitney wanted her to "understand what she was struggling with so that Krissi wouldn't wander down the same path when the time came."

Two months after Whitney returned from the Caribbean, the first episode of *Being Bobby Brown* aired on Bravo. And if the public didn't already regard her as a train wreck, the show confirmed it.

The first episode opens with Bobby's release from jail after yet another of his many incarcerations—this one after a thirty-day stint for a parole violation in Atlanta. Not long after he gets home, he is seen heading into the bedroom with Whitney as Bobbi pounds on the door, begging to be allowed in. "Be right back. Daddy tryin' to make a baby," Whitney yells out. It was a harbinger of what was to come. The series contains many such unseemly private moments, including one memorable scene in which Bobby recalls having to "dig a doodie bubble" from his wife's butt, prompting her to shout, "That's black love." In another scene, Bobby tells his wife "to bring that ass in quick. I'm going to show you what I'm going to do with it." The eleven episodes follow the couple and their children on family vacations, picnics, Christmas gatherings, and jaunts around town and capture many seemingly candid moments.

The show's most lasting contribution to popular culture is Whitney's repeated use of the phrase "Hell to the no," which almost immediately entered the lexicon of popular culture. She also frequently told her husband to "kiss my ass."

Throughout the show, Whitney is obviously high on drugs, and her skeletal appearance made it clear she still had a problem.

The *Today* show's Hollywood correspondent, Barry Garron, called the show "undoubtedly the most disgusting and execrable series ever to ooze its way onto television" and complained that the show robbed Whitney of "any last shreds of dignity."

But apart from the few undignified moments, the series also shows a very touching side to the couple, especially in their loving interactions with the children. Bobby repeatedly calls Bobbi "baby girl," and demonstrates a playful side that is very endearing. Between the buffoonish moments, the show occasionally offered a telling glimpse into the human side of both singers, who had long since become caricatures in the public eye.

Nevertheless, the media weren't kind and wondered why Whitney would have agreed to participate in such an exercise. A friend of Whitney's told the *Huffington Post* that her family and handlers are particularly worried that the raw unedited footage—owned by Bravo—may one day surface and further tarnish her legacy.

"They want to preserve her image as the greatest singer of our generation, not as the troubled wife of Bobby Brown, who turned her from an icon into a joke," the friend said.

Throughout 2006, reports emerged that Bobby was womanizing openly and had all but abandoned the marriage, while Whitney was back on drugs, following her latest rehab stint and acting as erratically as ever. Reports circulated that he was having an affair with a twenty-eight-year-old hip-hop model named Karrine Steffans, who had bragged about sleeping with him in her 2005 book, *Confessions of a Video Vixen*. Steffans, however, denied being a "home wrecker." When *People* confronted Bobby about a rumor that he planned to divorce Whitney, he denied it. "She's my friend," he insisted. "She's the better half of me. They say opposites attract, but we're not opposites. We're one person. We're loving life, and we're just trying to be as good to each other as possible." A few months later, he was asked about reports that Whitney was still using and that the marriage was on the brink. Again, he denied that anything was amiss. "We are happily married. . . . We are going to stand for each other for as long as we live. I adore that woman. She helps me see God. I look in her eyes and I see God."

In April, Bobby's sister Tina told the *National Enquirer* that she had done crack with Whitney on several occasions and revealed that Whitney's drug use was much worse than anybody had let on. She described regular deliveries of marijuana, powder cocaine, and crack to the Atlanta house and claimed that Whitney was completely dependent on drugs. She revealed that her sister-in-law would purchase eightballs of crack—pieces of rock cocaine weighing an eighth of an ounce each. She'd then cut open a cigar, remove the tobacco, put in marijuana and the entire piece of crack, and then smoke it.

"She saw demons when she got high," Tina told the paper. "She'd point to the floor and say, 'See that demon. I'm telling you somebody's messing with Bobby.'" She also sold photos of a room strewn with Whitney's drug paraphernalia, including crack pipes and spoons. Tina also said, "It's common knowledge among family members" that Whitney has had affairs with women. "I saw her with a woman a couple of times," she revealed.

Whitney's attorney, Phaedra Parks, later told a reporter that Tina's

decision to betray her secrets was a "turning point" for the belea-
guered singer.

"Whitney felt very betrayed," said Parks. "She obviously considered Tina to be family, and for her to release a story like that with
such derogatory comments and allegations—it broke her heart."

It was easy for some people to dismiss what they read in the
National Enquirer because of the nature of the publication, but one
of America's most respected newsmagazines, *Newsweek*, also revealed
that they had spoken to somebody with close ties to Whitney who
confirmed much of what Tina had said.

The source described shocking drug-fueled behavior that went all
the way back to the early nineties.

"Ironically, Houston's drug use only grew worse after the birth of
her beloved Bobbi Kristina, who arrived after several earlier miscar-
riages," the magazine reported. 'She loved that little girl with all her
heart, but she was far too sick by the time her baby came to be the
kind of mother she needed to be,' says a family friend. 'Sometimes
Whitney would be so out of it, the baby wouldn't be changed for days
at a time. That's what drugs will do to you, and it doesn't matter how
rich you are. An addict is an addict.'"

When another member of Whitney's former entourage, Kevin
Ammons, released an insider's account, *Good Girl, Bad Girl*, he
claimed that Whitney called those who worked for her "the Royal
Family." *Vanity Fair*'s Mark Seal described how the exposé opened the
lid on the behind-the-scenes machinations of those she surrounded
herself with during this period. "Everyone wants a piece of the action
of the increasingly stressed and distant diva," he writes. "When their
golden goose is abducted by Bobby, the Royal Family resorts to
manipulation, fistfights, and threats of violence to protect their interests and remain on the gravy train." Whitney evidently regarded the
book itself as just one more act of betrayal, according to Ammons's
collaborator Nancy Bacon. "As soon as Whitney heard I was writing
the book, someone sent me a package," she told Seal. "I opened it up,

and it was a snake. It didn't smell—it had obviously been sent to me alive. She told Kevin I was like a snake in the grass, because I was writing bad things about her."

Not long after Tina's horrifying revelations appeared—an account that would, by the singer's own admission, prove remarkably accurate—Whitney headed back to rehab.

In September 2006, she made an unexpected appearance at a Beverly Hilton Hotel event honoring the singer Johnny Mathis. As she arrived with Clive Davis and Dionne Warwick, guests were surprised to see her looking healthier than she had in years. Davis had told MTV a few days earlier that he and Whitney were working on a "comeback album."

The next day, Nancy Seltzer issued a statement revealing that Whitney had split from Bobby and had served him with legal separation papers as a step toward divorce. Soon afterward, Whitney filed for and received sole custody of Bobbi, though Bobby would be granted visitation rights. Because of their prenup, he was entitled to no financial settlement.

Cissy recalls that after the split, Bobbi was sent for a time to stay with Pat and Gary.

"By now, Krissi was thirteen, old enough to understand that all this mess was going on," she wrote. "I was always worried about her—not because Nippy wasn't a good and loving mother, but because I knew it had to be hard on Krissi to be in a home situation that could sometimes be unstable. And I know she always looked out for Krissi the best she could. Always."

CHAPTER **TWENTY-TWO**

If Bobbi Kristina had really given up all drugs except Xanax after her mother's death, as Zach told the *Daily Mail*, it means that just about everybody I met in Atlanta and Miami who claims to have known her is lying. That's not outside the realm of possibility, because I know from experience that people are often desperate to cloak themselves in the aura of celebrity by exaggerating their associations with the famous or infamous.

And just as some of the media was starting to buy Zach's claims, another one of the snakes associated with the couple crawled out from under his rock and shared a story that completely contradicted Zach's account.

A man named Steve Stepho, who claimed to have lived with the couple for a time, told the London *Sun* that he sold both Bobbi and Nick narcotics, though he insisted that he wasn't their "main dealer."

"Bobbi and Nick would spend a lot on drugs every day, it just depended on how much money they had," he told the paper. "It wasn't unusual for them to spend $1,000 a day on drugs. There were times when it got really bad—they would be completely passed out for hours, just lying there on the bed. There were times when she would be so knocked out she would burn herself with a cigarette and not even notice. She was always covered in cigarette burns."

He repeated a story I had heard a number of times before from people who claimed to have known Bobbi's fiancé.

"Nick has a really short fuse and would often lose his temper with her. He is not a good person," Stepho said. "She'd do whatever he told her. He was very manipulative and would even use the drugs to control her. They would argue a lot and there were times when he would be violent with her and push her around."

As with many of the characters who have emerged in this drama, Stepho has a lengthy police record, including two heroin busts. I obtained a police report from an arrest on October 23, 2013, when Stepho and another man were pulled over by Roswell police in his Pontiac Bonneville because of an outstanding FBI warrant for a parole violation in Dallas. They found 5.8 grams of heroin and charged him with trafficking. Only two weeks before Bobbi was found unconscious, he was pulled over again by Roswell police, driving a black Toyota. The arresting officer observed that he "appeared to be under the influence of a drug." A search of his pockets discovered no contraband, but as he stood outside the vehicle, a Baggie fell from his shorts, and he was arrested for possession of heroin.

Although Stepho was undoubtedly a lowlife, I wasn't sure I trusted his account about dealing drugs to Bobbi, especially since, like Zach, he chose to sell the story to a British tabloid.

Still, the sheer volume of friends and hangers-on of Bobbi and Nick who have told me variations of the same story appears to reveal a pattern.

A clubgoer who calls herself "Lady" told me she met Bobbi Kristina at a party at a club in West Hollywood a couple years ago.

"She looked like she was a party girl, the center of attention, doing lines of coke all night, drinking like a fish. I saw her in the bathroom doing serious lines of blow. She was out of it, looked like she had a serious problem."

When we stopped for lunch at a Mexican restaurant called Moe's Southwest Grill, we got into a conversation with the server, who said that Nick and Bobbi frequented the restaurant on occasion. "They always seemed to be in a rush," she said. "And they always seemed to be high. They were weird; they certainly stood out. They weren't disruptive, but they always made a scene, even if it was unconsciously."

In Miami, I met a former New York City hairstylist named David Hill, who frequented the diner where Nick and Bobbi breakfasted when they were in town.

"I used to go to the same midtown diner as her for breakfast," he told me. "She was in town shooting her reality show. Whenever I saw her I'd go up to her. She was very receptive, very humble. Always had a big beaming smile. But she did appear to be on something. She was too bubbly, she looked high; her eyes were usually red. When I saw her with her boyfriend, the two of them seemed high. Clearly, she had secrets."

At Atlanta's Halo lounge, a supposed acquaintance of Bobbi told me, "Bobbi Kristina is a tragedy. We all tried to help her but she only listens to one person, Nick Gordon. I met her buddies Nick and Max a few times. They're one word—trouble. I just wish someone could have done something to get her away from that scene."

A young woman named Bree told me she knows Gordon from the Atlanta club scene and that he used to flirt with her "whenever Bobbi Kristina was not around. He's quite feisty. He loves to be the center of attention. I can't believe she was with him for so long. I really feel sorry for her. She deserved better."

Before long, it's like a broken record. For all I know, none of these people even knew the couple. One of the few people I met who encountered the couple is Aziza Letherwood, the sales manager of the Sunglass Hut in Atlanta's North Point Mall. This is where I'm told the couple purchased sunglasses shortly before they dropped by Kay Jewelers to drop off Bobbi's engagement ring for repair.

"She came in here," Aziza confirmed. "I'm a big Whitney Houston fan so I recognized her right away. Then I recognized Nick. She was saying her diamond was missing on her ring. They bought two pairs of Ray-Bans. She seemed kind of jittery. I'm a real big fan of her mother. I'm thirty-six, from her generation. Whitney was Beyoncé to me. I just wanted to hug her and tell her 'Your mother wouldn't have wanted this for you.' Both of them appeared to have issues. They didn't seem normal."

So far, it's clearly obvious that the relationship was volatile, and both Nick and Bobbi were abusing substances of some kind or another. But the same can be said about just about every couple I saw on the dance floors at the hip Atlanta clubs where I was searching for clues each night after Sheila and I finished our investigation.

I could have discovered most of this information at my desk in Miami. I resolved to stop wasting time trying to gain insight into Bobbi and Nick and the nature of their relationship. None of that, I realized, was going to answer the question of what went down on January 31.

Instead, I am anxious to delve deeper into the possibility of attempted suicide. It is the conclusion of just about everybody I met in Atlanta, including those who knew her and those who didn't.

When I first spoke to the former homicide detective turned private investigator in February, the subject of suicide did in fact come up. But for him the facts didn't add up. He had immediately homed in on reports that the bathwater in which Bobbi was found was ice-cold.

"Nobody takes a cold bath in winter," he insisted.

I raised the possibility that it started out hot but that she was in the bathtub for so long that it eventually turned cold. He told me that was one of the things the police would undoubtedly be investigating. But they weren't sharing, and I didn't have time to wait for the eventual results of their investigation. And so I did what I assumed my favorite TV detective, Columbo, would have done. I ran a bath.

I filled the bathtub with water that I considered hot but not too hot, bringing it to a temperature that most people would likely find comfortable. And then I waited. An hour later, I checked it. It was still lukewarm. Forty-five minutes after that, I checked again. It was mildly tepid. Thirty minutes later it was definitely on the cool side. After yet another half hour, I tested it again. For the first time since I ran the water, I would probably describe the temperature as cold, though not ice-cold. Still, for the sake of argument and since one person's definition of ice-cold might not be the same as mine, I think it's safe to conclude that a hot-water bath takes a minimum of two and a half hours to turn cold. But Bobbi survived—barely—so we know that she probably couldn't have been facedown in the water for more than a few minutes.

Columbo probably could have made something of this knowledge—more likely the team from *CSI Miami*—but I was still stumped. Nonetheless, it gave me something to go on. The fact that she was lying in a cold-water bath, however, wasn't the only thing reported about Bobbi's condition when she was found in the bathtub that morning.

CHAPTER **TWENTY-THREE**

Seeking a fresh start after the divorce, Whitney moved Bobbi and her dog, Doogie, to Laguna Hills, California in 2006, where she filed for divorce from Bobby in Orange County superior court. The Nellie Gail Ranch where she and her daughter resided for more than a year was rented for her by an addiction specialist named Warren Boyd, who has worked with a number of drug-addicted celebrities, including Courtney Love and Robert Downey Jr.

"It was very quiet. We were a very respectful community," recalled her Laguna Hills neighbor Susan Shoultz. "She was very polite to everybody." Another neighbor, Nancy Martindale, says she often saw Whitney and Bobbi together on walks.

It was during this period when Bobbi first gained a wild-child reputation.

A friend would later tell *Hollywood Life*, "Bobbi Kristina was really nice. People liked her, but she was known as a problem child." Calling her a "party animal," the friend claims she "didn't have much supervision" and was "living life on the edge."

Working with Boyd during her time in Orange County appeared to be paying off, at least for the time being. But if Whitney was back on her feet, the same couldn't be said for Bobby, who attempted in court to overturn the terms of their prenup and receive spousal support. It appeared that without Whitney's money he had fallen on hard financial times as evidenced by his court filing, which claimed he had been footing the bills associated with one of her rehab stays.

"Whitney took Bobbi Kris without my prior knowledge or consent, and moved to Orange County, California, where Whitney received treatment for her drug addiction," the court filing reads. "Although I was having severe financial problems, I did all I could to see my daughter. I came to California to be near Bobbi Kris. I also paid approximately $10,000 for Whitney and Bobbi Kris to live in a nice hotel while Whitney was going through rehab. At the same time, I basically lived out of my car."

Whitney's counterfiling was blunt, blaming her ex's problems on his lifestyle.

"Bobby is fully capable of working and earning substantial sums of money if he would control his personal behavior. It is his personal conduct that keeps him from earning substantial amounts of money," she stated.

In the end, the judge rejected his claims on a technicality.

Meanwhile, Whitney announced she was ready to tour again in advance of a brand-new studio album to be overseen by her old mentor, Clive Davis. It appeared that shedding Bobby and his baggage was just what she needed to get her life back on track and jump-start her career.

But the comeback hit a snag almost immediately when she launched her new tour at a jazz festival in Tobago. Receiving a whopping $3 million for the appearance, she hit the stage to a tumultuous ovation. But right from the start, things did not go as planned. First, she repeatedly shouted, "I love you, Trinidad" only to have the crowd respond in a full-throated roar, "This is Tobago." Ignoring them, she delivered only seven songs and she wasn't finished with the first before it was evident her voice was shot. The next day's review, headlined, "Houston, there's a problem," complained, "By her third song,

'Saving All My Love,' the once soprano's newfound tenor tone was in full rasp." *Ebony Jet*, once her biggest cheerleader, noted that her "flat, hoarse and listless voice was a big disappointment."

In 2007, Whitney sold the Alpharetta, Georgia, house on the outskirts of Atlanta where she had lived with Bobby for just under $1.2 million. Not long afterward, she purchased the town house and moved back to Atlanta with Bobbi, where she could lay down tracks for a new album at Patchwerk Studios.

Yet those who expected Bobby's departure to bring stability to Whitney's domestic life hadn't counted on the effect that being in the middle of their dysfunctional relationship had to have had on their daughter all those years. In February 2008, reports circulated that Bobbi had been committed to the Peachford Psychiatric Hospital for observation. According to Ann Davis—who is related to Bobby's mother, Carole Brown—Bobbi tried to stab Whitney during a heated argument two weeks before her fifteenth birthday and then slashed her wrists in a suicide attempt.

"Bobbi Kristina had been running around drinking and partying, doing what she wants to do," Davis claimed. "She and her mother had been arguing a lot."

It was a few months later that she asked Whitney if her eighteen-year-old high school friend Nick Gordon—who had been kicked out of the house by his own mother—could stay with them occasionally while he landed on his feet.

Meanwhile, Whitney had been actively involved in working on the album that she believed would signal to the world that she was back after what she termed a "hiatus."

Among her collaborators on the album was the R&B songwriter/producer Akon, who had recorded a duet with Whitney. Afterward, he told *Billboard*, "The voice is there; I don't think anyone could ever take that from her. As long as we apply that voice to hit records, she'll be right back where she left off." It would be another two years before the album would see the light of day, but his words were reassuring to the many observers who prayed the old Whitney would reemerge now that she was free of Bobby's influence.

The first chance people had to judge for themselves came at Clive Davis's annual pre-Grammy bash in February 2009, where Davis had hinted she would show up and perform. Sure enough, Whitney took the stage and proceeded to belt out some of her old repertoire as the crowd listened in hushed tones to see whether she still had it. The verdict was mixed. On the one hand, she hadn't embarrassed herself or exhibited any of the diva behavior people had come to expect over the last decade. On the other, her once-stunning gift from God had eluded her. The *LA Times* was guarded in its praise, noting that "she hit her cues and delivered the songs with confidence," but alas, it wasn't the Whitney of old, because, "The voice that once seemed able to topple mountains had grown more subdued, and the high notes just weren't there."

Still, it was a promising start. With the album finally finished, Whitney agreed to give her first interview in years, and when Oprah Winfrey announced that she had scored the exclusive, America held its breath in anticipation. Would she provide the answers to the questions people had been asking for years?

After she sat down with Oprah in a two-part interview to be aired in mid-September, she taped a performance at Central Park to be broadcast on *Good Morning America* the next day. It did not go well. Her voice was shot during the four-song concert, but it didn't stop fans from singing along and cheering her on.

"It brought tears to my eyes," said one fan. "She's been through so much in her life. She's been working very hard, and it's a lot to do. And she's been doing it well."

Another fan wasn't so understanding. "I expected it to be longer. She couldn't sing. She was really damaged," Jao Andrade told the *Daily News*. "I'm a little disappointed. I think she was brave to come out with no voice."

But most fans forgave the raspy voice and were just thrilled that she was back. "Everyone falls down and everyone stumbles. It's how we pick it up and keep going," thirty-two-year-old Ky Davis told the paper.

The highlight of the performance was when sixteen-year-old Bobbi Kristina—looking in good spirits—joined her mother on a duet of "My Love Is Your Love," in which she had made her debut as a five-year-old, saying, "Sing, Mommy." This time, she tried to sing along, although both mother and daughter appeared to be having trouble remembering the lyrics.

Two weeks later, the first part of the Oprah interview aired, and the world was floored by what they heard.

From the start, Oprah makes it clear that she is among the vast majority who assumed that Bobby Brown was responsible for Whitney's downfall. She asked, "What is the princess doing with this guy?"

To Oprah's surprise, however, she came to her ex's defense. "They don't have any idea about that sweet, gentle tenderness about him that nobody knew," she said. "He was a very quiet person."

Eventually, Oprah turned to the subject that everybody had been waiting for.

"Tell me, how bad did it get, the drugs?" she asked.

Whitney then proceeded to reveal that before the making of *The Bodyguard* her drug use was "light," but after the film took off and Bobbi was born, it got heavier, and by 1996, the drugs were "an everyday thing . . . I wasn't happy by that point in time. I was losing myself."

Whitney then described how she would spend long periods of time with Bobby in the same house without talking, just freebasing cocaine.

"We weren't buying twenty-dollar jumbos. We were paying money. We were buying kilos and ounces and ounces. We would have our stash," she said, revealing that at one point she would spend seven months in her pajamas without going out while the two did drugs.

When Oprah asked her whether Tina's *National Enquirer* account—claiming that Whitney had locked herself in her room for days to do drugs—was accurate, she confirmed it. She also revealed that when he was high, Bobby "would smash things, break things in the home. Glass. We had a big, big giant portrait of me and him and my child. He cut my head off the picture. Stuff like that."

When Oprah asked whether he was violent, Whitney at first denies it. "Emotionally, he was abusive. Physically, no way. Because first of all, I was raised with two boys, and I will fight you back. I will fight you back with anything I can find."

Does that mean he never touched her, Oprah asked.

"No."

He never laid his hands on you," she persisted.

"He slapped me once, but he got hit over the head three times," Whitney replied. "Because I was, like, 'Okay, you're going too far.'"

Asked what the worst thing he ever said or did was, Whitney revealed that he once spit on her.

"And my daughter was coming down the stairs, and she saw it. That was pretty intense." She tells the talk show host that the incident left a lasting impression on the young girl, which is one of the reasons Whitney finally decided to divorce him.

"It was enough. She saw enough. The spitting in the face was enough. She said, 'Mom, did he spit in your face?' And I looked in her eyes and she looked in mine and I said: 'Yes. But it's all right.' And she said: 'No, it's not. No, it's not. It's not, Mom. It's not all right.' I said: 'If you can do me a favor. Just do this for Mommy. I'm going to put my trust in God. You put your trust in me. You may not understand it now, but just trust me. I'm not letting you go. I will hold on to you with my dear life. Just trust me. And we will get up out of this. And we'll be happier for it. And then as you get older, I'll tell you little by little as to why things are happening and why Mommy has to go.'"

She revealed that when they moved to California, Bobbi was "very angry" and did not understand why she left her dad.

"She fought me. But I kept coming back with love. I kept holding her in my arms. I kept knocking on that door and I kept getting on my knees. I kept praying. Telling her I loved her."

Asked how Bobbi was faring at that time, Whitney told Oprah she was fine.

"I don't know how to describe her. She's more and more like me every day."

When Oprah noted that she was starting to look like her, Whitney agreed.

"She does. When she was a kid, she was looking so much like her father—her body frame, her face, her skin."

Oprah asked if Whitney could see traces of herself in her daughter.

"Oh, all over her," she replied. "She writes creatively all the time. She writes. And she sings. She's really starting to sing really well now."

Is she good? Oprah wanted to know.

"Yeah, she is. I want her to take her time. I don't want anybody to touch her. I want to groom her." Whitney told Oprah that she'd be okay if Bobbi decided to follow her into the business.

"But I will be there. Like my mom was there with me. When I was just getting in the business, and they came for me when I was fourteen and wanted to sign me, my mother said: 'No way. Whitney's got a lot more to learn.'"

Asked if she enjoyed being a mom, Whitney was unequivocal.

"I love it. I love being a mother and watching her become a woman. There are times where she's going through that young womanhood where there's the boys, and there are little things and you got her little feelings being hurt. I love her to come to me, and she trusts me. She trusts me and I can tell her the truth and say, 'Listen. It's going to happen, but we're going to get through it. We're going to make it.' That kind of thing. I love that. She's proud of me. And I'm proud of her. She got into bed with me this morning and she said: 'Mama, can I just tell you how much I love you and how proud I am of you? Your record's kicking tail all over the world. I'm just proud of you. We did it, Mom. We did it.'"

The revelations on the show about the drug-crazed hell that had once been her life made worldwide headlines, but they were tempered by the seeming assurance that those episodes were all in the past and that Whitney was getting ready to resume her once-enviable career.

People love a story of redemption. And when the album was released in August 2009, it looked like she had finally put her troubles behind her as *I Look to You* shot to the top of the *Billboard* charts with the best first-week sales of her career.

Most critics welcomed the new Whitney, giving the album high marks. "Happily, it appears that 'I Look to You,' the pop diva's first album in seven years, marks the end of her 'crack is whack' era," heralded the *Washington Times*.

More credibly, *Rolling Stone* was impressed; lavishing the most praise they had ever delivered for one of her releases even if recognizing that her voice was no longer the four-octave wonder of two decades earlier. "Close your eyes, open your ears, and you're back in 1992," they declared. "At 46, Houston is not the singer she once was. Time and hard living have shaved some notes off that amazing range; the clear, bright voice that dominated radio has given way to a huskier tone—less powerful but more sultry."

At the American Music Awards, she wowed the audience and received a standing ovation from the appreciative crowd. Awarding her performance an A-, the *LA Times* noted, "If her instrument isn't what it once was, it can still silence a room."

As the singer prepared to embark on a world tour to capitalize on the success of the album, it appeared her career had come full circle. It wasn't long, however, before the same questions reared their ugly head when she canceled a series of European dates. When she did show up, the performances were often punctuated by long breaks midshow, and Whitney often rambled to the audience instead of singing. Reviewers noted large portions of the audience booing or walking out at nearly every show.

The Birmingham *Sunday Mercury* complained that her show "spiralled into shambolics."

Nor were critics kind on the Australian leg of the tour.

"Her acoustic set of old favorites unfortunately could not hide the very obvious problems with her voice," noted one Brisbane critic, describing streams of "disappointed, saddened and angry fans" heading for the doors in the middle of the show.

The *Daily Telegraph* critic was also put off by her antics, but impressed by her delivery.

"Some of her behavior here, it's true, petered between the eccentric and the charmingly kooky," wrote Cathy McCabe, who was gratified to hear that Whitney's live version of many numbers sounded as good as the recorded versions. "She chattered ramblingly between songs, signed an autograph from the stage, started sentences and didn't finish them—but the proof of her sanity was in her singing."

Reports from Europe of canceled shows and bizarre onstage behavior had many wondering if Whitney had once again lapsed into her old habits.

In April 2010, *People* took note that speculation was growing about whether Whitney was once again "in a downward drug spiral."

Whitney called such reports "ridiculous," saying, "At this point, I just don't respond. I don't even read it."

The tour ended on a sour note with a slew of new cancellations and furious Australian promoters bemoaning millions of dollars in losses. The much-heralded comeback was anything but a success, despite a successful album. And if 2010 ended on a sour note professionally, 2011 saw dark clouds on the home front.

While her mother toured the world, seventeen-year-old Bobbi was left to her own devices in Atlanta, where she had taken up with a hard-partying crowd, including the boy who had moved into her house three years earlier, Nick Gordon. And while the media began once again openly speculating about Whitney's drug use, it was Bobbi whose name was splashed across the headline when her ex-boyfriend Zach Jafarzadeh sold a photo to the *National Enquirer* of Bobbi snorting lines of cocaine at two separate parties. "Krissi is addicted to cocaine," Zach told the paper. "I've tried to stop her, but all she said was, 'I'm just like my mother!'"

Responding to the report on Twitter, Bobbi tweeted:

"It's really not what it looks like."

Whitney reportedly ordered her daughter to rehab and canceled plans for a lavish eighteenth birthday party planned at the Atlantis resort in the Bahamas in March.

In May, Whitney did another stint at rehab, this time with her troubled daughter, who was already showing signs of following in her parents' footsteps.

Despite the troubles at home, Whitney was eager to move forward with her career. As a teenager growing up in the seventies, her favorite movie was *Sparkle*—the 1976 film set in Harlem about a girl group in the late fifties and early sixties loosely based on the Supremes. Cissy remembers her daughter going to see it over and over because she found the story inspirational.

"As a young girl back in the 70s there was the black-exploitation movie thing," she would recall. "This was a positive reinforcement for young African-American women. For anyone who wanted to pursue their dream and present their gifts. It just appealed to me."

Following the success of *The Bodyguard*, Whitney had eyed a remake and had secured the rights from Warner Bros. in 1995. But the project had remained on hold, and it looked like it would never see the light of day. But when the African-American husband-and-wife production team Mara and Salim Akil approached her with a screenplay they had written, she jumped at the opportunity. Too old to play the lead role, Whitney agreed to play the mother of the three girls, while *American Idol* winner Jordin Sparks would star.

Apprehensive because of recent renewed speculation about whether she was back on drugs, everybody involved with the production was relieved that she appeared sober. There were no tantrums, no late arrivals, no diva demands. There was, however, a lot of praying. It appeared that Whitney's recovery was helped by what those around her had described as a "religious revival" in recent years. Whitney, who grew up in a deeply religious household, had always talked in interviews about the power of God, but she had been receiving spiritual counseling, and it appeared to many as if she had had a genuine religious awakening.

The production's makeup artist, Kym Lee, recalled that every three-hour makeup session with Whitney started with a prayer.

"She came in. She stakes a claim and she said, 'Hey, this is how I start my day,'" Lee recalled to the Christian Broadcast Network. "And she put on Fred Hammond. And we started off with worship, and it was incredible, because she set the tone."

And while onlookers bemoaned Sparks's noticeable lack of acting talent, Whitney proved the consummate professional who had come a long way since her labored performance in *The Bodyguard*.

"I found Whitney Houston to be very professional on the set," recalled producer T. D. Jakes. "She was an excellent actress. She was very, very effective, obviously as a singer."

But if her drug use had been severely curtailed since her marriage ended, she couldn't give up the habit entirely, as one of her former dealers told me when we met for drinks. The man, who gave up dealing in 2012, claims he sold Whitney "smoke and blow" whenever she was in LA, including during 2011 when she was filming *Sparkle*—and during post-production.

"We became friends, good friends," said the man, who claimed he wasn't her only dealer and that she likely had other sources when

Sparkle was shooting on location in Detroit for part of that period. "She trusted me. I gave her the best quality of whatever she wanted." He recalled that, unlike many celebrities he dealt to, Whitney had a "human element about her."

"About six years ago I was in the hospital for a couple weeks," he recalled. "I had a heart condition and had a stent procedure. Whitney sent me a card and flowers. She told me if I needed anything she was there for me. She really cared, there was nothing put on about her, she was real people."

Cissy suspected something was wrong when her daughter canceled an invitation to join her in Detroit after shooting was completed. Her daughter-in-law Donna was the one who told her Whitney had decided to fly to Atlanta instead. A month later, Whitney showed up unexpectedly in New York with Bobbi and invited her mother and brother Michael to join them at her Manhattan hotel, where they spent the day together.

Cissy begged them to come to New Jersey—only thirty minutes away—for a visit, but Whitney declined. She promised to visit after Clive Davis's annual pre-Grammy gala in February.

Cissy had been looking forward to the promised visit. But on Saturday, February 11, she received a call from Gary that would mark "the end of life as I had known it."

Whitney had arrived in LA a few days before Davis's party, at which she had been scheduled to perform. To avoid the paparazzi, she always used a pseudonym when she traveled. This time, she checked into a junior suite at the Beverly Hilton—room 434—under the name "Elizabeth Collins," with an entourage that included Bobbi, a hairdresser, two bodyguards, and a stylist.

Bobbi had brought Nick along on the trip, although few knew they were already romantically involved.

A few months earlier, Whitney had granted an interview to a reporter from the entertainment website *Global Grind* when she was in Detroit shooting *Sparkle*. When the reporter asked her how she had been balancing her personal life while she was away from home, she talked about Bobbi and made the first and only reference ever to Nick Gordon, although she never mentioned him by name.

"That's a good question," said Whitney. "I have priorities. Maintaining my daughter is my first. She also has it in her blood too. She's doing her acting classes and her vocal coaching. I keep her busy with that and she's very happy with that. She's 18 now. She's going to be a young woman, going to be a woman, Lord have mercy. But I also have my godson; he is going to be 22, a well-balanced young man."

Whitney had been seen at various events with the singer Ray J, the younger brother of her *Cinderella* costar Brandy, whom she had known since he was ten. Ray J, in fact, had quite a reputation as a womanizer and had starred in the infamous 2007 sex tape with Kim Kardashian that helped put her on the map. Whitney had been seen having dinner with him on a number of occasions since the divorce, but there's no evidence that the two ever dated, and he has always denied it. "That's my friend, I've been knowing her for years and years . . . she's a friend of the family," he told a reporter. Although there was speculation that he and Whitney were romantically linked, friends of the singer later claimed he was using Whitney to pitch a reality show. Ray J was best known for two previous TV shows, the dating show *For the Love of Ray J*, and the 2010 reality show with Brandy and their parents, *Brandy and Ray J: A Family Business*.

"He was just using her like many people did, to get a deal," a friend of his told *The Daily Beast* in 2012. Indeed, he had been following her around with a TV crew and had pitched the show to a number of producers in early 2012.

While she was in LA, Whitney rarely ventured out of the hotel, although Bobbi and Nick were frequently seen around town. On Thursday morning, Whitney ventured down to the hotel ballroom, where singers Brandy and Monica were rehearsing for their scheduled performances at Davis's gala.

LA Times music critic Gerrick Kennedy happened to be present when she popped her head in to offer coaching to the young singers. When he saw her, he knew something was amiss.

"Though Houston greeted people with a warm smile," Kennedy recalled, "she appeared disheveled in mismatched clothes and hair that was dripping wet with either sweat or water." Describing her appearance as "visibly bloated," he claims that Whitney "displayed erratic behavior throughout the afternoon—flailing her hands frenetically as she spoke to Brandy and Monica, skipping around the ballroom in a child-like fashion and wandering aimlessly about the lobby." Hotel security later received reports that she had been doing handstands by the pool.

Later, Kennedy was present when she returned to the ballroom in the afternoon with Bobbi to watch Davis give TV interviews to promote the show. As Davis was being interviewed by E!, Whitney stood just out of camera range, dancing and trying to make her mentor laugh. Turning to Brandy and Monica, she started talking about what she was going to wear to the gala.

"I don't wear no blue," she ranted. "I don't want no goddamn blue." Watching her mother's antics, Bobbi finally led her out of the ballroom.

Later the same evening, Whitney showed up to a party at LA's trendy nightclub Tru Hollywood, where she performed a duet of gospel hymns with Kelly Price. According to onlookers, her voice was shaky, but the crowd didn't seem to mind as they watched in awe and broke out in applause. Although Ray J was in LA the week she was there, he did not stay with her at the Hilton. Whitney was in the VIP section of the club with former *X Factor* contestant Stacy Francis, who was with her boyfriend, when Ray J arrived. She and Francis, who had both performed at a tribute to the late Etta James, had been getting along well and were chatting cordially earlier. When Ray J arrived, he spotted Francis and started chatting. By that time,

Whitney was visibly drunk—having guzzled significant quantities of tequila and champagne, according to onlookers.

Francis later claimed that while she was talking to Ray J, Whitney suddenly came over and demanded of him, "Who's the bitch?"

"She was out of control," Francis recalled. "She put her hand in my face. She was screaming at me and called me a bitch. She just went crazy—like Jekyll and Hyde. I turned to look at her and she pushed my forehead and turned my face away. I grabbed her hand and said, 'Please don't do this. You're everything to me. You're my idol, you're a legend.'"

Later, Whitney was seen leaving the club with a cut on her wrist and blood running down her leg. Her hairdresser, Tiffanie Dixon, claims that when Whitney returned, she saw her reading the Bible in her hotel room. "Her glasses were broken, but she read by holding the little single lens. She had marked pages—Exodus, Mark, and Matthew," she told *Vanity Fair*. "The last thing I remember her saying was 'I just want to love and be loved. I want to love like Jesus did. Unconditionally.'" Whitney had told Oprah in 2009 that when she locked herself in her room for days at a time doing drugs, she spent much of the time reading the Bible.

The next day, she remained in her room all day until the evening, when she ventured with a group of friends down to the bar where she spent a long time drinking.

On Saturday morning, her cousin Dionne Warwick spoke to Whitney on the phone about seating arrangements for Davis's gala that night and said she sounded fine.

At around three thirty that afternoon, her personal assistant, Mary Jones, decided to check on Whitney. After an hour, she became concerned and knocked on the door repeatedly, receiving no response. Entering, she let out a scream, which brought one of the bodyguards running. Hearing the screams, Pat Houston saw Whitney's hairstylist on her knees in the hallway, saying, "Oh my God!" Numb, she made her way to the room, where she found Jones in hysterics. Entering, she found her brother, Ray, who worked as Whitney's security guard, trying to revive the singer. As the paramedics arrived, Ray turned to Pat and said, somberly, "I tried."

When she was found in the bath, Whitney's face was under the water as though "she had slid down the back of the tub." Her head was described as "facing west." It's interesting to note that the autopsy report would later reveal the temperature of the water was "extremely hot," measured at 93.5 degrees Fahrenheit well after she was found. Investigators found a "plethora" of prescription medication bottles as well as a "small spoon with a white crystal like substance in it" and a mirror with a white powdery substance on its base.

While the bodyguard attempted CPR, somebody alerted a hotel security guard, who called 911 about a forty-eight-year-old woman who was "apparently not breathing," though he was not sure if the unidentified woman "fell, or if she was in the bathroom with the water." Paramedics arrived soon afterward and attempted to revive the singer, but Whitney was pronounced dead at 3:55 PM.

Meanwhile, her entourage had gathered outside the hotel room but were kept out by bodyguards. There is no indication that Nick Gordon was present at any time and it's clear from both the police and autopsy reports that he did not administer CPR as his mother claimed to Dr. Phil. It appears that neither Bobbi nor Nick were even in the hotel at the time of the incident, because Bobbi was reported to have arrived a full two hours after her mother was found, demanding to be let in the room—where the body was being examined—and arguing loudly with police. Dionne Warwick also arrived some time after the body was discovered but was also denied access. Ray J was away in San Diego when Whitney died, although he would later arrive at the hotel while her body was still in the room.

At eleven PM, Bobbi was so distraught that she was taken to Cedars-Sinai Medical Center and sedated. A press release sent to ABC News that evening said she was "awake and alert." She was released later that night. The next day, she was again brought to Cedars-Sinai where she was reported to be "hysterical, exhausted and inconsolable." The Associated Press reported that night that she had been "treated and released for stress and anxiety."

News of his ex-wife's sudden death was reported to have also hit Bobby Brown hard. He had reunited with New Edition and was performing that night in Mississippi, where he was reported to have had "crying fits" upon learning the news. During the performance, he pointed to the sky and declared, "I love you, Whitney." He later flew to LA to be with his daughter. In a media statement about his daughter's condition, he said, "Obviously the death of her mother is affecting her, however, we will get through this tragedy as a family. Again, I ask for privacy during this time."

The world was reeling from the news as tributes poured in far and wide from fans and celebrity friends wondering how it could have all gone so wrong.

Many were quick to assign blame, and most believed they knew exactly who had caused the singer's downfall, as Bobby Brown was vilified in all quarters of the globe. But it is interesting to note those who knew her best went out of their way to stress that Bobby was not to blame for Whitney's problems, perhaps because they knew that it wasn't Bobby who introduced her to drugs, as many still suspected.

Her mentor, Clive Davis, was one of the first to rise to Bobby's defense, even though he did not have much of a personal or professional relationship with him.

"I don't believe it was Bobby Brown," he would say. "I think they did have a co-dependent, unhealthy relationship with each other. But I would never point to him. I have no idea who her enabler was."

Even her family believed that Bobby had been unfairly blamed. Not long after Whitney's death, Pat Houston told Oprah Winfrey, "Bobby and I had a good relationship. She [Whitney] would say, 'You're always trying to protect him.' I said, 'No, I'm protecting truth. I can't do it any other way.' Their reality was everyone else's, and it's

very difficult if you've got family members that are demanding certain things from you, then the world demanding certain things from
you. In all of that congestion, how can you make it work?"

Even Cissy would exonerate Bobby when she went on the *Today*
show and insisted that her daughter was responsible for her own
problems. "I don't blame Bobby Brown," Cissy said. "I know he didn't
help her . . . But everybody's responsible for their own actions up to
a point."

The British activist and parliamentary candidate Peter Tatchell,
who had known Whitney and Robyn from the 1991 Reach Out and
Touch UK HIV/AIDS Vigil, and had seen them holding hands in the
back of their car "like teenage sweethearts," claimed he believed he
knew what caused Whitney's tragic demise and was one of the first
to publicly link her downward spiral to her decision to remain in the
closet.

"Whitney was happiest and at the peak of her career when she
was with Robyn," Tatchell wrote in the London *Mail on Sunday* soon
after her death. "Sadly, she suffered family and church pressure to
end her greatest love of all. She was fearful of the effects that lesbian
rumors might have on her family, reputation and career. Eventually
she succumbed. The result? A surprise marriage to Bobby Brown."

Whitney's life, he argued, started to go downhill soon afterward—
evidence of what he called "a troubled personal life and much unhappiness."

"It seems likely that the split with Robyn contributed to her substance abuse and decline," he argued. "There is a known correlation
between denial of one's sexuality and a propensity to self-destructive
behavior. Homophobia undoubtedly added to the pressures on Whitney and hastened her demise."

Roseanne star Sandra Bernhard—who had been one of the first
Hollywood personalities to come out—echoed these sentiments on
The Rosie Show soon afterward when she said that Whitney's down-
fall stemmed from her "inability to accept her sexuality."

This theory has been hotly debated in the three years since Whitney's passing, but for me it has a particularly unique resonance.

When I first heard the news on the radio on that Saturday afternoon in February 2012, I immediately had a chilling sense of déjà vu. Less than three years earlier, I had published a book about the last days of Michael Jackson in which I had infiltrated his camp to discover the behind-the-scenes life of the King of Pop. I became so intimately acquainted with his deterioration during those final years that I gave an interview publicly predicting in December 2008 that MJ would be dead within six months. When he died six months later to the day, my prediction got some attention.

However, the book was not a salacious account of Jackson's life, nor an exposé. Instead, I focused largely on the most damaging chapter of Jackson's life and one which virtually destroyed his career—the child molestation accusations leveled by two different boys.

In my book, I meticulously tore apart the so-called evidence in both cases and proved almost beyond any doubt that Jackson was innocent of the heinous allegations that had inexorably destroyed his legacy. Instead, I argued that both families were ruthlessly exploiting their children to obtain money from the singer and that there was no credible proof he ever molested children. In other words, my book may have singlehandedly redeemed his severely tarnished reputation.

However, during the course of my research, I also discovered evidence that, although Jackson wasn't a pedophile, he was in fact gay. I encountered two separate adult males who showed me evidence that they had engaged in affairs with the singer.

When my book, *Unmasked*, was published shortly after Jackson's June 2009 death, the reaction was not at all what I expected. Although it was well received and spent two weeks on top of the *New York Times* bestseller list, the reaction from Jackson's legions of worldwide fans was nothing short of vicious. Rather than celebrate the fact that I had exonerated their idol from the unspeakable accusations against him, I was attacked with the fury of a thousand suns. Fan clubs all over the world called for a boycott of my book; I was accused of defaming and smearing Michael's reputation and declared public enemy number one. I even received two death threats and countless threats of physical violence.

"If I ever meet you face to face, I'll cut your balls off," wrote a Jackson fan from Holland. My crime? Daring to suggest that MJ was gay. The threats against me from many Jackson fans, in fact, were far worse than those against the families that accused him of molestation. In their eyes, it appeared, accusing somebody of being homosexual is even worse than accusing him of being a pedophile.

Soon after my book appeared, a man named Jason Pfeiffer—the office manager for Jackson's longtime doctor, Arnie Klein—came forward and claimed he had a two-month affair with the singer at the end of his life. He described how their relationship began.

"We were just sitting there and we both started to cry and I got up and went over to him and said it's going to be okay, Michael. . . . We hugged," he told *Women's Day* magazine.

"It was kind of then that the hug was a little bit more . . . It wasn't until a few months later that it was obvious that Michael had feelings for me as well. I just assumed that he was probably bisexual. I know we loved each other. I know he told me all the time. I believe he was probably my soul mate."

When Pfeiffer's story and credibility were questioned, Klein publicly told both *Extra* and *TMZ* that the affair had taken place, revealing that he had once walked in on the two men, both shirtless.

"When you see two people looking at each other you know what's happening. I was just very happy for both of them," he said.

It is a revelation that Klein said had sparked a number of death threats against him. Two years later, just before April Fool's Day, a letter purporting to be from Klein briefly appeared on his Facebook page for about an hour claiming that Pfeiffer's allegations were fabricated by a ghostwriter, but the letter disappeared almost immediately, and, if true, there was no explanation of why Klein had supplied an eyewitness account of the affair to *Extra*.

Considering the unleashed scorn that Klein and I faced for simply telling the truth about Michael, I can certainly understand why Whitney chose to remain in the closet and hide her own bisexuality.

Shortly after Michael died in 2009, Whitney told Oprah that seeing Michael at his 2001 tribute concert had made her take stock of her own life.

"I was getting scared," she said. "I was looking at myself going, 'No, I don't want this to be like this. This can't happen. Not both of us.'"

After she eventually suffered the same fate as her onetime idol, I couldn't help examine some of the parallels between the two that Whitney herself must have been well aware of.

They were both raised by deeply religious and homophobic mothers. La Toya Jackson once revealed that Katherine Jackson—a devout Jehovah's Witness—had referred to her son as a "damn faggot." When Oprah asked Cissy Houston in 2013 "Would it have bothered you if your daughter Whitney was gay?" Cissy's response was unequivocal. "Absolutely," she replied.

"You would not have liked that?" asked the talk show host.

"Not at all," Whitney's mother confessed.

Apart from the homophobia of their parents, both singers were acutely aware that large segments of their fan base would have been deeply offended by the truth, in part because of the widespread belief that public figures are role models and their "immoral" actions might "influence" children. It is probably safe to say that neither Whitney nor Michael would have attained iconic status had they been honest about their sexuality, notwithstanding their phenomenal talent.

And, of course, as both singers spent their careers in the closet, they developed devastating drug habits that would eventually contribute to their demise. Does that prove Tatchell's theory—that denying one's sexuality leads to self-destructive behavior? Did living in the vinyl closet kill two of the greatest superstars of the twentieth century?

For me, the jury is still out. It is a little simplistic to simply give a pat answer about what led to their tragic fates. Certainly there are some convincing parallels. But there are a number of heterosexual superstars who also suffered a similar fate. Elvis and Marilyn Monroe immediately come to mind. Still, it is certainly worth asking whether the price of fame is worth living a lie.

I have no doubt that I will be accused of smearing Whitney's reputation, as happened when I told the truth about Michael. Many will undoubtedly argue that there is no evidence to even prove Whitney was bisexual and that unless Robyn Crawford confirms the two had a sexual relationship, we must accept Whitney's many vehement denials.

After Robyn moved on, she eventually entered into a long relationship with *Esquire* magazine editor Lisa Hintelmann, with whom she lives today in New Jersey with their adopted twins. Robyn, who would later go to work at ESPN, has never spoken publicly about whether she and Whitney were ever a couple, but she did pen a poignant tribute in *Esquire* the day after Whitney's death.

In the piece, she recalled how she and Whitney first met at an East Orange community center. She writes that shortly after they met, her new friend told her, "Stick with me, and I'll take you around the world." Sure enough, they traveled everywhere together and always first-class. Robyn appears to allude to her despair about the fact that they never again spoke after her departure.

"She could not pick up the phone, and that meant it was too painful," she wrote. But if people expected Robyn to finally come clean about the nature of their relationship, they would be disappointed.

"I have never spoken about her until now," she explained, "and she knew I wouldn't. She was a loyal friend, and she knew I was never going to be disloyal to her. I was never going to betray her."

But if Robyn wasn't going to spill any secrets, the same couldn't be said about Bobby Brown, who had already revealed in his 2008 memoir, *Bobby Brown: The Truth, The Whole Truth and Nothing But . . .* , that Whitney may have married him as a smoke screen to deflect the lesbian rumors.

> *I think we got married for all the wrong reasons. Now, I realize Whitney had a different agenda than I did when we got married. . . . I believe her agenda was to clean up her image, while mine was to be loved and have children. The media was accusing her of having a bisexual relationship with her assistant, Robyn Crawford. Since she was the American Sweetheart and all, that didn't go too well with her image. . . . In Whitney's situation, the only solution was to get married and have kids. That would kill all speculation, whether it was true or not.*

When the funeral took place on February 18 at the New Hope Baptist Church, where Whitney had developed her talents singing in the choir, both Bobby and Robyn were in attendance. But while Robyn sat quietly in the back and didn't draw attention to herself, Bobby ended up immersed in a controversy that invoked memories of the couple's stormy marriage.

Tellingly, among the performers at the funeral was the "ex-gay" pastor, Donnie McClurkin, who in 2002 claimed God had delivered him from "the curse of homosexuality" and likes to compare homosexuality to pedophilia because he was raped by an uncle when he was eight. Also in the lineup that day were the duo Debbie and Angie Winans, whose notorious 1997 song "Not Natural" is an anti-gay anthem written in response to the famous coming-out episode of Ellen DeGeneres's sitcom, *Ellen*. Debbie Winans had told *Jet* magazine, "It was written that day after [DeGeneres came out]. The Lord inspired the song . . . because you can't turn on the TV without something being pushed down your throat that's contrary to God." She explained that the song reflects a "holy anger because if your kids see that, they're going to mimic that."

The media would later report that Bobby stormed out of the funeral service when security refused to let his entourage sit with him. In fact, he arrived with his three children, but when security told him they couldn't sit with him in the church, he was infuriated and ended up leaving the service. Onlookers reported that he appeared emotionally distraught and on the verge of tears as he walked up the aisle.

Before he departed, however, he approached the casket and kissed it before leaving with his children. He would later claim that security also barred him from attempting to see Bobbi, who was sitting in the front row with the family. Despite media reports, however, he never caused a scene.

For many attendees, the highlight of the memorial service was the eulogy delivered by Whitney's *Bodyguard* costar, Kevin Costner:

"The Whitney I knew, despite her success and worldwide fame, still wondered, am I good enough? Am I pretty enough? Will they like me? It was the burden that made her great, and the part that caused her to stumble in the end," he said.

There was one other notable guest at the funeral that day. Nick Gordon had been added to the program as a pallbearer at Bobbi's request. It was the first time most of the mourners, including the family, had seen the young man, and many wondered aloud who he was.

CHAPTER **TWENTY-FOUR**

Only a month after Whitney's death, Bobbi Kristina agreed to sit down with Oprah and talk about the impact of her mother's passing. Many had wondered how the teenage girl was coping, especially after reports of her two breakdowns and hospitalizations that weekend.

The autopsy report had not yet been released. When it was, it would reveal the cause of death as accidental drowning, with "heart disease" and "cocaine use" listed as contributing factors.

As Oprah greeted Bobbi in the living room of the Atlanta town house, the host asked how she was doing. "I'm doing as good as I possibly can at this point," Bobbi told her. "I'm just trying to keep going." She said her family was helping her get through it.

It is clear that she was still reeling from the death of the woman she called her "best friend, a sister, a comforter." She told Oprah that she woke at five AM every morning and felt her mother's presence in the house.

"I can hear her voice in spirit talking to me, 'Keep talking to me. I got you,'" she said. "She's always with me. I can always feel her. I can always feel her with me. She always asked me, 'Do you need me?' And I caught myself, out of nowhere, I didn't even know I said it, I said, 'I'll always need you.'"

Bobbi had been named sole heir of her mother's estate, but it was still unclear how much money that involved. Some estimates put Whitney's net worth at $115 million, while others had her in the red. In the days following her death, it was revealed she had squandered most of her fortune and was actually in debt at the time of her death, despite earning an estimated $250 million throughout her career. The *Daily Mail* reported that Clive Davis even had to loan her $1.5 million to settle her debts before her last stint in rehab.

She had been locked in a very nasty battle with her stepmother, Barbara Houston—John's former housekeeper—over her father's million-dollar life insurance policy that he had left to Whitney. The fact that she was fighting tooth and nail over such a relatively small sum indicated to many that she desperately needed the money.

Michael Jackson's estate had raked in a staggering $279 million in sales in the year following his 2009 death, but since Whitney didn't write her own music, she didn't have the same earning power as the King of Pop. Still, in the days following her death, a number of her albums returned to the charts, and the estate was clearly raking it in. iTunes immediately raised the price of her songs from ninety-nine cents to $1.29 to capitalize on the new demand. "I Will Always Love You" was downloaded 100,000 times the day after her body was found, and other Whitney Houston hits also enjoyed robust sales.

Whatever financial straits she had fallen into before her death, these sales would guarantee the estate untold millions. In the three years since, the general consensus is that Bobbi Kristina's inheritance hovers around $20 million, with untold millions more to come.

Yet Whitney's will was structured in such a way that her daughter would only receive the money in installments, while the remainder would be placed in trust.

The first installment came due on Bobbi's twenty-first birthday in March 2014. An additional twenty-five percent was due when she turned twenty-five, with the balance coming to her when she turned thirty. As executor of the estate, Pat Houston had agreed to pay Bobbi a monthly allowance until she turned twenty-one, though it's uncertain whether those sums were deducted from her first installment or, more likely, taken from any interest earned on the trust's capital.

The fact that she wasn't due to collect her first installment for another two years may have been the contributing factor in Bobbi's decision to participate in a Lifetime reality show—*The Houstons: On Our Own*—only weeks after her mother was buried. Billed as a series chronicling "the lives of Whitney Houston's family as they move on after her death," shooting started in May 2012.

When the series premiered in October, it was the first time many had heard of the existence of Nick Gordon, other than Whitney's brief reference to her godson and his participation as a pallbearer at the funeral. It is still uncertain how the misinformation circulated that Nick was an orphaned boy taken in by Whitney when he was twelve and Bobbi was eight. It was a falsehood that was circulated by ABC News in March 2012, claiming "Houston invited Gordon to live with her more than 10 years ago after learning that his birth mother could no longer care for him. She raised him alongside her daughter." Surprisingly, the respected news network cited the celebrity website *TMZ* as the source of their information. The site had claimed to get their information from "sources close to the family." When ABC contacted Nick to ask him about his relationship with Whitney, he coyly replied, "Everything that me and her went through will go to the grave with me."

The falsehood quickly gained steam from there and was even cited as fact by *Vanity Fair* in their June 2012 investigation into Whitney's death—surprising, considering the vast fact-checking team at the magazine's disposal. The article, entitled "The Devils in the Diva," discusses the move to Alpharetta and reveals that, besides Bobbi Kristina, the family sometimes included Bobby's three children as well as "Nick Gordon, an orphaned boy Whitney had taken in two years earlier, when he was 12."

During the first episode of the series, Nick tells the camera, "My name is Nick Gordon. My life changed dramatically when I met Krissi and Whitney. I was going to high school. My mom had kicked me out of the house. Krissi being my friend, I got to know Whitney. She took me in." As it turned out, he was telling the truth. What he didn't share was that he was eighteen when he got kicked out, not twelve.

Bobbi then adds, "We were best friends a long long time ago." Then she shares a revelation that would create considerable buzz for months to come. "And now I'm in love with him."

This is a story line the series had been hyping for weeks to promote the show. It's conceivable that it was the Lifetime publicity team that first exaggerated the nature of the relationship and made it seem as if Nick and Bobbi had been raised almost as brother and sister from childhood. It had the public and media immediately talking about "incest." It was this story line that everybody focused on and the one that had people tuning in.

Still, nobody overtly lied about the history of the relationship. But other family members certainly played along. Promoting the show, Bobbi's aunt Pat revealed to Oprah that she was disturbed by the sudden romantic turn. "It didn't sit right with me," she told the talk show host. "I always saw them as the brother and sister type. We weren't happy about it. No not at all."

Strangely, nobody could find many photos of Nick with Whitney over the years and few recalled the young man who had supposedly been raised by Whitney as a son. Leolah Brown publicly declared she had never heard of him. Similarly, *The Houstons: On Our Own* features a scene in which Nick meets Pat's cousin, and he asks Pat, "Who is this young man right here?," making it clear that the cousin of the woman who had been closer to Whitney than anybody since Robyn left had no idea who he was.

Michelle Gordon's interview with Dr. Phil in March revealed that Nick was prone to exaggerate—even lie—about his close ties to Whitney, even falsely claiming to have administered CPR as she lay dying on the bathroom floor.

Still, we know that Nick spent an unspecified amount of time living in the Atlanta town house after he turned eighteen and definitely
traveled with Whitney and Bobbi in 2010 and 2011, but even his
mother didn't seem to know when exactly he moved in.

We do know that the first of Nick's many brushes with the law
occurred when Whitney was still alive, and it involved both Bobbi
and Max Lomas, the young man who eventually discovered her in
the bathtub.

On April 1, 2011, at approximately four in the morning, police
received a report that a number of people "armed with guns and shotguns" were involved in a fight in the parking lot of a Chevron gas
station in Roswell. When a policewoman, Genevieve Myrand, arrived
on the scene, she discovered Nick, Bobbi, Max, Zach Jafarzadeh, his
brother Matteen, and a friend named Justin Walls standing outside a
Honda and an SUV.

The officer ordered everybody to lie on the ground, then requested
backup. Waiting for help, she began questioning those present. According to her incident report, "NICHOLAS stated he and his friend MAX
LOMAS followed [the occupants of the Honda] to the Chevron
because GORDON's sister [Bobbi Kristina] was in the Honda with
ZACH JAFARZADEH."

Nick told her he and Max "did not particularly like" Zach and that
Max had recently broken up with Bobbi Kristina.

Justin Walls then told the officer that the incident started as
they were leaving the Ellard Village complex where Bobbi lived. He
claimed Max approached the car and "tried to punch him in the face"
while they were stopped at a light. When they got to the Chevron station, things turned violent when everybody got out of their vehicles.

Walls claimed that Max came toward him and hit him in the
face repeatedly. "I observed Walls' face and he was bleeding from the
mouth and appeared to have a chipped tooth," the officer wrote. Zach
then tried to pull Max off of Walls and "was struck several times in
the head by LOMAS."

The officer reported that she observed Zach's face "and his fore-head was bruised and starting to swell. [Zach] also had a red mark above his left eye brow."

When the officer asked Nick if he had any guns in his possession, he told her he had a black handgun in his glove compartment. She located a Glock 19 and two loaded Glock magazines. When she asked Nick what happened with the gun, "he stated that he waved the gun in the air in an attempt to stop the fight."

When two backup officers arrived, they proceeded to handcuff all six participants. Max started throwing up but refused medical attention. He said he had been drinking. Revealing that Bobbi, Zach, and Walls also smelled of alcohol, Officer Myrand administered a Breathalyzer test to all three.

Bobbi blew .0215, well above the legal limit, though she hadn't been driving. Police confiscated the black Glock 19 and charged Nick with "pointing a pistol at another." Meanwhile, Bobbi—who had turned eighteen a month earlier—was cited for "being a minor in possession of alcohol." Max was charged with two counts of battery and being a minor in possession of alcohol.

Despite Nick's assertion that he was only waving the gun to break up the fight, a Chevron employee who had called police told Officer Myrand that Nick had been "threatening to shoot the gun at the other subjects in the parking lot."

Eventually, Bobbi left the scene in Nick's car with Max even though she was dating Zach at the time, and it was Max who had appeared to instigate the confrontation in a jealous rage. When questioned by police, Nick described Bobbi as his "sister."

The incident took place only weeks after Whitney had canceled Bobbi's Bahamas eighteenth birthday celebration and brought her to rehab because of the photos that appeared in the *National Enquirer* showing her snorting coke under the headline, "Whitney's daughter hooked on cocaine and booze." It would later emerge that it was Zach who had sold the photos to the magazine.

Eight months later, on December 26, 2011, Bobbi posted a photo of Nick sitting between her and Whitney in the back of a car, along with a tweet:

"Mom, @ndgordon (: & I on the way to the airport friday! (: #NYCBABYYYYY home home home."

This was the Christmas trip to New York, where Whitney and Bobbi spent the day at the hotel with Cissy—the last time mother and daughter would ever see each other. Six weeks later, Whitney would be dead.

In a March 2012 tweet—less than a month after Whitney's passing—Nick responded to a growing chorus of social media vilification. Many were complaining that his relationship with Bobbi was unseemly and that Whitney would have disapproved of a relationship with his "sister." Responding to these accusations, he tweeted:

"For the stupid ppl out there she gave birth to 1 child. And she trusted me with EVERYTHING!!!!!!!!!!!!!"

It was only a few months earlier that Whitney had referred to him as her "godson" in a Detroit interview.

Michelle told Dr. Phil that the couple had met "in school." That was my starting point. But try as we might, neither Sheila, my private investigator, nor I could uncover any evidence that Bobbi had ever attended high school in Atlanta. If they didn't meet in school, how did they first become friends?

Inspired by *Being Bobby Brown*, and people's unquenchable thirst for their fifteen minutes of fame, I announced to a lineup of twenty-somethings outside an Atlanta club one evening that I was a producer for a new reality series to be set in Atlanta's club scene. I said I would be looking for six participants to follow as part of my new show. I asked if anyone were interested.

Several hands shot up. I explained that since Atlanta was in the news because of Bobbi Kristina's near drowning, I wanted to include at least one person who knew her. "Does anybody here qualify?" I asked. Nobody responded. But a woman named Lee-Anne told me that she has a friend who went to the same middle school with Bobbi. What school? "Taylor Road." She gave me a cell number and her friend's name—Alex.

The next morning, I called the number and told Alex who I was. Would she be interested in participating in my show? "Not a chance," she told me. "I'm too shy." The conversation shifted to Bobbi. She confirmed that Bobbi attended Taylor Road for a year in 2007. "I wasn't part of her clique," she told me, but she had friends who were.

What high school did Bobbi attend after Taylor Road? I asked. "She didn't go to high school, she was privately homeschooled with tutors and stuff." I told her that Michelle claimed Bobbi met Nick in high school. Bobbi had also once described Nick as her "high school sweetheart" in a tweet.

"No, they never went to school together, he was dating her really good friend. That's how they met. I have no idea how they hooked up," she told me.

She gave me some names and numbers of two people who know Bobbi better, one of whom is the apparent source of the information she had just shared. She told me it was all anybody was talking about since Bobbi's bathtub incident. When I called, however, neither woman had any interest in talking to me. One of them hung up almost immediately.

I had discovered that Nick—who had moved with his mother and stepfather to Atlanta from Toledo, Ohio, when he was young—had attended Chattahoochee High School, which is only a few hundred yards down the road from Taylor Road Middle School, so it's possible that this is the common link.

If I was a little closer to determining how Bobbi and Nick connected for the first time, I was still uncertain how Nick had linked up with Max Lomas.

Max had a long history of trouble. He had been charged with two counts of battery at the Chevron station when he and Nick confronted Zach in April 2011.

Two months later, in June, Max was once again arrested with four other people in a wooded area in Dawson County, Georgia. Police confiscated three rifles and a significant amount of marijuana. They charged Max, who sported a Mohawk at the time, with "consumption of alcohol on a wildlife management area, possession with intent to distribute marijuana and possession of a firearm in the commission of a crime." A year later, he was charged with a probation violation stemming from the previous incident.

In June 2013, Max and Nick were back in trouble once again when police responded to a report that they had beat up a man named Steven Stepho in his apartment in an attempt to get money. Stepho would later tell the London *Sun* that he sold narcotics to both Nick and Bobbi.

"Bobbi and Nick would spend a lot on drugs every day, it just depended on how much money they had," he told the paper. "It wasn't unusual for them to spend $1,000 a day on drugs."

A month later, on July 8, 2013, somebody called 911 to report trouble at the couple's town house. When police arrived, Nick told them that Bobbi had fallen on the floor and was "unresponsive." According to the police report, "GORDON described it as a seizure. BROWN said she has no history of medical conditions and has never had seizures before. BROWN was disoriented and transported to Emory Johns Creek Hospital by RMA."

On the evening of June 6, 2014, Roswell police responded to a 911 call at an extended stay hotel called "Studio Six." When they arrived, they were informed by a man named Garry Grace that his friend Max Lomas had "possibly overdosed on some type of controlled substance," according to the police report. Max was transported to

North Fulton Hospital and police confiscated "drug related objects." The report describes a tattoo on Max's left elbow. It reads: "LAUGH NOW CRY LATER."

On August 28, 2014, Nick was in trouble yet again when he was arrested on a Thursday morning not far from the town house. According to a Roswell police spokesperson, he was behind the wheel of a BMW sedan that struck a curb while changing lanes. The car overturned and hit a fire hydrant. Nick was charged with a DUI, failure to maintain a lane, and driving with a suspended license.

His license had been suspended back in December 2012 when he was caught driving eighty-two miles per hour in a residential zone in Alpharetta. "The danger of that particular incident lies in the fact of 82 MPH in a very busy area within our city," said a spokesperson from the Department of Public Safety after the incident. When he was pulled over, there was loud music blaring from the speakers. The song playing? Whitney's "I Will Always Love You." The officer who stopped him revealed that Nick asked, "Is there any way I can not go to jail."

"Not for that, not for that speed," the officer replied.

And in January 2015, two weeks before Bobbi was discovered, Danyela's mother, Marlene Bradley, called Roswell police, who were dispatched to a motel room on Hembree Road on suspicion that Max Lomas was forcibly confining Danyela against her will.

Max was arrested for possession of a firearm/knife, possession of marijuana with intent to distribute, and possession of Xanax. Police found a "large quantity of marijuana" and thousands of Baggies "commonly used to package marijuana" and a scale, along with a loaded Glock with a bullet in the chamber under the blanket.

The other man present was Duane Tyrone Hall, who Danyela's mother revealed to Sharon Churcher had allegedly been present in the house when Bobbi was discovered.

Three days after that, Roswell police pulled over a gray Toyota Camry for a lane violation. When they searched the car, they found marijuana residue in the center console, though no charges were filed. The occupants of the vehicle happened to be Nick Gordon and Duane Tyrone Hall.

It is clear from this pattern of police incidents that in the almost three years following her mother's death, both Nick and Max were cavorting with some shady characters. Without giving credence to dubious secondhand accounts from those who claim to have known them, it's just as clear that they were heavily immersed in the local drug scene.

But if the multiple police incidents indicate that Bobbi was surrounded by drug dealers, narcotics, and thugs, there is no clearer evidence that she was immersed in the local drug crowd—at least by association—than what happened to the woman she described as her "best friend in the world."

In March 2014, twenty-year-old Chelsea Bennett began partying with two men in an Alpharetta apartment. At the time, Chelsea and Bobbi were very close. A month earlier, Bobbi had posted a photo of the two of them on her Instagram with the caption:

"I love you chels! So much fun with you & have been friends with you since I can remember! Thanks for always being there for me . . . Ahh adore you mamacita! XO"

On that March evening when Chelsea—a longtime heroin addict—needed her fix, one of the men helped inject her. But heroin needs to be cut and this dose turned out to be extra pure. Chelsea overdosed almost immediately. Rather than phoning for help, the two men instead tried a variety of methods to revive her and waited to see if she would wake up. Only when she died ten hours later did they finally call 911.

Four months later, a grand jury returned a felony murder indictment against the man accused of selling her the heroin, Kevin McCaffrey, and the man who injected her, Cory Ben-Hanania. The other man in the apartment was charged with concealing a death. While it's unclear whether Bobbi knew him, Ben-Hanania happens to be Facebook friends with Mason Whitaker, who is so close to Nick that he describes him on Facebook as a "family member" and who was with Nick when he overturned his vehicle after striking a fire hydrant in August 2014.

Forty-three-year-old Paige Thompson was another friend of the couple who frequently posted photos of her friends Nick and Bobbi, even though she was much older than them. Her mother, Ophelia Ward, told reporters, "Paige looked at [Bobbi] like a daughter." In January 2014, Thompson was arrested for heroin possession with intent to sell. A year later, in February 2015, she granted a jailhouse interview to *Radar Online* defending Nick against the accusations swirling around him.

"You'll never convince me that Nick had anything to do with hurting her," she insisted. "People fight and argue; sometimes it gets physical, but as far as hurting her in a way . . . and killing her . . . no way! He would have nothing to gain really. I would not believe it. I don't believe Nick had anything to do with this."

This was the couple's motley circle of friends.

It is safe to assume that, as with her mother's tragic fate, whatever happened to Bobbi Kristina Brown on the morning of January 31, 2015, was somehow connected to drugs.

When Whitney drowned in a bathtub three years earlier, it took a coroner's report and several weeks to verify a drug connection to the death. With Bobbi still lying in a coma, I was determined not to wait that long to find out what happened—especially since I held out hope, however remote, that she would escape her mother's fate and that a coroner would be unnecessary.

———

When Bobbi Kristina sat down with Oprah only a month after her mother's death, the talk show queen asked her what she planned to do with her life.

"I have to carry on her legacy," she answered. "We're going to do the singing thing. Some acting . . . I still have a voice."

Only a month after the funeral, producer Tyler Perry—who was very close to both Bobby and Whitney—announced that he was casting Bobbi Kristina in his TBS sitcom *For Better or Worse* "in a recurring role." The show was produced in Atlanta, so she didn't have to travel far when she reported to the set for the series' second season in May. That same month, *Radar Online* reported that she had "walked off the set."

"She thought she was ready for this, but she wasn't," a production insider told the site. "She was crying and said she needed a minute, she needed a break to get herself together. But then she decided she couldn't handle doing the show right now. She's still mourning her mom."

Perry was quick to deny that she had left the set.

"Were there tough days for her?" he said. "Yes of course. Not because of the acting or any job-related issues but because of the fact that she had just lost her mother. So yes she was grieving, but grief aside, she managed to finish her obligation and did a great job at the same time."

But when the series aired, Bobbi appeared in only one episode, and her acting was very labored. Cast members tried to put on a brave face, saying she had done "a great job," but watching her acting debut is quite painful. It was immediately evident that Hollywood would not be beating down her door.

That left her long-standing dream of following in her mother's singing footsteps. On one of the episodes of her reality show *The Houstons: On Our Own*, Bobbi met with Whitney's former musical director Rickey Minor, who gave her some singing tips. "I have a really versatile voice, so I don't really know yet what genre I'm going to be in," she tells him, admitting that she had been smoking a lot, which had affected her singing.

"Singing is an extension of you," Minor advised her. "And so it really has to be something you connect to."

He warned her that she would inevitably be compared to her parents and grandmother.

"Of course I'm going to be compared to my mother," she agreed. "Being her daughter is a huge blessing, but also a curse at times."

Minor askes her to sing "I'm Your Baby Tonight," which she admitted put her under "a lot of pressure." She proceeded to sing a passable a cappella version of Whitney's classic, which demonstrated that she could carry a tune but that she didn't come close to possessing her mother's vocal range or phenomenal talent.

Yet it is clear from her social media postings that she still had great hopes for a musical career. In one 2013 tweet, shortly before the one-year anniversary of her mother's death, Bobbi hinted that she would be recording in the near future, tweeting:

> "Hiworld :)(: yes I am a night owl, this is when my creative side come's out. ALLTHETIME! I need2be in the studio RITE-NOW! #SOONverySOON"

In February 2015, as Bobbi lay in a coma, her cousin Jerod Brown revealed that he had spent the last six months working with her, intending to head into the studio "soon." He said they had been working on a single called "Guilty of a Love Song"—a track about "spreading love."

Jerod claimed to have had high hopes for the recording. "That record was going to touch the world," he said. "To her it was a very personal song of what her love life was about. She's excited. She was real focused. She was ecstatic about her new journey that she was embarking on . . . you could see it on Instagram when she commented on it with the fans as well. She was ready to do this and let the world see what she was working on."

But if singing was still her main ambition, it was clear that Bobbi had not yet given up hope for an acting career, despite her less than stellar debut.

In May 2014, Whitney's former *Waiting to Exhale* costar Angela Bassett announced that she was planning to direct a TV biopic about Whitney Houston for Lifetime and that the film would chronicle the good times and bad, including her rise to fame and her tumultuous marriage to Bobby Brown.

Bassett insisted that she had great respect for Whitney and that the film wouldn't tarnish her legacy, as many fans feared. "We worked together. We had a wonderful time working together," she said. "She was amazing to be around. She broke through this glass ceiling of what a sister was paid, what a woman was paid for starring in a movie. We had a mutual admiration for each other."

When news that the film would include Robyn Crawford as a character, many were nervous that Bassett planned to out the singer. None more so than Whitney's family, who made it clear that the film was "unauthorized" and that they disapproved of the production.

At least one family member, however, was excited about the prospect of a film about Whitney's life. When Bobbi heard that a movie was planned about her mother, she knew there was only one person who could do justice to the leading role—herself.

Within months of Whitney's death—as rumors first swirled that Hollywood was anxious to portray the diva's life on film—Bobbi had been lobbying for the part.

"Bobbi feels like she is the perfect person to play the part of Whitney—telling friends that no one knew her better," a friend told *TMZ* in April 2012.

"That would be something I would have to give my entire life to do, because I would really want to pull it off," Bobbi told the *Daily Mail*. "Whoever does it has to do a good job." Rihanna and Jennifer Hudson were also reportedly lobbying for the part.

In early 2014, Bassett announced that she had cast Yaya DaCosta in the role of Whitney. When *Entertainment Weekly* asked her in June 2014 whether she had ever considered casting Bobbi Kristina—who had made it known she wanted the role—Bassett was unequivocal.

"No, I did not think about that," she said. "I did not think about casting her. And probably for a number of reasons, you know. One being that she's not an actress. I know she's acted here and there. I know she's been on their family's reality show, but she's not an actress, and acting is a craft. It's an attempt to illuminate the complexities of human behavior and life. And this is a very fast-paced schedule; we have just 21 days to tell this story. It's more than just saying lines and turning the light on. You have to drive the story—there's a technical aspect."

The perceived snub did not sit well with Bobbi, who immediately took to Twitter to vent her rage, tweeting two separate broadsides at Bassett:

> "Ha MsAng "bassketcase" has such a damn nerve my lord, at least the world doesn't mistake me for the wrong sex . . . she has some #XtraEquipment."
>
> "When I win my first Grammy or Oscar, *Shrugs* hmm whichever comes 1st, I'll be sure 2shout URname out b-tch! Hah UrTestResults = Male. Lmao."

If Bobbi's career wasn't going as she expected in the three years following her mother's death, her personal life wasn't faring much better. As far back as late 2012, the world first learned that she and Nick were a couple on an episode of *The Houstons: On Our Own.* Before long, they suddenly announce their engagement in an episode where Bobbi displays a ring that belonged to Whitney and announces to her family, "We're engaged."

Pat Houston makes it clear she doesn't approve, calling the engagement "unacceptable." Nick reveals to the camera that Cissy doesn't particularly like him. For her part, Bobbi's grandmother says, "I don't know Nick that well. Let us pray that everybody finds their way."

Pat reveals she was wary of Nick from the start. "Many people told Whitney it was the wrong decision to bring Nicholas into the household," she tells the camera. She then makes it clear that she was one of those people. "But don't let me have to say 'I told you so.'"

Finally, toward the end of the series, Bobbi revealed that the engagement was off.

"He said after he proposed to me, like, it was a mistake," Bobbi tells somebody on the phone. "So we're not engaged anymore. We're just brother and sister again." Later, Nick is seen at an event, flirting with another woman, as Bobbi looks on, distraught. "You gotta give me your number before you get outta here," he tells the object of his affection.

On November 18, Nick confirmed the news, tweeting:

"@REALbkBrown and I are not engaged or dating. Just close like we have always been"

Pat Houston's eighty-two-year-old mother, Ella Mae Watson, would later reveal that it was actually Bobbi who first fell for Nick, claiming she was distraught that her love was unrequited.

"I told Krissi, 'You can't buy his love,'" she told the *Daily Mail* in February 2015. "The baby girl was crying on my shoulder about the boy. She said he told her that he loved her as a sister and that was all. I told her it didn't matter how many things she gave him she could not buy his love. That was after her mother died."

It was difficult to determine whether the romantic relationship had simply been a publicity stunt to hype the ratings or whether it was genuine. By the time the series aired in the fall, Bobbi and Nick were referring to each other on social media as "brudda" and "little sis."

Soon after the series aired, they moved out of the Atlanta town house where they had both continued to live after Whitney's death and into their own apartment in Alpharetta not far away. This marked a period where the two would gain a notorious reputation for throwing wild drug-fueled parties lasting into the wee hours of the morning.

A young couple with a baby was living below them and filed at least ten noise complaints in the six months that Nick and Bobbi lived there. Finally, in June 2013, Bobbi and Nick reportedly received an eviction notice because of their disruptive behavior.

Before they left, however, the neighbor who lived in the apartment below—Joshua Morse, the man who had filed the multiple noise complaints—revealed that he had received a caustic handwritten note from Bobbi on his doorstep:

> *Thanks.*
> *You are shit at the bottom of my shoe.*
> *Thank you for making a hard year harder.*
> *You are a miserable couple, and always will be.*
> *You were honored to have us living above you and you couldn't stand such a young beautiful couple being far more successful than you will ever be. I pray your misery doesn't rub off on your innocent little baby.*

When reports emerged about the eviction, Bobbi claimed she and Nick had voluntarily chosen to leave to get away from Morse, tweeting:

> *"Awoke2CrazyNeighborStory ha Those pplR [people are] insane! nickdgordon & I choose2move THEY were the nightmare."*

Then in July 2013, a month after they moved back into the town house, Bobbi confirmed on Facebook that she and Nick were once again together.

> *"Yes, me and Nick are engaged. I'm tired of hearing people say, 'Eww your engaged to your brother.' My mom never adopted him."*

Nick would later post a photo of his engagement ring. It is this ring—the one that Nick dropped off for repair but later forgot about—that I tried on at Kay Jewelers in March while Bobbi lay in a coma.

Six months later, on January 9, 2014, Bobbi posted the infamous tweet announcing that the couple were #HappilyMarried.

At the time, Bobby Brown denied that his daughter was married to Nick, telling *TMZ*, "She's still single." When the website asked, "You don't approve of him?" Bobby replied, "It's not a question you know when your daughter gets married it's different. Whether or not you like him or not, it's 'damn, my daughter's getting married.' That's what it is." Asked if he thinks he could grow to "be down" with the marriage, Bobby replied, "Well, when he calls me I'll figure it out."

Coincidentally or not, the wedding announcement came only two months before Bobbi was due to receive the first installment of Whitney's estate trust, which had stipulated that she would receive ten percent of the money when she turned twenty-one.

Not long after her twenty-first birthday in March—when Bobbi was due to come into an estimated $2 million—Pat Houston, the trust's executor, filed an application for a restraining order against Nick. In her petition to the Fulton County Court, she claimed that Nick "made threatening comments and posted photos of guns with the intention of making petitioner fearful for her personal safety. Respondent then posted more photos of guns later and has sent harassing texts."

She revealed that Nick had been posting a series of "terrorist threats" aimed at her. Among them, he had tweeted, "I got guns bigger than you" and "crawl your head in that noose." Other tweets had mentioned Pat by name:

> *"Everybody got so fake after Mom passed away. Specially Pat."*
> *"Fuck that Pat bitch."*

Bobbi herself would also turn on Pat around the same time, tweeting:

"Ba hah PAT GARLAND.. (she will NEVER be a Houston) is a fucking coward !!!!!! Lmfao oh boy, you wanted this, so U got it bitch!!! #GameON"

A police report about the incident that sparked the filing notes that Bobbi and Nick "are not pleased with [Pat] controlling Whitney Houston's estate." The officer reported on his interaction with Pat, whose real name is Marion.

"Marion informed me that Mr. Gordon wants Ms. Brown's monthly allowance increased," the report said. "Marion refused to relinquish the money. Marion stated that Mr. Gordon has turned Krissi against the family and in the process has said threatening statements to Marion and other family members."

The petition requested that Nick be barred from approaching within two hundred yards of Pat and that he be compelled to undergo "appropriate psychiatric or psychological services."

Police declined to press charges against Nick, but the court granted the restraining order—a "Default Stalking Twelve-Month Protective Order"—that forbid Nick from having any contact with Pat and Houston's "immediate family."

This order, which expired on April 13, 2015, was in effect when Bobbi was found unconscious and it is believed to have been one of the reasons Nick has not been allowed to visit the hospital where Pat and her family have gathered daily.

When I spoke to one of Pat's former employees who spends the winter in Miami, she told me that Pat is "above reproach" and completely trustworthy.

"Pat always looked out for Whitney's interests when she worked for her," she explained. "That wasn't always an easy task, there were some hard times, but Pat really tried. Her husband [Whitney's brother Gary] had his own issues, so she knew a thing or two about navigating around Whitney's stuff but it was hard on her. If anybody knows the skeletons, it's Pat but she'll never tell. She also did a lot for Krissi after her mother died. Pat was determined to look out for her but Krissi kept pushing back. I haven't been around and I don't know Nick but I think it's been really hard on Pat and Cissy to see Krissi go down that path. I can't imagine how they must be feeling about what happened, like revisiting a nightmare."

Indeed, I have been impressed watching the Houston family handle the circus that has revolved around Bobbi since the day she was found. It is a refreshing contrast to the antics of Bobby Brown's buffoonish clan, even though I have been equally impressed by Bobby's quiet dignity as he maintains his daily bedside vigil. It seems apparent that he has finally overcome his long battle with substance abuse and alcohol. It is a reminder of what might have been—both personally and professionally—had he and Whitney not succumbed to the addictions that plagued them both.

Nick's fight over Whitney's money, in fact, brings up the specter of what might happen to the trust should Bobbi succumb. Whitney's original will has caused some confusion because of its stipulation that her money would go to Cissy should Bobbi predecease her mother. Many media outlets have interpreted this provision to mean Cissy is entitled to the trust—ninety percent of which has not yet been distributed—if Bobbi dies. However, my legal sources assure me this is not the case. Under Georgia law, the estate of Bobbi Kristina Brown will go to her next of kin. Unless Nick can provide evidence that the couple were legally wed, her father, Bobby Brown, will inherit everything. I can only imagine that this is why his embarrassing family is hovering like vultures and publicly leveling accusations against both Nick and Pat.

———

There are many conflicting reports about what happened in the weeks and days leading up to January 31. Almost everything reported on entertainment sites purporting to come from "sources close to the family" is either deeply suspect or provably wrong.

We know for a fact that security called 911 on January 23 to report a domestic dispute inside the town house. However, nobody appears to know what happened or how it was resolved because the neighbor who reported the incident declined to call 911.

We know that four days later, on January 27, Bobbi was driving her Jeep Liberty late in the afternoon in Roswell when she lost control of the vehicle and crossed a lane, colliding with a Ford Taurus coming in the other direction. Riding with her was Danyela Bradley, the young woman who was present four days later when she was found in the tub. Bobbi and the other driver, forty-one-year-old Russell Eckerman, were brought to the hospital. Bobbi was treated for minor injuries, but Eckerman was listed as in critical condition.

Bobbi had been pulled over by the police on September 9, 2014, for "driving with expired tags." The day after the January 27 accident, a bench warrant was issued against her because she hadn't shown up in Alpharetta Municipal Court to answer that charge.

There are unconfirmed reports that Bobbi and Nick had been fighting and that they had called off their supposed engagement. But the last thing we know for sure is that on January 29, Bobbi had posted the tweet: "On My Own."

Other than that, almost everything is secondhand.

———

I knew I couldn't rely on the dubious accounts of those who claim to know the couple at the circle of this mystery. I needed to somehow worm my way into the Atlanta drug circles that I assumed held secrets that could shed light on the events of January 31. But I had no idea how to go about it.

Twenty years earlier, I had spent more than a month in Seattle, immersing myself in the city's notorious drug scene while I researched a book about the final days of Kurt Cobain. In the midst of my investigation, I spent considerable time with my coauthor hanging out in heroin "shooting galleries," places where junkies go to shoot up. It was on one of these undercover ventures, in fact, where I got my first real break—meeting Kurt's best friend, Dylan Carlson, the musician who bought the shotgun that killed the rock icon. Unaware that I was an undercover journalist, he shared some crucial information as we jammed together before he excused himself to shoot up.

The most difficult thing about that adventure was spending hours at a time in the sordid conditions of these run-down houses surrounded by junkies without drawing attention to the fact that I wasn't one myself. But I was much younger then, and I had caught a lucky break when a Bulgarian musician I had played with offered an entrée.

A local shooting gallery was exactly the kind of locale where I might find the kind of information I was seeking. But I had no idea how to go about finding one in Atlanta and gaining access. My investigator informed me which sections of the city were notorious for heroin. Indeed, when I patrolled these neighborhoods' streets, they were certainly very seamy and didn't at all resemble the neighborhoods where I had hung out in Seattle on a similar quest twenty years before.

And although I saw at least a couple dozen denizens who looked as if they spent a fair amount of time in shooting galleries, I knew I couldn't just approach one to ask directions. For one thing, no matter how I dressed, I feared that a middle-aged pudgy guy like me would have screamed "Cop."

Alas, two days of sniffing around got me nowhere. When I consulted a friend in Miami who has worked with addicts, she suggested I locate a methadone clinic and try my luck there. It was a good suggestion, but three hours outside two separate clinics yielded zero results. Nobody wanted to talk to me. It was disheartening and a little embarrassing to know that my much-vaunted investigative skills were failing me.

Then my friend had another suggestion. "Why don't you go to a Narcotics Anonymous meeting," she said. "You might just find potheads but you'll definitely find some people who know the drug scene, and you won't stand out."

She told me that Narcotics Anonymous is roughly similar to Alcoholics Anonymous and follows the same twelve-step principles. It sounded worth trying. It took me only fifteen minutes online to find a meeting taking place that night at a local church. When I got there, my only fear was that I'd have to talk about what brought me there. I came up with a story about my coke habit and how I'd been clean for four years and attended regular meetings in Miami which is, after all, the coke capital of America.

When I got there, however, I was fifteen minutes early, and I found a slew of people smoking outside the church. I discovered they were waiting for the meeting to begin, and all but one were regulars. As it turned out, I was not the least bit conspicuous, because they were older than I had expected. They were all male. The only thing conspicuous about me was that I don't actually smoke. But I quickly bummed a cigarette and started a conversation.

I told them I was from Miami, and within a minute I had managed to bring up Bobbi Kristina. Alas, none of them knew her or Nick or anybody that knows them, although they all seemed to have an opinion on the case. Most believed it was a suicide. One man thought Nick had been "acting suspicious." A couple of minutes into the conversation, I brought up the temperature of the bathwater to see if somebody could enlighten me about what that might mean. That's when one of my new acquaintances—a man with a goatee who looked to be in his early forties and who had actually theorized that Bobbi attempted suicide—said, "She probably took the plunge."

I had no idea what that meant, and I still don't know why any of these people are in NA. But it's evident from the way he spoke that he was a former junkie. He told me that when somebody "drops"— which seems to be a term for an OD—there are all kinds of ways to revive them.

"I've never seen it done with a bath," he said to me, "but I sort of helped bring somebody around with a cold shower. You stick them under the cold water and you slap them to bring them around. I didn't do the hitting, but I held somebody up while a buddy did. It worked." He told me he'd heard of the same method being used in a cold bath.

He explained that "hopheads"—slang for *junkies*—use all kinds of remedies to bring somebody around when they drop. Some of them are "stupid," he explained, like [injecting] "salt water." It was a little hard to follow but he seemed to imply that he wasn't necessarily talking about heroin overdoses, or at least not exclusively. Overdoses can be caused by any number of other drugs. He told me that his drug buddies used to use something that is very effective when he OD'ed, but he used a technical name that I couldn't remember afterward. What surprised me most was his explanation that overdoses are much more common than I thought and that most people survive the experience. He said he had dropped at least three times, and that's one of the reasons he's in NA, but he never told me what drug or drugs he was addicted to, and I never asked. The meeting was about to start, or I would have persisted in my questioning. In the end, I decided I had gotten what I needed and left without going inside—still nervous that I would have to deliver my phony story to a roomful of seasoned addicts.

What intrigued me as much as his story about cold baths is his description of "slapping" the overdose victim. Could this be how Bobbi sustained the facial bruises that paramedics reportedly found that morning? Is this why the water was ice-cold?

Eager to test out my new theory, I begin searching. Within fifteen minutes, I find scores of sites related to drug abuse or treatment that address the idea of a cold-water bath for overdose victims. Each one goes out of its way to warn *against* this method, indicating that it must be very common. Many other sites list cold-water baths in a list of the most common myths and old wives' tales about reviving overdose victims.

The North Carolina Harm Reduction Coalition, for example,

warns, "Do Not put the person in an ice-cold bath, it could put them into shock, or they could drown."

According to Medical Assisted Treatment of America, "If you put someone who has overdosed in a shower or bath, you could send them into shock by changing their body temperature too quickly. They could also drown if their lungs get filled with water."

And despite the countless warnings against this dangerous practice, I find a staggering amount of people on drug abuse forums advising people to use the cold-water method and slap the victim's face or revealing that they have used this method themselves. Although it would obviously be safer to call 911 and seek medical help, they admit they go out of their way not to alert the authorities, for fear of being arrested for felony drug possession. That is why these home remedies are so common.

I also found a telling passage from the memoir of a former junkie, *Once an Addict*, in which the author, Barry Woodward, discusses one of his overdoses.

> *I went blue in the face and my eyes rolled into the back of my head. Any heroin overdose has the potential to be fatal, and the best remedy is to put the person in a bath of cold water, or inject them with salt water. Joey freaked out because he had never seen anything like this before, but Lisa was there and she knew what to do. She ran into the bathroom and turned the cold water tap on full; she then told Joey to slap me in the face.*

In an Arizona newspaper, the *Cronkite News*, I find an account describing the demise of a twenty-eight-year-old overdose victim named Natasha Gates who died in 2012: "Passed out from the heroin, her friend and his roommate partially undressed her and put her in a bathtub filled with cold water to help suppress Natasha's overdose symptoms. Both fell asleep and when they woke, she was dead," the article states.

Can these accounts solve the mystery of why Bobbi was found in a cold-water bath and why she had unexplained bruises on her face?

I call Calvin Whitehead, a substance Abuse Therapist at the Greenleaf drug treatment center in Valdosta, Georgia, to run the theory by him.

Whitehead tells me that he has heard of the cold-water revival method and slapping the overdose victim but stresses that

It's not anything we would suggest in response to an overdose, it's such an emergency type of situation. The nature of an overdose is that the drug is affecting your brain to the point where it's affecting your brain stem, which is affecting your breathing so if the drug is impacting your brain stem to the point that it's shutting down your respiratory system, cold water and slapping will have limited effect.

I follow up with a call to Dr. Christopher La Tourette La Riche, medical director of Florida's Lucida Treatment Center, asking him if the cold-water bath method might have any effect.

When someone ODs, what happens is that somebody stops breathing. Cold water might just give them a sensory shock and arouse them but it wouldn't reverse the opiate block on their receptors, it wouldn't do that. But if they're in the gray area where it's not a full-on overdose, they're just sedated and just fading, something as shocking as an ice-water bath might make them a little more alert. But if they're in full-on overdose I can't see what it would do. But if they're in the gray area I can see it.

The cold-water bath theory—if correct—would answer some of the pressing questions about the circumstances that led to Bobbi being found almost drowned in a bath of ice-cold water. Most significantly, it would likely rule out foul play. But it would also raise a number of other questions that only the police can answer and still doesn't let Bobbi's friends off the hook. Did one of them leave her alone in the bathtub to answer the door for the cable technician? Or did they both panic when the doorbell rang and leave the bathroom to clean up drug paraphernalia and residue? How did Bobbi end up facedown? Might she have flailed in shock when the water revived her and landed facedown in the water after she was left alone?

When I asked the former homicide detective about the various scenarios, he told me he thinks the police are very unlikely to lay charges if Bobbi survives. If she dies, however, he believes somebody will be charged.

"If they find narcotics in her system, or even pills she obtained without a prescription, they're going to be looking at how and where she got the drugs," he said. "They probably already know a lot and they're just sitting on it to see whether she survives. This is a big case, it involves a celebrity; they're going to want to find a culprit. I assume somebody's going down."

Of course, the cold-water bath theory doesn't rule out suicide. It's possible that Bobbi—depressed about the upcoming anniversary or her breakup with Nick—ingested a large quantity of Xanax and was on the verge of blacking out when her friends discovered her. Trying to revive her from a pill-induced stupor, they could have immersed her in cold water and slapped her, causing the facial bruises. But if so, why have both men been so reluctant to cooperate with the police? Indeed, they both immediately lawyered up.

Who gave Bobbi the drugs? Was Nick attempting to conceal evidence if he cleaned up the scene before authorities arrived, as Max reportedly alleged? Is Max's own extensive drug record the reason why police haven't offered him immunity, for fear that they may be letting the guilty party off the hook?

These questions invoke the call I received only four days after Bobbi's body was found. The caller is not tied to the Roswell PD, which is investigating the circumstances of Bobbi's case. But, although not a cop himself, he does have a direct tie to the Atlanta Police Department. He told me that, from the information he had garnered from colleagues soon after Bobbi was found, "It looks like we have another Natalie Wood."

When he told me this, I assumed he was referring to the fact that it was another unexplained celebrity drowning. As I delved into the facts of Bobbi's case, however, I discovered some remarkable parallels.

In 1981, the legendary star of *West Side Story* and *Miracle on 34th Street* was on a weekend boat trip to Santa Catalina Island in California with her husband, Robert Wagner, and the costar of her most recent film, Christopher Walken. Around eight in the morning of November 29, Wood's body was discovered drowned a mile away from the boat. Wagner reported that when he went to bed the night before, his wife wasn't there. The autopsy report would later reveal that the star had bruises on her arms and an abrasion on her cheek when she was found. The coroner ruled the death an accidental drowning.

But thirty years later, the only other person on board that weekend—the captain, Dennis Davern—confessed that he had lied to the police during the initial investigation. He told the *Today* show he had heard Wood and Wagner arguing the evening before and he now believed that Wagner was responsible for his wife's death. However, Walken was also on board and Davern couldn't account for his whereabouts on the night in question. There were simply too many unanswered questions and so nobody was ever charged. The cause of death, however, was changed from drowning to "undetermined."

The parallels to the Bobbi Kristina case are indeed strikingly obvious, including unexplained bruises and more than one person present in the house who may or may not have been involved. Only the toxicology report—or in the worst-case scenario, an autopsy—can definitively answer the question about which, if any, drugs Bobbi Kristina had in her body at the time she was found. It's possible that authorities will unveil new evidence that discredits the cold-water bath theory completely.

It's also possible that, like the drowning of Wood, we may never know what happened that morning.

However she ended up unconscious in the tub, some will argue that Bobbi Kristina's fate was sealed years earlier, growing up at the center of the world's most famous dysfunctional couple. Others have already argued that Whitney's own fate was inevitable, given the unhappiness of hiding her sexuality for the sake of stardom.

In the end, neither pop psychology nor amateur sleuthing can probably answer these pressing questions. I'm especially struck and saddened by what Cissy Houston wrote in her 2013 memoir comparing her daughter's problems with that of her then-struggling granddaughter:

> *Some people believed that Nippy was public property, because of her voice and her fame. But Krissi wasn't then, and she isn't now. She was a young girl who saw her mother go through some very tough times. All I know is, Nippy loved her daughter fiercely, and whatever Krissi went through at this time is her business to tell, if she ever chooses to do it. So I'll leave it at that.*

EPILOGUE

As Bobbi continued to lay unresponsive, there had been no medical news for weeks from the rehabilitation facility where she had been moved in March. It appeared to outsiders that any prospect for a recovery was increasingly bleak. The family continued to pray for a miracle.

On April 18, it appeared that miracle had come to pass when Bobby Brown stunned the crowd at a Los Angeles festival where he was appearing.

"I can say today that my baby's awake. She's watching me," he announced. His sister Tina Brown followed up on this shocking revelation the following day when she posted on Facebook, "[Bobbi] woke up and is no longer on life support!!!!!:):)God is good!!thanks for your prayers,,still a process,but she is going to be ok:):):):)."

As the public and media stirred at the unexpected turn of events, sources close to the family quickly doused the reports, letting it be known that, despite Bobby's revelation, Bobbi's condition remained unchanged.

Indeed, the false hopes finally inspired Cissy Houston to set the record straight on April 20 and provide the first ever-public medical prognosis about Bobbi's condition. It wasn't good.

Her granddaughter, she revealed, has "global and irreversible brain damage and remains unresponsive."

Bobby was quick to clarify his previous misleading comments, explaining that he was in an "emotional state" when he implied that Bobbi had recovered.

The good news, if it can be called that, is that Bobbi is no longer in a medically induced coma or fighting for her life. It is conceivable that she can live in this state for decades.

"Meeting with the doctors and understanding that she can live in this condition for a lifetime truly saddens me," Cissy stated. "We can only trust in God for a miracle at this time."

And if the news now extinguishes any remaining possibility that Bobbi will carry on her mother's legacy, Whitney's spirit will continue to live on in her music and in my memory of that encounter with her one night in 1988 when the Houston family demons had not yet made their appearance.

ACKNOWLEDGMENTS

Thank you doesn't begin to adequately express my gratitude to my editor, Jeremie Ruby-Strauss. The same goes for Jennifer Bergstrom, Jennifer Robinson, Nina Cordes, Elisa Rivlin, and my entire family at Simon & Schuster. You are the most incredible, inspiring, thorough and supportive team an author could hope to have.

Chris Casuccio and John Pearce at WCA were invaluable in helping to shape the book in all stages of development.

My longtime friend Max Wallace brought a sharp eye to the book and kept it grounded.

Words can't express the appreciation and respect I have for the brave friends and family members who spoke on and off the record. At their request, I've changed the name of some sources to protect their identity.

Special thanks to:

Rob Dolinski, Taylor Reid, Cassandra Simon, Rhahime Bell, Les Weitzman, Arik Roshanzamir, Ron Deckelbaum, Tony Dixon, Alicia Banton, Rob Polishook, Eric Kirshner, Dr. Eva Ritvo, Seth Zane, Claude Lussier, Martin Rouillard, Rory and Diana Conforti, Hardy Hill, Dr. Christopher La Tourette, John Houston, Dany Houle, Martine Albert, Eric Clark, Marc Andre Lord, Sheldon Neuberger,

Carol Lagace, Stephane Fiset, Sebastien Roy, Barbara Sax, Henry Horowitz, "Kid" Desmond, Esmond Choueke, Le Roi Medelgi, Annie Rose, Rob Polishook, Stuart Nulman, Mike Cohen, Minelle Mahtani, Jonathan Ollat, Louise Gardiner, Sherman Young, Fulton County Courthouse, the Atlanta Police Department, the Roswell Police Department, Uber, Richard Peddie, Colleen Peddie, Tracy Davis, Paivi Helmio, Clover Sky, Stan Bernstein, Ken Bell, David Gavrilchuk, Kris Kostov, Michael Peshev, Dimitra and Tom Papadapoulos, Caity and Rodriquez, Zaya Star, Jimmy Bollettieri, Dwayne Williams, Kevin Stevens, Steven Milner, Cathy Montanez, Jan Rucidlo, Paivi Mattila, Vince Cauchon, Severi Pyysalo, Jarno Venho, Jo Piazza, Eric Dulac, Gabriel Auclair, Henry Yang, Malcolm Reinhold, Jeffrey Kennedy, P.I. Sheila McPhilamy, Harvey Baylor, Irwin Zelnicker, Michael Friedlieb, Emily Toney, Carl Mathieu, Katherine Kennedy, Judith Regan, Jarred Weisfeld, Tiki Melvin, Elsa Mays, Rhonda Starr, Trixy, Dr. Charles Small, Dylan Howard, Claire Newman, "Kid Atlanta," Sirius XM, Olivier O'Mahony, Jesse Tyler, Roxanne West, Ian Hamilton, Eddie Payne, Travis Tefft, Herb Morton, Bruce Richman, Sauli Hietala, Alice Martinez, Ted Hathaway, Corey Jones, Fred Cabrera, Mack Anderson, the Atlanta Board of Education, and a courageous Hollywood A-lister who provided me with key leads.